Female Sexuality

Female Sexuality

NEW PSYCHOANALYTIC VIEWS

By Janine Chasseguet-Smirgel

with

C.-J. Luquet-Parat, Béla Grunberger,
Joyce McDougall, Maria Torok, Christian David

Foreword by Frederick Wyatt

Ann Arbor
The University of Michigan Press

Foreword

Frederick Wyatt

Considering the amount of time human beings commonly spend on the twin subjects of love and sex, one might think that psychology would, as a matter of course, regard them as its foremost concern. But this is not so. We have more systematic knowledge of the mating behavior of most animals than of the analogous enterprise in man. So much of the latter is mental, that is, subjectively experienced as impulse and affect, and mostly enjoined by fantasy. It goes on either without any corollary behavior, or with widely divergent ones. It is not surprising, then, that the literary imagination has dealt so often with the varieties of love, but we still have reason to wonder how psychology managed until recently to have so little to say about it.

One of the abiding contributions of psychoanalysis to the human condition is, indeed, that it finally came to grips with the subject, providing us with a systematic theory of sexual development. Psychoanalysis for the first time put some order into the profusion of sexual aims and their possible objects, showing us how they derive from a plural convergence between the child's instinctual needs and fantasies, his inherent individual dispositions, and the pressures of his environment.

Psychoanalysis had less to say about love. Even if it is not considered a subject too sublime for it (as some critics have maintained), it will not be grasped either if regarded merely as a by-product of sexuality, a kind of sentimentalized decoy for a gullible public, as some psychoanalysts hold. There is no principal reason why love can not be understood within the scope of psychoanalysis. What psychoanalysts will then have to say about it may still not be as uncannily perceptive as poets and writers so often have been; but, by proceeding more systematically, psychoanalysis might give us at last a more comprehensive and steady understanding of the subject than we have had so far.

However, no psychology of love is without a psychology of sex. The involvement of the sexes and the subterfuges and inversions of this involvement have been commonly discussed by psychoanalysts in terms of instinctual needs and their arrest and distortion through conflict. The development of male sexuality was studied first, and perhaps for that reason as well as because of its relative simplicity, it became a model for all subsequent investigation. Freud's one-sided approach to the psychology of women has been criticized so much that it will be in order here to reflect on what the situation now is. Those familiar with the literature know, of course, that major revisions of Freud's view on female sexuality have already taken place. Further revisions are needed. There are simply too many facets in the psychology of woman which are not yet sufficiently understood. As clinicians we meet continuously with breaks and discontinuities of the life history too readily put down as symptoms. Sometimes we can seize upon some of their meaning intuitively, but we cannot consistently fit them into our conceptual framework and so explain them. The endless ambiguities of women with regard to themselves belong here—the common envy of the male's prerogatives and of his presumable advantages. We are continuously struck by the greater psychological vulnerability of women, strangely coupled with greater biological sturdiness, and by the very widespread disabilities in sexual responsiveness. All these features create a penumbra of problems both personal and social which is not lighted up by insisting that we have already a complete theory to provide all the answers. Freud's writings on the subject, in spite of some jostling with female psychoanalytic critics, leave no doubt that he was fully aware of the limits of his own explanations. Of course, we do not help matters either if we dismiss psychoanalytic propositions about feminine sexuality altogether. No better theory is in sight anywhere, and the promise of the psychoanalytic approach is so obvious and in so many respects not yet realized that we should first of all strive to work it out. The point now is to explore and vary our frame of reference systematically. We may well have carried along a set of theoretical expectations, a grid for the ordering of our observations, which from time to time detracts us from links and patterns of development which may yet lead to more effective explanations. What is needed, then, is a willingness to alter viewpoints. To provide us with such a change in perspective is the prominent contribution of this book.

The divergence of this book from the classical psychoanalytic position can be schematically stated in this way: the authors agree on the overwhelming importance of the mother for the personality and later sexual adjustment of the little girl. The significance of this early relationship can best be demonstrated by its failures and by the pathological twists following upon them. In these instances the child has never succeeded in freeing herself from the mother. At least in her own perception of herself she has remained beholden to her. In effect she thinks of herself as merely a part of the mother's body, or total presence, and must not have wishes and an individuality of her own. The various pathologies of which the authors offer impressive case examples represent attempts of the girl, now grown into womanhood, to free herself from the image of that possessive but often unprepossessing mother. Appropriate to the origin of that image are the girl's attempts at overcoming it— they are, as a rule, as devious and irrational as they are futile and self-limiting.

In their conception of the impact and scale of these events in early childhood the authors tend toward the views developed by Melanie Klein and frequently promulgated by Ernest Jones. According to this position the drama of early childhood goes on very much inside, consisting as it does of fantasies insinuating the usurpation of genitals and other properties of the parents' bodies, and of the guilt the child accumulates by participating in these games in his imagination.

Melanie Klein's ideas have had much less influence on the development of psychoanalysis in this country than they continue to have in England, in France, and, for that matter, in South America. The question at this point cannot be whether they are right or not. Being reconstructions rather than propositions based on readily accessible observation, they are not verifiable in the strict sense of the word. They must be judged, above all, in terms of what they can do for us by enabling us to organize observations in a novel and productive way. The authors of *Female Sexuality* show what use can be made of the Klein-Jones frame of reference by demonstrating its efficacy in the organization of clinical materials and in the formulation of productive hypotheses. They throw light on some of the perennial queries of the clinical investigator and therapist concerning that ubiquitous and much debated motif penis envy, on the stuff of which men and women make up their fantasies of each other, on the rather universal roots of female homosexuality, and on many other topics.

This book differs not only in its conceptual framework, but in its emphasis on what in the psychoanalytic image of man matters most. It stresses primary process, impulse, and affect before ego organization. There is in this way not much room for the autonomy of the ego, which for many of us has become the center of psychoanalytic theory. Nevertheless, the authors of this book again vigorously remind us of what can still be gained from expanding on psychoanalysis's earlier stress on instinct and the unconscious. The authors are by no means unaware of the collective behind the individual—of the motive-orienting force of culture and social norms, and their indispensable part in the reconstruction of normal and pathological developments. To advance our understanding of the casting of the sexes we shall have to draw much more on anthropology and sociology—and ethology—than we have done so far. But that is the prospect for psychoanalytic psychology at large. The merit of the studies assembled in this book seems to me to consist in organizing observations more comprehensively and with fewer strings left dangling than before. It consists in answering some questions and in cutting back others to essentials, so that the problem can be approached more efficiently in the next round. The authors of this book suggest new ways of looking at an age-old problem, and in doing so give us also a welcome demonstration of the French point of view in psychoanalysis. The reader who follows their exposition with an open mind will find the excursion most rewarding.

Contents

Introduction

J. Chasseguet-Smirgel

Preliminary Remarks

If one considers psychoanalytical literature on female sexuality one cannot but notice a disproportion between the importance this subject necessarily commands in clinical experience—half the people analyzed are women—and the very modest role it plays in theoretical studies. This disproportion is all the more remarkable if one goes on to compare it with the anthropological ambitions of psychoanalysis.

One could argue that Freud's discoveries in this domain are definitive, but that would be to exaggerate greatly Freud's own estimation of his work on female psychology. Indeed, Freud was always reticent about the "dark continent" of femininity, and constantly stressed the incomplete nature of his discoveries. Although he maintained his theories on female sexuality he nevertheless left the question open. Thus, at the end of his lecture on "Femininity," one of the last works in which he discussed this problem, he says: "If you want to know more about femininity, enquire from your own experiences of life, or turn to the poets, or wait until science can give you deeper and more coherent information."

The debate is long-standing, Freud's first works on femininity having already provoked strong opposition even among "orthodox" analysts; by following Freudian methods of exploring the unconscious, they often arrived at conclusions different from Freud's own. Many analysts published the clinical experiences which led to their new hypotheses. On the other hand others followed Freud's ideas closely, trying to confirm them or enrich them by personal contributions.

The position adopted by Ernest Jones, one of the first and most faithful disciples of Freud, his biographer, and the founder of the English psychoanalytic movement, was startling. Far from agreeing with the Freudian hypotheses, he aligned himself with the views of the "opposition" and expressed in his own conclusions his deep, but respectful, disagreement with Freud. The study of the psychoanalytical texts which reflect these divergences is interesting inasmuch as it provides a basis for reflection as well as represents an important moment in the history of psychoanalysis. But these debates, however rich and animated they may have been, never resulted in a fruitful clash of opinion, nor in a synthesis which might take into account the positive aspects of both sides. The discussion ended in deadlock. Of all the analysts who opposed Freud's views on female sexuality, only Karen Horney broke away from Freud. Yet it is difficult to assess exactly how far she really disagreed with Freud in her final views on this topic. The Kleinians have, of course, adhered to Melanie Klein's views on the little girl's development as an intrinsic part of her whole theoretical system. As for "independent" analysts, that is to say the majority, some follow Freud—as much in theory as in practice—but many others, without adopting definitive doctrinaire positions, develop a variety of ideas following from their personal clinical experience.

Since the last echoes of the discussion on female sexuality died down some thirty years ago, analysts have continued to analyze women, and rich and abundant clinical material has accumulated, yet studies of female sexuality have become rarer, more sporadic, more fragmented. Certain reasons may be found for this relative gap in psychoanalytical research. The rigidity of theoretical positions probably influences subjective experience; didactic analysis does not prevent an analyst from being personally biased in a domain which, for reasons that we shall try to explain in this book, revives emotions and frightening representations as much in the theoreticians as in those with whom the theories are concerned.

It would be relatively easy to reconsider many established theories on femininity in the light of what we know about unconscious fantasies of femininity itself. It is obvious that an analyst who reflects upon such problems and develops his own views is also directly and personally involved. He must confront a number of internal and external difficulties, challenges which the first psychoanalysts, those of the twenties and thirties, did not hesitate to accept. Since then, psychoanalysis has entered a phase of maturity; psychoanalysts are no longer pioneers. They have become established. In order to achieve this they left behind the theoretical differences which could have disrupted a new movement. Undoubtedly, the fact that Freud's ideas will be questioned in this book is not unconnected with that period of inactivity. But the time at which this attitude was important is now gone; to prolong it would be sterile and complacent. The vitality of any doctrine depends on the possibility of rethinking certain aspects without disrupting the whole structure.

The authors of the present book are united in their desire to reexamine the theories of female sexuality, using the Freudian approach to the unconscious. They hope to avoid the misleading theoretical path which attempts to approach the problems of femininity through the study of male sexuality.[1] Such an approach (whose deeper motivation I hope to examine later in this book) is detrimental to any understanding of the essence of femininity.

The present authors have attempted as far as possible to free their theoretical ideas and their clinical interpretations from the unconscious fantasies which distort scientific objectivity. Thus, Christian David tries, through the use of a clinical history, to study masculine myths about femininity. Catherine Luquet-Parat approaches "the change of object" in a personal way, attributing an important role to female masochism in the little girl's attempt to change from the maternal object to the paternal one; Béla Grunberger examines the origins of female narcissism; Joyce McDougall shows that female homosexuality cannot be understood simply as a perversion, or a flight from man, or a rivalry with him: it must also be considered as a component of woman's development which must be normally integrated in order to achieve a harmonious feminine nature. Maria Torok gives masculinity wishes and penis envy a role and meaning which offer a possible explanation of this problem. For my part I shall try to describe the girl's relation with her father and discuss aspects of this relation which contribute an important dimension to female guilt.[2] Yet this identity in method is not an identity in theory; each of the authors contributes to this research in his own way and according to his own personal experience.

We felt that a brief historical review of Freud's main studies on femininity, and those of his disciples as well as those of his opponents, might provide a helpful introduction. Only the most significant and the most controversial theoretical positions will be considered.

Freud's Views on Female Sexuality

THREE ESSAYS ON THE THEORY OF SEXUALITY
(1905)

(Additions made in the following editions: 1910, 1915, 1920, 1922, and 1924)

In his *Three Essays on the Theory of Sexuality* [3] Freud lays the main bases for his conception of femininity, that is to say, the existence of a *sexual monism* for both sexes until puberty. "The assumption that all human beings have the same (male) form of genital is the first of the many remarkable and momentous sexual theories of children." This concept is fundamental to the development of female sexuality inasmuch as the male sex organ is the only one which is acknowledged by children of both sexes: the penis for the boy, and for the girl its corresponding organ: the clitoris. In Freud's view the clitoris is a little penis. Boys and girls believe that the world is created in their image and ignore the existence of the vagina. "The sexuality of little girls is of a wholly masculine character." Not only is the vagina nonexistent but the role of the clitoris is an exclusive one, even in regard to other external parts of the genital area. Boys and girls both pass through three essential phases in masturbation: the nursing period, the four-year-old stage (coinciding with the height of the Oedipal complex), and puberty.

However, there comes a time that Freud seems to identify with the second phase of infantile masturbation (at the age of four), when the male child realizes that girls are not made like him, since they have no penis, while the girl realizes that she has something *missing*. The boy, frightened by the missing penis, sees it as a castration and fears that the same thing may happen to him; from then on he despises women. The girl also thinks she has been castrated and wishes she were a boy.

In the *Three Essays*, therefore, Freud postulates the existence of the *castration complex* in both sexes and of *penis envy* in girls. Yet until puberty there is no real difference between the sexes. There is no "masculine," and no "feminine." At puberty "the penis, which has become erectile, presses forward insistently toward the new sexual aim of penetration into a cavity. . . ." At the same time the girl represses her clitoral sexuality, that is, the masculine element of her sexuality; both sexes discover the vagina.

Although Freud stated in *The Interpretation of Dreams*⁴ that the Oedipus complex was the nucleus of all neuroses, yet he was still unsure as to the relation between this complex and the castration complex. He speaks of the incest barrier, but not until the 1914 article "On Narcissism, An Introduction," ⁵ did he mention the superego. However, the importance of the maternal object in early childhood and its importance for women had already been stated.

The concept of sexual monism is asserted: the little girl is a little man until the castration complex. From then till puberty all she has is a castrated penis: she remains unaware of the existence of her vagina.

THE INFANTILE GENITAL ORGANIZATION OF THE LIBIDO (1923)

(A Supplement to the Theory of Sexuality) ⁶

In this article Freud completes the views of infantile sexuality expressed in the *Three Essays*. After many years of experience and observation he concluded that there was little difference in the organization of child and adult sexuality. Both imply the choice of an object and instinctual investment in this object. The difference lies in that adult sexuality is *genital* whereas child sexuality is *phallic*. Only one genital organ is known: the male one. Therefore, it is only in boys that one can study the consequences of this, "as far as the girl is concerned, they are little known."

At the phallic stage the boy certainly recognizes that there is a difference between men and women, but he does not see this difference as a sexual one. He believes that everybody has a penis similar to his and tries to find this penis in things and beings. When he discovers it does not exist in a little girl of his own age, he denies this fact, but later is compelled to accept it; he then thinks this is due to castration, which leads him to fear that this might happen to him, too. The castration complex comes into being and can only be understood in relation to the primacy of the phallic phase.

The little boy, nevertheless, believes that not all women have been castrated, only those who have the same guilty desires as he. The belief in the mother's penis and in that of women he admires continues for a long time. When he realizes that only women can bear children he gives up this idea. The observation that women do not have a penis frequently leads the boy to despise them, to be disgusted with them, or even to become homosexual. It is only at puberty that the genital stage is reached. Until then the vagina is not discovered.

Maleness signifies "subject, activity and possession of the penis"; femaleness signifies "object and passivity."

The infantile and adult genital organization is identical with regard to the object. Until puberty "male" and "female" signify respectively "phallic" and "castrated." The vagina is not known.

THE DISSOLUTION OF THE OEDIPUS COMPLEX (1924)[7]

In this article Freud studies the motives and the forms of the passing of the Oedipus complex for both sexes. The existence of a phallic libidinal stage with exclusion of the vagina for both is once more asserted, and its role in the structuring of the Oedipus complex is emphasized.

Freud still maintains that true genital structure only occurs at puberty. The dissolution of the boy's Oedipal conflict is instigated by the castration complex. Real traumas are presumed to be at the origin of this complex; first of all, the male child fears he will lose his penis if he masturbates, this threat being attributed to his mother. Since the sexual excitement that leads him to masturbation is linked with his Oedipal desires, the threat of castration is associated with them. Yet this threat has no immediate effect; it is only the sight of the female genital that gives reality to the fear of castration. This becomes all the more credible as the boy can relate it to earlier experiences: the loss of the breast, and the daily loss of feces, have acquainted him with the loss of precious parts of the body (the breast being regarded initially as part of the child's body). The male child has to face a conflict between his libidinal desires (which in the positive Oedipal position are directed toward the mother), and his narcissistic interest in his penis. Normally, the *narcissistic interest* prevails. The little girl's castration complex is brought into being by the sight of the boy's penis; this makes her feel inferior, and she compensates for her deficiency by penis envy (masculinity complex). Far from making her give up her Oedipal desires (as with the boy) the castration complex makes her turn toward her father in an attempt to replace the penis she lacks with a child; *the desire to have a child by the father, as a substitute for the penis, is therefore the dynamic factor in the female Oedipus complex.*

It seems as though the girl slowly turns away from the father because this desire is not fulfilled. The Oedipus complex does not end abruptly. Being already castrated, the girl does not fear castration. This plays an important role in the theory of the superego, particularly in regard to its origins and its strength. In the boy the castration complex results in the introjection of paternal or parental authority which forms the basis of the superego. The abandoned object cathexes are replaced by an identification with paternal prohibitions (in particular the prohibition of incest wishes). This process intended to save the penis has at the same time suspended its function. The child enters the latency period.

Although he acknowledges the existence of a superego in girls, Freud believes it is formed with some difficulty because of the lack of castration fear. External factors such as education, intimidation, the fear of no longer being loved, must be invoked, in contradistinction to the internalized prohibitions which form the boy's superego.

Whereas the dissolution of the Oedipus complex is marked by the castration complex in boys, in girls the castration complex initiates the Oedipus complex. During the Oedipal phase the boy has no desire to penetrate his mother, as he is not aware of the existence of the vagina. The mother's vagina is never sexually cathected by the little boy. (The Oedipus complex occurs simultaneously with the phallic stage.) The woman's superego is much less strong than the boy's.

SOME PHYSICAL CONSEQUENCES OF
THE ANATOMICAL DISTINCTION
BETWEEN THE SEXES (1925)[8]

The boy's Oedipus complex is easily revealed and understood; the mother is the object of his desires while he is nursing as well as during the following stages of his development. Freud recalls once more the description already given of the dissolution of the Oedipus complex. Yet, even in boys, there is a double Oedipus situation (active and passive), due to bisexuality; the boy at one point wants to take the mother's place with the father (feminine position).

The prehistory of the Oedipus complex is less clear; it is as though the male child goes through a period of tender identification with the father, without having any feeling of rivalry with regard to the mother.

Freud believes that the little boy's masturbation is not necessarily connected with his Oedipal desires. He considers the role of the child's observation of parental intercourse and of "primal fantasies" in both versions (positive and negative) of the Oedipus complex.

For the little girl the Oedipus complex gives rise to an additional problem: how does she give up her early attachment to the mother and how does she then choose the father as object? The girl wants to have a child by the father, but this stage of development has a long prehistory. Freud wonders if the discovery of the genital zone (clitoris or penis) is not linked with the loss of the maternal breast, in an attempt to replace one source of pleasure by another. Fellatio fantasies seem to indicate this, but Freud thought that psychic content need not necessarily accompany early stimulation of the genital zone. The crucial moment in the girl's development is the discovery of a sexual organ superior to her own in her brothers or their friends. Whereas the boy is at first indifferent to the girl's sexual organ and is worried about it only when he has established a link between the threat of castration and the sight of the female genital (from which he then turns away in "horror" or with "triumphant contempt"), the little girl on the contrary, as in a flash, "sees it, knows that she is without it and wants to have it."

This process is at the origin of both her castration and her masculinity complex. Several possibilities are open to her. She can keep the hope of one day acquiring a penis or she can deny her castration and persuade herself that she really has a penis. The resultant narcissistic wound leads to inferiority feelings. She first thinks that she has been punished, then, realizing that her condition is that of all women she wishes to become a man.

Penis envy may give rise to the feminine character trait of jealousy. The little girl starts to resent her mother for having made her without a penis. She also accuses her mother of loving the other children (those with a penis) more and takes advantage of this excuse to reject her. Masturbation ceases because she is disappointed in her clitoris.

For Freud masturbation is generally a masculine activity. Therefore, the acknowledgment of the difference between the sexes obliges the little girl to give up masculinity and turn to femininity. Till then there is no trace of the Oedipus complex, but now the girl gives up the desire for a penis and replaces it by the desire for a child (child = penis) and *to this end* she turns to her father. The mother is then set up as a rival, and the little girl has become a woman.

The female Oedipus complex is a *secondary* formation in Freud's opinion. He reiterates that "whereas in boys the Oedipus complex is destroyed by the castration complex, in girls it is made possible and initiated by the castration complex." In both cases the castration complex *"inhibits and limits masculinity and encourages femininity."* The differential effect of the masculine and feminine castration complex is due to anatomical differences.

In girls castration has already occurred, and can no longer be feared. In boys it is a threat, leading *not only to repression* of Oedipal desire; the Oedipus complex is broken up by the shock of the threatened castration, the libidinal cathexes are abandoned, desexualized, and in part, sublimated; the *objects* are incorporated into the ego where they form the basis of the *superego*.

"In the normal, or rather in the ideal case, the Oedipal complex exists no longer, not even in the unconscious; the superego has become its heir." This whole process occurs in the boy because of the narcissistic cathexis of the penis. In the girl the motive for the destruction of the Oedipus complex is missing because castration has already occurred. Therefore it slowly disappears or becomes repressed or even persists during the woman's entire life. The female superego "is never so inexorable, so impersonal, so independent of its emotional origins as that of the man."

Freud criticizes the feminists who "are anxious to force us to regard the two sexes as completely equal in position and worth," but adds that male and female bisexuality adds nuances to their principal positions.

In boys the Oedipus complex is a primary formation. In girls it is a secondary formation: the girl first desires her mother, then a penis, then a child by the father, the desire for a child being merely a substitute for the desire for a penis, and the attachment to the father merely a consequence of penis envy.

FEMALE SEXUALITY (1931)[9]

Chapter I
This work is mainly concerned with the importance of the *pre-Oedipal phase in girls*. The female Oedipal problem is dominated by the necessity for a *change of object* (when and why does she give up the fixation to her mother?) and a *change of organ* (how does she pass from the clitoris to the vagina?).

Preceding the father attachment there is a strong attachment to the mother. In many cases this continues beyond the age of four or five: "We had to give due weight to the possibility that a number of women remain arrested at the original mother-attachment and never properly achieve the change-over to men." The existence of the pre-Oedipal phase in women is much more important than Freud had supposed: "It seems that we shall have to retract the universality of the dictum that the Oedipus complex is the nucleus of neurosis . . . we can give due recognition to our new findings by saying that women reach the normal, positive Oedipus situation only after surmounting a first phase dominated by the negative complex." During the period of attachment to the mother (negative Oedipus complex) the father is a rival for the girl even though she is not as aggressive toward him as is the boy. There is no parallel between the female and the male Oedipus complex. The girl's primitive fixation to the mother is difficult to understand analytically, as it is an archaic, mysterious fixation, which seems to be inexorably repressed. This phase seems to provide the fixation point for female hysteria and paranoia in women.

Chapter II
Bisexuality is more obvious in woman than in man as the clitoris is the homologue of the male organ; the vagina is psychically inexistent until puberty, and has most probably no sensation. Female sexuality goes through two phases: a male one and a female one, a complication arising through the fact that the clitoris can continue to function actively during the woman's sexual life. Women, therefore, change their sex at the same time as they change their object. Freud decided not to use the term "Electra complex" (because the female and male Oedipus complexes are not analogous). *"It is only in male children that there occurs a fateful simultaneous conjunction of love for the one parent and hatred of the other as rival."* In boys the sight of the female genital is the basis of the castration complex and its consequences, the destruction of the Oedipus complex, the decathexis of the mother, the creation of the superego and "all the processes that culminate in enrolling the individual in civilized society." One residue of man's castration complex is his depreciation of women as castrated beings. The girl acknowledges her castration and man's superiority, but protests against this state of affairs. She has the choice between: giving up her sexuality, claiming a penis or accepting her femininity. The castration complex determines woman's social role.

The woman turns away from her mother for several reasons:

—she is jealous of those whom the mother loves;

—this relationship has no real aim and cannot be satisfactory;

—the mother forbids masturbation;

—at the time of the castration complex the girl despises the castrated mother and femininity in general;

—she reproaches her mother for not having given her a penis and for having seduced her.

The relation between daughter and mother is necessarily ambivalent whereas the boy is able to displace his hatred onto his father.

Chapter III
The little girl's sexual wishes toward her mother are active or passive, according to the libidinal phase. In all domains (including nonsexual ones) a sensation passively received leads to activity. The child tries to do actively what was done to him. The aim is to master the external world and may even lead to the repetition of painful experiences. Games are also used to master what was experienced passively by activity (the doctor-game). Here Freud identifies "activity-passivity" and "masculinity-femininity"; the child's first sexual experiences are of course passive, at the hands of his mother. Yet the child's libido soon expresses itself actively; thus "sucking" is substituted for "being suckled." The child tries to turn *the mother into an object,* while he becomes an active *subject.* "This last reaction which comes into play in the form of real activity, I long held to be incredible until experience removed all my doubts on the subject." It is as though the child says "now let's play that I am the mother and you are the child." But it is mostly in doll-play that these active tendencies can be observed. ". . . it is the *active* side of femininity which finds expression here. In games with dolls only the attachment to the mother is important; the father has no part.

The little girl experiences oral, sadistic, and phallic impulses toward her mother. Freud noted that women who were strongly attached to their mothers often mentioned the fits of rage associated with the administration of enemas by the mother. Freud believes, like Ruth Mack Brunswick, that these are the equivalent of orgasm. The passive desires of the phallic stage incite girls to accuse their mothers of seduction. In fact the mother first seduces the child by her physical care. The active impulses of the phallic stage are the same for girls and boys. The frustration of active tendencies helps to establish the primacy of the passive tendencies, but if they are too severely frustrated, the little girl's sexuality is more or less totally inhibited. One must not forget that there is only one libido whether its aims be active or passive.

Chapter I V
In this last chapter Freud discusses the theories of other psychoanalysts. He agrees with Abraham (1921) on the manifestations of the castration complex in women, but regrets that the exclusive attachment of the girl to her mother is not mentioned. He believes Jeanne Lampl de Groot (1927) had correctly observed the little girl's pre-Oedipal phase, but had not insisted enough on the hostile aspect of it. Helene Deutsch emphasized the hostility but was not able to free herself from the Oedipal schema and saw the girl's phallic activity as an identification with the father. He does not agree with Melanie Klein's (1928) concept of an early Oedipus complex but thinks there may be exceptional cases. Karen Horney (1926) held that the importance of penis envy was exaggerated; she believed it to be *secondary* and used to conceal feelings about the father. "This does not agree with the impressions I myself have formed," says Freud. "And if the defence against femininity is so vigorous, from what other source can it derive its strength than from that striving for masculinity which found its earliest expression in the child's penis envy and might well take its name from this?"

Jones (1927) thought that the female phallic stage was secondary, a reactive and not an authentic phase in development. "This does not correspond to either the dynamic or the chronological conditions."

The female Oedipus complex is not the homologue of the male Oedipus complex. The pre-Oedipal attachment to the mother plays an important part in the girl's development.

FEMININITY (1932)[10]

(in *New Introductory Lectures in Psychoanalysis*)

In this text Freud discusses the problem of bisexuality. Anatomically a person is neither totally male nor totally female. Only the sexual products sperm or ovum are unambiguous. Psychology has shown that "masculine" and "feminine" are names applied to behavior according to anatomy and convention. "Masculine" is thus often synonymous with "active," and "feminine" with "passive." Masculinity is aggressivity. But the habits of certain animals contradict this. "Even in the sphere of human sexual life you soon see how inadequate it is to make masculine behavior coincide with activity and feminine with passivity." Thus, in the mother-child relation the mother is the active element. To equate femininity with passivity and masculinity with activity is an error.

"One might consider characterizing femininity psychologically as giving preference to passive aims," but this is not the same as passivity. Indeed, sometimes a great deal of activity is needed to obtain certain passive aims. "But we must beware in this of underestimating the influence of social customs, which similarly force women into passive situations. All this is still far from being cleared up. . . ." "The suppression of women's aggressiveness which is prescribed for men constitutionally and imposed on them socially, favors the development of powerful masochistic impulses, which succeed, as we know, in binding erotically the destructive trends which have been diverted inwards. Thus masochism, as people say, is truly feminine."

The problem facing Freud is then: how does this bisexual person, the little girl, become a woman?

Even though the girl is less aggressive and more dependent than the boy, she goes through the first stages of her development in exactly the same way as he does. Thus during the anal-sadistic phase her aggressive impulses are just as violent as those of boys, as the analysis of children's games reveals. At the beginning of the phallic stage there is no difference between boys and girls: *"We are now obliged to recognize that the little girl is a little man."* (My italics.) At this stage masturbation is phallic for both sexes. The vagina does not exist for either sex.

Female masturbation therefore requires a change of erogenous zone, that is, from clitoris to vagina. This change of zone coincides with a change of object; the little girl gives up her early attachment to her mother and chooses her father.

Freud denies the instinctive character of attraction to the opposite sex: "We scarcely know whether we are to believe seriously in the power of which poets talk so much and with such enthusiasm but which cannot be further dissected analytically." Accordingly, the father is for the girl a rival at the beginning of her development; the fixation to the mother may extend beyond the age of four. The pre-Oedipal attachment to the mother is crucial for the little girl's development. She takes on the characteristics of the stages she goes through: oral, anal, phallic, active, passive. She is markedly ambivalent. The nature of her sexual desires toward her mother is difficult to define. At the phallic stage her desire is to make a child for the mother and to have a child by her. This is the fixation point for paranoia in women.

After the phallic stage the girl experiences intense hatred toward her mother and this induces the change of object. The leading and most typically feminine factor in this hatred is the *castration complex*. The little girl at the sight of male genital organs, source of her castration complex, reproaches the mother for not having given her a penis. Thus, penis envy arises and persists during the girl's entire life. One of the reasons for going into analysis is the desire to acquire a penis. The advantages a woman hopes for from analysis (like the possibility of exercising an intellectual profession) are often sublimated forms of this repressed desire.

Freud disagrees with the analysts who see penis envy as a *secondary formation. "The discovery that she is castrated"* is a crucial point in the girl's development, it leads her either into neurosis (with sexual inhibitions), or to character problems (masculinity complex), or to normal sexuality. It also influences her detachment from the mother because her love was directed to a phallic and not castrated mother. "As a result of the discovery of women's lack of a penis they are debased in value for girls just as they are for boys and later perhaps for men."

The discovery of her castration makes the little girl give up clitoral masturbation and therefore phallic activity. This leads her to passivity and toward a relationship with her father. At first the desire for the father is linked with penis envy, that is, with the desire to have the penis, but the normal Oedipus situation "is only established, however, if the wish for a penis is replaced by one for a baby . . . (which) . . . takes the place of a penis."

At the beginning the doll represents a possibility of identifying with the active mother and later represents the father's child. In adult life penis envy is fulfilled by the birth of a child, especially a male one. The Oedipus situation therefore is initiated by the castration complex, a "position of rest" for the little girl. "The castration complex prepares for the Oedipus complex instead of destroying it; the girl is driven out of her attachment to her mother through the influence of her envy for the penis and *she enters the Oedipus situation as though into a haven of refuge."* (My italics.)

But, according to Freud, the little girl whose castration is a fact, does not fear it, as does the boy for whom this fear is the main motive of the dissolution of his Oedipus complex. She remains for a long time, or maybe forever, fixated to the Oedipus situation and does not therefore have a *powerful and independent* superego.

Bisexuality attaches some women to their mothers; they become homosexual or alternate in character between masculinity and femininity. Nevertheless, the libido is always masculine because it is active even though it sometimes has passive aims. Frigidity seems to be a massive repression of the libido in the service of female functions.

Freud believes that many feminine characteristics are due to woman's "original sexual inferiority," her "genital deficiency" and the need to overcome these facts and to hide them. She is fully satisfied only when she has a son, thus compensating for her penis envy and her feeling of inferiority. Her married life follows the same pattern: "Even a marriage is not made secure until the wife has succeeded in making her husband her child as well. . . ." Freud ends his article by remarking that women in analysis show a special libidinal rigidity. "A man of about thirty strikes us as a youthful, somewhat unformed individual, whom we expect to make powerful use of the possibilities for development opened up to him by analysis. A woman of the same age, however, often frightens us by her psychic rigidity and unchangeability . . . . There are no paths open to further development, it is as though the whole process had already run its course and remains thenceforward insusceptible to influence—as though, indeed, the difficult development to femininity had exhausted the possibilities of the person concerned."

In his last article on femininity, Freud restates all his previous viewpoints on the psychosexual development of woman, and emphasizes even more strongly the important role played by the castration complex.

Psychoanalytical Views on Female Sexuality Similar to Those of Freud

J. LAMPL DE GROOT

THE EVOLUTION OF THE OEDIPUS COMPLEX IN WOMEN (1927)[11]

According to J. Lampl de Groot, until the phallic phase the little girl behaves physically exactly like the little boy. It is also assumed that children of both sexes follow the same psychic development.

The girl enters the Oedipus complex and the phallic stage, like the boy, taking the mother as the object of desire, and trying to eliminate the father, seen as a rival, in order to obtain exclusive possession of the mother.

The sight of the boy's penis gives rise at this stage to feelings of inferiority in the girl. She believes she once had a penis and that it was taken away because of her forbidden desires toward the mother. The castration complex has the same effect on her as it has on the boy, because not only does she feel narcissistically wounded by her physical inferiority, but also obliged to renounce any hope of fulfilling her desire for the mother. In both cases the castration complex ends by the dissolution of the Oedipus complex (negative for the girl); however, while castration is merely a threat for the boy, for the girl it is a fact.

The libidinal relation with the mother is replaced by an identification with her. She then turns to the father, previously a rival, and chooses him as her love object. Her aim is to replace the lost penis by a child from the father. The little girl's narcissism is healed because childbearing is exclusively a woman's privilege. At the same time clitoral masturbation as well as the active and conquering aspect of the libido are given up. Yet the negative complex in girls does not always have a normal dissolution. The little girl may remain attached to her mother and deny castration. If she is disappointed by the father, she may turn away from him and return to her previous position, to her masculine attitude. In extreme cases this leads to homosexuality, as Freud showed in his paper on "The Psychogenesis of a Case of Homosexuality in a Woman." [12]

In most cases "the little girl does not entirely deny the fact of castration," but tries to compensate for her bodily inferiority in a nonsexual field, by professional activity for example, in which she will be in competition with men. At the same time she gives up her sexuality. She may turn toward men but will remain frigid as the true object is still the mother.

J. Lampl de Groot agrees with Freud that the castration complex leads the girl to the Oedipus complex, but she believes that it is a secondary formation, as it follows the negative Oedipus complex, which is similar to the boy's in its origin (excitation of the clitoris), in its object (the mother), and in its aim (active, sexual).

This article by J. Lampl de Groot was published four years before Freud's article "Female Sexuality," and contains the elements of Freud's views on the girl's pre-Oedipal phase.

CONTRIBUTION TO THE PROBLEM OF
FEMININITY (1933)[13]

The main difference between men and women lies in the opposition
between activity and passivity: the person who attacks and conquers
the object is active, the one who gives himself to his partner is
passive. It is not only in the sexual field that one speaks of passivity
and activity. As Freud said, in every field of psychic life a child
tends to react actively to impressions received passively. In love relations there is the same opposition between "active" and "passive":
men love and women *let themselves be loved.*

Man normally overcomes his narcissistic wounds and his castration complex in order to succeed in his object relations. He uses
and sublimates his aggressiveness to win a woman. He subordinates
his passive tendencies to his active ones.

Women's sexuality normally requires passivity. Her aggressive
instincts are turned inward in a masochistic way; the sexual events
of a woman's life such as defloration or giving birth are usually
painful; Helene Deutsch said that the feminine *passive woman
shows little overt aggression.* Lampl de Groot repeats the point that
there is only one libido for both sexes and asks why women's attitudes are passive and men's active.

The little girl's early life is active like the boy's. Her object is
the mother and her attitude toward this object is as active as the
boy's. How does she come to give up this activity and what happens
then to these tendencies? She has actively loved her mother until
the age of five and even later. This changes around the age of six
when she enters the Oedipal phase and turns to her father; until
then her relation with the father has been no different from her
relation with other people in the house, sometimes friendly, sometimes not, according to her mood.

If her love shifts from the mother to the father this is due to
narcissistic disappointment (absence of penis), which leads her to
withdraw her libido from the maternal object. Thus, narcissistic retreat pushes her into the desire to be passively loved by the father.

The psychic difference between boys and girls begins only
when they discover the difference between the sexes. The little girl
is disappointed at not have a penis with which to possess the
mother; she has no libido left for her active tendencies; her aggressive expression is paralyzed, and partly internalized (the masochistic
fantasies and behavior studied by Helene Deutsch).

What relation is there between active and passive libidinal tendencies in the sexual and other fields? How does psychoanalysis explain the biological fact that male sexual life is fulfilled by active tendencies, the female one by passive tendencies? In everyday life we give the same meaning to active and passive behavior as we do in sexuality; a person is passive if he allows external impressions and excitations to act upon him, and he is active if he reacts to the external world by attempting to master or conquer it. The first sexual feelings are perceived *passively* by the child, who is responsive to agreeable sensations and tries to repeat them. The ego has a libidinal object-relation with the mother. The passive feelings therefore provoke active reactions, the object being cathected by the libido (which is active by definition) with the help of aggressive impulses.

The individual tends actively toward object-relations. In that case why are men more active than women? Man's sexuality is linked with the biological need to put a fertilizing sperm into the woman (activity) while she passively receives it.

"In the truly feminine woman's attitude towards men there is no room for activity." "Feminine love is passive and narcissistic." "The feminine woman does not love, she lets herself be loved." "Whenever she realizes object love, this is the result of her active libidinal components."

Thus, women who love men are masculine. Their maternal love is active also and therefore linked with masculinity. Women who work with children professionally find in this activity a masculine satisfaction. "Good mothers are frigid wives." A surplus of narcissistic libido is used for active aims and for object-libido.

The superego based on introjection is therefore linked to the first oral object-relation; the introjection of the object is an aggressive and active process, in which passive components play no part. In boys the dissolution of the Oedipus complex is linked with the aggressive introjection of the hated paternal object; the libidinal tendencies provide for a continuation of the loved or admired paternal imago in the form of the superego. As the mother is no longer a rival there is no reason to destroy her, in other words, *there is no need to introject her.* She will remain a tenderly loved object in the external world. As the creation of the superego requires active and aggressive instinctual components, *passive and purely feminine women have no superego.*

Femininity is identified entirely with passivity and masculinity with activity.

HELENE DEUTSCH

PSYCHOLOGY OF WOMEN IN RELATION TO
THE FUNCTIONS OF REPRODUCTION (1925)[14]

Helene Deutsch's theories are summed up in her book *The Psychology of Women*. The article under discussion forms the central part of this book.

H. Deutsch remarks that once the boy has reached the phallic stage, he has only to continue along these lines and to construct his Oedipus situation. The girl must, in addition, give up the masculinity linked to the clitoris and progress from the phallic to the vaginal stage, that is, she must discover a new genital organ.

According to H. Deutsch, "the man attains his final stage of development when he discovers the vagina in the world outside himself and takes possession of it sadistically." "The woman has to discover the new sexual organ *in her own person,* a discovery she makes through a masochistic submission to the penis, thus becoming also the guide to this new source of pleasure."

Helene Deutsch tries to understand how the little girl effects this change of erogenic zone. She believes heterosexual libido to have archaic oral roots. In her unconscious the little girl makes an association between breast and penis; this equivalence gives rise to the common oral theory of sexual intercourse at this stage (fellatio) and also to oral fantasies of pregnancy. In the following anal-sadistic phase the penis loses it oral quality in order to become the organ of mastery. Sexual relations are then conceived as sadistic. Either the little girl identifies with the active father, or masochistically with the mother.

The pregnancy fantasy at this stage is that of the "anal-child." The anus acquires a passive role similar to the mouth in the oral phase; breast, penis, and feces are given active roles. Thus, the way is prepared to a passive cathexis of the vagina. But female bisexuality is an obstacle to this development, and the clitoris keeps its libidinal cathexis; therefore the transition from "phallic" to "vaginal" (postambivalent) is a difficult one. The vagina has no erogenic role until the first sexual relations.

The little girl also cathects her whole body libidinally. From her body and in particular from her clitoris she progresses to the libidinal cathexis of the vagina. The penis provides this link which invests libido in the vagina, just as the mother's breast did in the child's mouth. Thus, the vagina takes over the role of the mouth in the passive-oral function of suckling. The activity of the clitoris is given up for that of the penis, and the woman (her vagina) becomes active by identification with the partner's penis. The vagina's orgastic activity is similar to that of the penis (secretion and contraction). As with men there is an "amphimixis" (Ferenczi) of the anal and urethral tendencies. The identification of the functions of vagina and penis allow *castration trauma* to be overcome, the penis being regarded as part of the woman's body. The feminine, passive attitude of the vagina is a repetition on a postambivalent level of the preambivalent oral phase in which subject and object were united. Vaginal coitus helps the woman to overcome the *traumatic separation due to weaning*.

In the sexual act women repeat the mother-child relationship; at the same time the partner is identified with the father, who in fantasy is incorporated and becomes the child in the womb. H. Deutsch discusses Ferenczi's theory that in coitus man fulfills his desire to return to the mother's womb and adds that woman, too, identifies with the child in her own womb. Childbirth represents for the woman the active mastery of the original trauma of birth. The vagina becomes the container not of the penis but of the child, and in the unconscious it represents the child itself. "A woman who succeeds in establishing this maternal function of the vagina by giving up the claim of the clitoris to represent the penis, has reached the goal of feminine development, she *has become a woman.*"

The function of the male is fulfilled by one event: the emission of sperm, whereas that of the female proceeds in two stages. According to Helene Deutsch "the act of parturition contains the acme of sexual pleasure." She also believes that the pleasure felt during intercourse is due to the fact that intercourse is a prelude to parturition. Parturition is itself "an orgy of masochistic pleasure."

In fact the sexual act is not completed until parturition, which then becomes an erotic gratification similar to the moment when in masculine coitus body and seed separate. The child in the womb represents a part of the woman's ego and also *the incarnation of the paternal ego-ideal.* In this process the libido is desexualized and the child initiates a sublimatory process in the mother. Whereas man creates sublimations in social and intellectual fields, for the woman the child is in itself a sublimation. Although the child in the mother's womb is a part of her ego, he is also an object and therefore doubly cathected, first in a narcissistic and then in a conflictual way. Suckling restores the union broken at birth and represents a sexual act in which the breast is equivalent to the penis. Suckling is for the mother another way of overcoming *the trauma of weaning.*

All inherently feminine activity according to the author helps woman to overcome a series of traumata. She concludes: "But for the bisexual disposition of the human being, which is so problematic for the woman, but for the clitoris with its masculine strivings, how simple and clear would be her way to an untroubled mastery of existence."

The prototype of female genitality is orality, the mouth being the prototype of the vagina. Yet the vagina is not known until coitus (the penis functioning as guide). Sexuality and reproduction are inseparably linked in woman; they allow her to overcome a series of traumata. The clitoris plays a purely inhibitory role; it is a superfluous organ.

THE SIGNIFICANCE OF MASOCHISM IN THE MENTAL LIFE OF WOMEN (1930)[15]

"My aim in this paper is different: I want to examine the genesis of 'femininity,' by which I mean the feminine, passive-masochistic disposition in the mental life of women." Helene Deutsch seeks some solution to the problem of frigidity. She agrees with Freud's views about the castration complex at the age of four, about the necessity or decathecting the clitoris, and with the fact that children are unaware of the existence of the vagina until puberty. Like Freud she believes that the little girl gives up her penis envy for the desire to have a child by the father. This constitutes her Oedipus complex; but she goes on to question what happens to the active erotic component cathected in the clitoris. She thinks that the erotic active-sadistic instincts are transformed into masochistic ones, the narcissistic-masculine desire to have a penis is substituted by the desire to be castrated by the father, and fantasied as rape. A woman's life is therefore dominated by a *masochistic triad: castration = rape = parturition.* It corresponds with a definite developmental phase and is linked to the castration complex. Frigidity is due to masochistic tendencies. Consequent fears for the ego may then strengthen female narcissism. The identification with the father may represent a retreat in the face of the danger contained in a masochistic identification with the mother. The choice of an object may also be due to repressed masochistic tendencies. In certain cases sexual satisfaction being subordinated to irreducible masochistic fixations, an analysis must, according to the author, encourage the patient to give up sexual gratification and allow her to follow a "masculine" path. Patients whose feelings of inferiority are linked with penis envy are helped in analysis by converting this envy into the desire for a child.

Frigid patients have few neurotic symptoms, and the woman who comes into analysis at her husband's request (as he feels narcissistically concerned by his wife's frigidity) presents few conditions which could make the analysis succeed, her masochism having once and for all eliminated sexual satisfaction. Masochism can also be found in the relation of mother to child (of which the mater dolorosa is the epitome).

Female sexuality is closely connected with reproduction, as the woman sees the child in her father or her sexual partner. The little girl becomes (potentially) mother and woman when her masochistic tendencies appear; she wishes to be castrated and raped and to have a child by her father.

According to the author some women never experience orgasm during intercourse yet have a perfectly healthy psychic life. They maintain good relations to family and friends, and during sexual relations are happy to be the source of pleasure for their partner. They believe that intercourse is only important to men: "In it, as in other relations, the woman finds happiness in tender, maternal giving. . . . This type of woman is dying out and the modern woman seems to be neurotic when she is frigid." This change is attributed to an increase in masculine tendencies.

Helene Deutsch believes woman's masochism serves the preservation of the species and regards this as a sublimation in itself. She concludes by saying: "Woman would never have tolerated throughout history to be kept by social ordinances from the possibility of sublimation on the one hand, and from sexual gratifications on the other, if she had not found in the reproductive function magnificent gratification for both these urges."

Female masochism is due to the diverting of active instincts originally cathected in the clitoris. This opens the path to femininity but can also be the origin of frigidity, because it gives rise to fears for the ego's integrity.

SUMMARY OF SYMPOSIUM ON FRIGIDITY:
CHAIRMAN—*Helene Deutsch (New York, December, 1960).*

(H. Deutsch's discussion is reported by Dr. Burnes Moore in the *Journal of the American Psychoanalytic Association.*[16]

Helene Deutsch gives an account of her experience and further reflections since *The Psychology of Women* published in 1944.[17] "She was shocked by the high incidence of so-called frigidity in women and disappointed in the results of psychoanalytic treatment. Cases of very severe neurotic illness had been helped without eliminating this problem. She saw psychotic women and aggressive masculine women who experienced intense vaginal orgasm, while loving, giving, maternal, and happy women did not, even though they felt fully gratified."

"Intercourse and motherhood mobilize a struggle between the narcissistic elements of self-preservation and the object-directed demands of reproduction which constitute a danger for the security and solidity of the ego." "Helene Deutsch questioned whether the vagina was really created by nature for the sexual function we assume and demand for it. . . ." "The transition of sexual feeling from the clitoris to the vagina is a task performed largely by the active intervention of the man's sexual organ." "She was ready to reverse the burning question 'Why are women frigid?' to 'Why and how are some women endowed with vaginal orgasm?'" "The typical function of the vagina during intercourse is passive-receptive. Its movements have the character of sucking in a relaxing rhythm adjusted to that of the male partner."

"In the vast majority of women, if they are not disturbed, the sexual act does not culminate in a sphincter-like activity of the vagina, but is brought to a happy end in a mild, slow relaxation." She says that this is the most typical and the most feminine of female orgasms. . . . "Postcoital dreams observed in analysis often reveal anxiety after vaginal orgasm. In contrast to this phenomenon the gratification reached in a passive-receptive sucking function of the vagina usually brings a peaceful sleep typical for an adequate sexual release."

"If the more passive-receptive way of gratification for women is accepted as normal, Helene Deutsch believes that frigidity is not so common as assumed, nor is it on the increase. What has increased are the demands for a form of sexual gratification not fully in harmony with the constitutional purpose of the vagina. . . . Such sexual ambition may inhibit the normal function of the vagina."

Orgasm belongs to the male: A truly feminine woman has no orgastic climax. The vagina is the organ of reproduction; the clitoris is the organ of pleasure.

RUTH MACK BRUNSWICK

THE PRE-OEDIPAL PHASE OF THE LIBIDO
DEVELOPMENT (1940)[18]

I. *The Oedipus complex and the pre-Oedipal phase*
"Under Oedipus complex we understand not only the positive attachment of the child to the parent of the opposite sex, but above all the situation of the *triangle*." For both sexes the pre-Oedipal phase is the one in which the child is attached to his mother while the father is not yet a rival (dual relation).

In boys the pre-Oedipal phase is short. The attachment to the mother is made in an Oedipal mode, with the father as a rival. With the development of the castration complex the Oedipus complex is destroyed.

In girls the pre-Oedipal phase becomes an attachment to the mother, with the father as a rival, exactly as with boys. But the discovery of castration leads the little girl toward a passive positive Oedipus complex; she turns to her father and her mother becomes a rival.

"At the beginning of her life the little girl is to all intents and purposes a little boy. Her relation to her first love object, the mother, is precisely that of the boy, with similarly conflicting passive and active libidinal strivings. . . . Once she has attained the Oedipus complex (positive phase), the normal woman tends to remain with it. . . . The resistance of the female Oedipus complex to the powers of destruction accounts for the differences in structure of the male and female super-ego." The woman has two objects and two sexual organs, whereas the boy has to change his attitude only toward his mother. He must give up passivity in order to become active.

A child does not recognize sexual differences among people he knows. "Until approximately three years of age, the pregenital zones outweigh the genital in importance."

II. *The three antithetical pairs*
Childhood is dominated by two antithetical qualities: "active-passive" and "phallic-castrated." Adolescence is concerned with one antithesis only: "masculinity-femininity."

"Active-passive." In the beginning the child is passive. The development of activity is based on an identification with the active mother. Finally, the child plays the role of the mother toward himself, as well as toward the people he knows, and even to his own mother. The active-passive phase is prephallic; the child believes other people to be of the same sex that he is. The genital zones do not play a very important part. At this stage the mother's role is not feminine but active.

"Phallic-castrated." The little boy discovers the girl's castration. At the outset he still thinks that the mother is phallic. "With the final recognition of the mother's castration and the possibility of his own at the hands of the father, the Oedipus complex of the little boy is destroyed." The normal child gives up his attachment to the mother and thus avoids castration. The neurotic child does not manage to give up the attachment; or he may accept the fantasy of castration by the father, giving it a libidinal meaning and taking the father as a love object (the passive or negative Oedipus position).

In the "active-passive" antithesis, the child at the beginning of his life was passive toward his active mother. Normally, activity should prevail over passivity. "Whether the passivity remains, is given up, or is converted we do not know." Activity is much greater in boys than in girls. Identifying with the active mother is the most primitive form of identification. *As the child identifies increasingly with the mother's activity, he is able to do without her and thus becomes independent of her.* Activity won over from the mother is jealously defended. The mother's unwarranted interference provokes aggression. "Until her subsequent depreciation because of her castration, she is not only active, phallic but *omnipotent.*"

Ruth Mack Brunswick then outlines Freud's theory of the phallic phase in both sexes, of the castration complex, and its consequences for the dissolution of the Oedipus complex, the formation of the superego and of sublimation in boys, "aided undoubtedly by a mildly contemptuous attitude towards the castrated sex."

As for the girl, the discovery of the mother's castration puts an end to her hope of acquiring a penis. She then turns to her father, transferring her passive tendencies to him and identifying herself with the castrated mother. "The active strivings are sublimated at this time and only much later find their real scope in the relation of the woman to her own child, in her final and complete identification with the active mother." The *"masculine-feminine"* antithesis only appears at puberty, and "in the boy, the flood of masculine libido brings with it for the first time the desire to penetrate the newly discovered vagina."

III. *The pre-Oedipal period*
Ruth Mack Brunswick outlines her concept of the phallic mother: "Whereas both the active and the castrated mother exist in point of fact, the phallic mother is pure fantasy." This fantasy arises when the child is no longer certain about the mother's phallus. It is therefore by nature compensatory. But "we shall continue to use the 'phallic mother' . . . because . . . the term is one which best designates the all-powerful mother, the mother who is capable of everything and who possesses every valuable attribute."

Infantile masturbation is initiated by the mother's bodily care of her child. Even at the beginning of the phallic stage, the child wants his mother to touch his genital organs. Later, he will want to touch and see his mother's genital. The primal scene whether it be really observed or only a fantasy plays an important role in masturbation. The child's interest in the parents' intercourse is awakened at the same time as the Oedipus complex. But one must remember that at this stage there is no sexual difference between the parents. The fantasy of the primal scene may be oral, anal, or phallic. In the latter instance, the need for penetration does not exist, since the vagina is not known and the child imagines reciprocal "touching" between the parents.

IV. *The development of a wish for a baby and the wish for a penis*
The wish for a child, "contrary to our earlier ideas," precedes by far the wish for a penis. For both sexes this represents the desire to possess the attributes of the omnipotent mother, that is, above all, a baby.

Penis envy has both an *object-oriented cause* and a narcissistic one, since the little girl desires to have a penis not only for herself but also because she wants to possess the mother. She gives up her attachment to her mother when she realizes that without a penis she cannot make her pregnant.

V. *The girl's phallic masturbation*
"One of the greatest differences between the sexes is the enormous extent to which infantile sexuality is repressed in the girl." For

Freud, the repression of masturbation in girls is linked to the narcissistic wound of castration. But it is reasonable to assume that if the discovery of the mother's castration evokes "a normal contempt" in boys, it arouses something different in the girl: she cannot despise somebody who is like herself, but she abandons the attachment to her mother and the phallic masturbation connected with it. Apparently, there is an early sensitivity in the vagina which is of anal origin.

VI. *The break with the mother*
The discovery of the mother's castration amounts to a trauma for the little girl and awakens her hostility towards the mother whom she reproaches for having made her without a penis. In the face of this castration the boy conceives of the normal contempt for mother and for all women.

The girl turns to her father, and "making a virtue out of necessity," she awaits an erotized castration from him.

VII. *Pre-Oedipal influence upon later femininity*
The author believes that there are many women who *do not have a normal Oedipus complex.* They come to women analysts because they are incapable of any contact with men. Most women remain partly fixated to their mothers.

VIII. *The Pre-Oedipal phase of the male*
The pre-Oedipal phase is for the male shorter and less dramatic than for the female. The boy may have a passive attachment to his father, analogous to the girl's positive Oedipus complex, thus forming *"the typical masculine neurosis."* The main reason for this relation with the father is a "nucleus of passivity" the importance of which is due to constitutional factors. *Too much aggression toward the mother,* due to external factors as well as constitutional ones, reinforces the attachment to the father.

The inability to accept the mother's castration can lead to a homosexual object-choice. It can also create an identification with the castrated mother and at the same time a passive attitude toward the father. Such people have difficulty integrating their passivity, and this may lead to grave problems (paranoia, neurosis).

This article was written in collaboration with Freud. Yet one sees in it certain divergences from Freud's views:

The desire for a child precedes penis envy. It is related to the omnipotent mother. Penis envy also has object-oriented roots in the

little girl's attachment to her mother. The boy's pre-Oedipal rela-
tion to his mother may be strongly aggressive.

MARIE BONAPARTE

FEMALE SEXUALITY (1951)[19]

Marie Bonaparte proposes to study in this work the frequent failure
of erotic function in women. If her views on psychosexual development are similiar to those of Freud, she nevertheless has her own
views of femininity.

She stresses the importance of the *biological* origins of wom-
en's sexual problems—in particular the question of constitutional
bisexuality. For her, as for Freud and others whose views are most
like his, woman's "masculinity complex" is primary. It is based on
the anatomical existence of a mutilated organ, the clitoris. Following Maranon's theory, Marie Bonaparte holds that woman can be
considered as a man whose development is unfinished. The existence of the clitoris is most important for woman's future psychosexual development: Her greatest difficulties are due to the fact that
she has to give up the eroticism linked to this organ: "The clitoris,
woman's little phallus, must follow the fate of those temporary organs which, like the thymus, after having played their role for a
transitory moment, are destined to disappear." The girl must accomplish the work of *"mourning"* her clitoris. Yet, unlike Freud,
Bonaparte believes that the little girl has very early, a psychical
model of what will later become vaginal eroticism. She believes that
at the anal stage the girl passively cathects the *cloaca,* that is the vagina and the anus coenesthetically combined. The vagina does not
have a function until puberty but passive cloacal eroticism is the
prototype thereof. The girl, like the boy, is passive at the beginning
of life. She awaits satisfaction from her mother, be it clitoral or
cloacal. The clitoris is primarily passively cathected. Clitoral eroticism soon changes direction and the little girl's attachment to her
mother becomes active and penetration-oriented (negative Oedipus
complex). But this phase soon gives way to the *castration complex*.
This in turn initiates a second passive cloacal phase toward the
father with the exclusion of the clitoris; this is the positive Oedipus
complex. Finally, at puberty the vagina is cathected erotically instead of the cloaca. In order to reach the genital stage women must

overcome three obstacles. According to the author *women have less libido than men.* Yet the more complex development of women requires considerable libidinal expenditure. Therefore, women are easily blocked in their psychosexual development because of libidinal deficiency. Also woman's reproductive functions form a psychobiological nucleus, her care-taking role extending from the fetal stage to the postnatal life of her child, and finally to her whole family, thus marking her behavior and her libido with relative "dynamic inertia."

The libidinal deficiency of women can be defined as *"the typically feminine condition of female frigidity."* Their strong bisexuality makes it difficult for them to adapt to vaginal passivity and this leads to *"the typically masculine condition of female frigidity."*

Marie Bonaparte tries to examine in detail the facts and the consequences of bisexuality. The vaginal function with its *"concave"* eroticism comes into being due to "essential feminine masochism" which makes it possible to overcome the obstacles put up by the "convex" eroticism of the clitoris. Passivity must prevail over activity and over the sadism connected with the phallic clitoris. "The male must resist against passivity and masochism in general, which his biological constitution does not impose, whereas woman must accept them." Marie Bonaparte examines one interpretation of the fantasy discussed by Freud in "A child is being beaten": in the little girl's unconscious the beaten child represents her clitoris beaten by the father's penis. This is an important stage toward mature femininity: the clitoris returns to the phase of *passive* erotization but has changed its object. Then the fantasy expresses the desire to be castrated by the father, castration being at this stage eroticized. According to Marie Bonaparte erotic function and reproduction are both linked in woman to deep fears concerning the preservation of the body, meaning its narcissistic cathexis. The conversion of the active-sadistic components into passive-masochistic ones is the only factor which allows libidinal desires to prevail over the fear of "biological infringements" by creating a receptive attitude toward the "continual laceration of sexual intercourse." The author claims that women are less aggressive than men, but they also have greater difficulty in separating their aggressive from their libidinal impulses. The boy, because of his completely different Oedipus complex, directs most of his aggression toward his father, and his love toward his mother. His parricidal wishes are finally turned back upon himself, and after they have been internalized they form the superego. The process is different for the little girl because her active negative Oedipus complex lasts a very short time, so that her aggressive instincts do not attach themselves to the mother. The aggressive and libidinal instincts continue to be combined and during the establishment of the positive Oedipus complex are directed toward the same object, namely, the father. As aggression is an obstacle to the "concave" eroticization of the vagina, it has to be turned against the self and eroticized in a masochistic way. The libidinal development of women therefore follows three rules:

—an object-oriented rule: the equivalence of mother-father; the first passive impulses are the ones which later determine the feminine attitude toward the father.

—an instinctual rule: the equivalence of sadism-masochism.

—a zonal rule: the equivalence of clitoris-vagina.

These three rules determine the movement *from "convex" male eroticism to "concave" female eroticism.* In relation to the problem of bisexuality Marie Bonaparte also studies the custom of excising the clitoris in certain cultures. Her prognosis concerning vaginal frigidity in "clitoral women" is pessimistic.

Constitutional female bisexuality is the main obstacle to the development of normal sexuality.

———

Psychoanalytical Views on Female Sexuality; Opposed to Those of Freud

JOSINE MÜLLER

THE PROBLEM OF THE LIBIDINAL DEVELOPMENT OF THE GENITAL PHASE IN GIRLS (1925) (published in 1932) [20]

Josine Müller believes that the vagina is cathected very early in life and that it is the most important erogenous zone for the little girl. This is particularly true for women who become frigid or who give considerable importance to the clitoris or who suffer from a strong castration complex. Müller's observations of children as a general practitioner led her to the conviction that there are early sensations in the vagina and that these are linked to masturbation. She thinks this early cathexis is repressed and reinvested in the clitoris. Self-esteem is connected with the gratification of one's sexual impulses.

After the vaginal instinctual cathexes have been repressed, a narcissistic wound results which then nurtures and aggravates penis envy. Women who can libidinally cathect their vaginas have greater self-esteem and their penis envy tends to disappear.

The vagina is the first sexual organ to be libidinally cathected. The cathexis of the clitoris is secondary and defensive. Penis envy is linked to a narcissistic wound resulting from a lack of gratification of the repressed genital instincts.

K A R E N   H O R N E Y

T H E   D R E A D   O F   W O M E N   (1 9 3 2)[21]

Karen Horney considers a number of myths and legends which express fear and horror of women: the Lorelei, sirens, witches. . . . These fears are also found in symbols such as water, the ocean, etc., and in various taboos. Horney thinks that Freud's understanding of the taboo of virginity (as an answer to woman's unconscious desire to castrate man) is incomplete. Men's fears about women have deeper roots. The mother was the first object of the little boy's aggressive wishes. Her prohibitions and her role as an educator make it necessary for her to dominate and frustrate him. Also the little boy, whose phallic impulses make him want to penetrate something hollow, guesses (consciously, preconsciously, or unconsciously) that his object, the mother, has an organ complementary to his own. Yet he is humiliated at being small, impotent, and weak in comparison with her, and thus incapable of penetrating her. Therefore, he feels narcissistically wounded and this provokes strong feelings of inferiority and violently aggressive desires for revenge; at the same time he projects his hostility on the mother and therefore her vagina frightens him. At this point he decathects the vagina, making a phallic-narcissistic retreat and even represses the knowledge he has of the vagina's existence.

Phallic organization with exclusion of the vagina is, however, *secondary.* To compensate for his early feelings of failure with regard to his mother and to deny his fear, man will attempt the following solutions: he will idealize his object, try to depreciate it, or triumph over many women, or avoid all contact with them (choice of a homosexual object), or again may despise the female sex in general.

The so-called nonawareness of the vagina is linked to the fear of the mother because of projected aggressive wishes and of the narcissistic wound inherent in Oedipal wishes.

The phallic narcissistic phase is a secondary occurrence.

THE DENIAL OF THE VAGINA (1933) [22]

In this article Karen Horney presents her ideas, this time not from the masculine but from the feminine point of view. She tries to explain woman's fears connected with her own sexual organ.

Discussing Freud's theory of the phallic stage, she makes the following points: Even a normal woman would have to overcome masculine tendencies at each stage of her life (menstruation, sexual relations, pregnancy, parturition, menopause) if Freud's ideas are correct. Female homosexuality would be much more frequent than male homosexuality. Regression to female homosexuality would occur easily. Even maternity would be resented according to Freud, as *ersatz*, and not as an instinctual achievement. Woman's entire life would be marked by resentment.

But in fact, the female child is a woman from the start, and not only from puberty, as Freud thought. Also, corresponding to girl's penis envy, the boy expresses a desire to be able to have children and to possess other female attributes. These wishes do not exclude an attitude conforming to the child's own sex. Should one then consider them to be instinctual? One must distinguish between wishes expressed at an early stage in a playful fashion, and similar desires which manifest themselves in the latency period.

As for the belief that the vagina does not exist until puberty, the author, like Josine Müller, has had pediatric confirmation that vaginal masturbation is frequent in little girls and begins at a very early age. The supposed unawareness of the vagina must be doubted as much as pretended unawareness of the clitoris. One must remember that women who come to analysis have good reasons for not remembering their vaginal sensations. Masturbation fantasies and the dreams of little girls show that they have an intuitive knowledge of their vaginas.

As for frigidity, the question is not how the change from clitoral excitation to vaginal excitation is made but rather why the vaginal excitations have become repressed. The answer is to be found in the existence of castration wishes toward the father, linked with Oedipal frustration and fear of revenge.

These fears are similar to the boy's, but there are other fears which are more specifically feminine, for example, fear caused by the disproportion between the father's big penis and the girl's small genital. The boy is frightened of looking ridiculous in front of the mother with his tiny penis; the girl is frightened of being destroyed in Oedipal sexual congress. Menstruation, defloration, parturition, abortion reinforce the girl's bodily fears. The girl cannot reassure herself that her fears are unfounded, because her genital is invisible. For the little girl as for the little boy *"the undiscovered vagina is a vagina denied."*

The girl fears above all injuries inside her body. She re-presses her vaginal impulses and transfers them to her external sex-ual organ, the clitoris, for the purpose of defense.

M E L A N I E   K L E I N

P S Y C H O A N A L Y S I S   O F   C H I L D R E N   (1 9 3 2)[23]

The ideas summarized here are found in chapter XI of Melanie Klein's *The Psychoanalysis of Children,* entitled "The Effects of Early Anxiety Situations on the Sexual Development of the Girl." This chapter is itself a synthesis of her own ideas on the female sex-ual development, drawn by her from several previous articles. She bases her study on the problem of the *female equivalent of castra-tion-anxiety.*

In a 1928 article on "Early Stages of the Oedipus Conflict" [24] she had already described the girl's anxiety situation. The girl mainly fears attack to the inside of her body. After the first frustra-tions of the oral phase the little girl turns away from the breast and seeks satisfaction from the paternal penis by incorporating it orally; at the same time genital impulses toward the paternal penis also come into play. *The passage from the cathexis of the frustrating breast to that of the penis represents the nucleus of early Oedipal conflict.* But the father's penis is seen as belonging to the mother, who keeps it inside her body. The little girl wishes therefore to at-tack her mother sadistically in order to steal from her the object she desires for herself. She fears that the retributions of the mother will destroy her own internal organs.

According to Freud the castration complex leads the girl to hate her mother for not having given her a penis. Melanie Klein be-lieves the little girl hates her mother for the same reasons, but whereas *Freud thought the girl wanted a penis for herself* (her aim being a narcissistic one), Klein believes that she desires the penis *libidinally: "She is brought under the sway of her Oedipal impulses not indirectly, through her masculine tendencies and her penis-envy, but directly, as a result of her dominant feminine instinctual components."* (My italics.) Melanie Klein here agrees with Karen Horney. *The oral desire for the paternal penis becomes the prototype of the genital, vaginal desire for the penis.* The penis thus coveted is invested with magical qualities and is thought to be capable of satisfying all the impulses aroused by maternal oral frustration. But the penis can also be the object of intense aggression because of the frustration it causes the little girl, and this aggression, projected onto the penis, renders it dangerous, as it then becomes cruel and threatening. *The introjection of this penis forms the nucleus of the paternal superego (in both sexes)*; the sadism linked with this phase makes this early superego a terrifying one.

The little girl because of her receptive female instinctual impulses tends to incorporate and keep the father's penis, that is, the Oedipal object. Through submission to the introjected father the girl's superego becomes still more powerful and therefore *stronger and more severe* than that of the boy.

Her ambivalence toward the introjected penis might lead the girl, and later the woman, to have many sexual experiences (in reality or in fantasy), in order to introject the "good" penis and to fight the "bad" introjected penis. Sexual intercourse is then used to ward off anxiety. It can also function as a means of "testing" people. Indeed, because of her sadistic impulses the girl is afraid of being destroyed; she fears "aphanisis" (Jones). Intercourse can reassure her (as well as the birth of a healthy child, and the possibility of breast-feeding him with good milk). Female object-choice depends on how the infantile fears are structured. She may choose a "good" penis to mitigate her bodily fears. In this case the pleasure she gets from sexual intercourse is more than mere libidinal satisfaction, since it also diminishes her anxiety, thus "laying the foundations for lasting and satisfactory love relationships." [25]

If the internalized penis is too "bad," the woman may seek out in reality a sadistic penis to destroy her bad introjects. For Melanie Klein *female masochism* is woman's sadism turned not against herself but against *her bad internalized objects.* This need to put reality to a test may lead some women toward compulsive sexual activity. But an incapacity on the part of the ego to overcome the anxiety can lead to frigidity. Fears for the ego can be such that both the external penis and the internalized one are feared and all the destructive component instincts are at once mobilized. The little girl's attacks against her mother's body produce strong guilt feelings which lead her to make *acts of reparation* which become the *roots of sublimation* in women. She is also trying to escape retaliation. Because the little girl fears that her attacks against the inside of her mother's body will revert to herself she cannot, like the little boy, realize that her anxieties are unfounded. She does not possess a visible genital. The vagina is "repressed" in favor of the clitoris, or the vagina is invested with all fears concerning the inside of her body. Yet all girls have an early and at least unconscious knowledge of the vagina. The clitoris, as an external organ, profits from this "repression" but is immediately cathected in a feminine way; the fantasies which accompany clitoral masturbation show a desire to incorporate the paternal penis and also stimulate vaginal sensations. *The castration complex and penis envy* therefore have two main reasons: first, the little girl wants to have an organ which she can test in reality. Second, the dissatisfaction linked to her wish to incorporate the paternal penis forces her to make a sadistic identification with the paternal phallus in order to destroy the frustrating mother, the breast she refuses to give her, and the paternal penis which she keeps for herself. This period is often accompanied by enuresis (drowning and poisoning the mother's body by means of a sadistic penis). This forms the aggressive homosexual side of the girl's identification, but paternal identification can also have the aim of repairing the damage caused to the mother and of replacing the penis she has stolen from her. These positions may be decisive in the girl's sexual development. The girl's position with regard to her objects and the receptive function of the female genital organ (hence the great importance of oral impulses) cause the introjection of the superego to be so important in the little girl's development. The absence of an active penis only accentuates her submission to the superego. The boy cathects his own penis with narcissistic omnipotence, while the girl does the same with the introjected paternal penis. Feminine dependence on external as well as on internal objects leads her to be in intense fear of her superego. The little girl has to face more obstacles than the little boy in forming a superego through introjection of the parent of the same sex. "It is difficult for her to identify herself with her mother on the basis of an anatomical resemblance . . . because internal organs . . . do not admit of any investigation or reality testing." But one must not forget that the little girl's relation with her father and with her superego depends on her primal relation with her mother (with the maternal imago).

The little girl's Oedipus complex begins very early. It is established at the oral phase by a displacement from the mother's breast to the father's penis (desire for the penis). Fears about the inside of her body will lead her to fear her own femininity (penis envy). Penis envy is secondary. Oral and vaginal feminine receptivity are primary. The female superego is more severe than the male superego.

ERNEST JONES

THE EARLY DEVELOPMENT OF FEMALE
SEXUALITY (1927)[26]

Jones emphasizes the prejudices of analysts about female sexuality: men tend to have "phallo-centric" views and to underestimate the importance of female sex organs, while women tend to express an unconcealed preference for the male organ. Analysis should be able to throw some light on the reason for this prejudice.

Jones bases this article on the analyses of five cases of homosexuality in women. He tries to find answers to the following questions:

1. What in women corresponds to men's fear of castration?

2. What difference is there between the development of a homosexual woman and that of a heterosexual woman?

Both these questions are centered in the significance of the penis. Jones notes that women tend to project fears into the future which are more frightening than those of men. How can one explain this if they have already accepted castration as a fact? Jones thinks that the fear of losing the penis is certainly important, but it does not imply that sexuality will come to an end; thus some men wish to be castrated for erotic reasons. In fact, the fear of castration in both sexes conceals the fear of a total and definitive destruction of sexual desire, or "aphanisis"; the idea of losing the penis is only one expression of this fundamental fear. The fear of aphanisis manifests itself differently in each sex. Thus, women depend more, for physiological reasons, on men for their sexual satisfaction than men depend on women. Women more often fear aphanisis in the form of *separation-anxiety*, whence they derive the fear of being abandoned.

Jones believes that one can discover the genesis of the superego more readily in women than in men, that is, the *link between "lack" and "guilt."* The child, according to Jones, creates his superego in order to project onto the external world the reason of his own deficiency. Deficiency or frustration alone is sufficient to give rise to guilt and to the formation of the superego, with the aim of sparing the child the stress of deficiency and of frustration. In short the *superego attacks in particular those desires which are not destined to be gratified.*

Referring to the stages of the girl's development, Jones agrees with Melanie Klein that there is direct transition from orality to the Oedipus complex. The little girl passes from her oral relation with the breast to a fantasied oral relation with the penis (fellatio fantasies) and to clitoral masturbation for autoerotic substitute satisfaction. Normal development toward heterosexuality requires the sadistic phase to develop later, lest the sadistic cathexis of the clitoris lead to masculine penetration desires of a violent kind or to fellatio fantasies tinged with strong oral castration-aggression.

Jones agrees with Freud that the cathexis of the oral erogenous zone is displaced to the anal orifice. At this stage close and complex links are established between *anal and vaginal cathexes,* the details of which arc still obscure. *This phase is sadistic but clearly also Oedipal.* At this stage of "mouth-anus-vagina," the little girl identifies with her mother. At first the oral relation with the penis is totally positive. But soon penis envy appears. Jones agrees with Karen Horney's ideas on the autoerotic motivation behind this wish, connected as it is with scopophilic, urinary, exhibitionistic, and masturbatory activities. He insists, like Melanie Klein, Karen Horney, and Helene Deutsch, that one must distinguish between the pre-Oedipal autoerotic penis envy and the Oedipal and erotic version (we might say, between envy and desire), the latter representing the wish to share possession of the penis during oral, anal, or vaginal coitus. Jones thinks that penis envy (that is, envy for a penis of her own), is merely a regressive defense in the face of the wish for the penis during intercourse with the Oedipal father. Oedipal disappointment may revive regressively the little girl's desire to have a penis of her own. Guilt and the establishment of the superego are the first and most important defenses against the unbearable Oedipal frustration which produces the fear of aphanisis. At this stage the little girl must either change her object or her desire. Either she must give up her father or her vagina (including its pregenital representations). In the first case she may find a happy solution to her femininity on an adult level which includes the vagina in her sexuality, her libidinal interest being displaced from the father to other men. In the second case she remains tied to her father by identifying with him (penis complex).

The situation is the same for the boy who has to give up either his penis or his incestuous desires. *It is the nongratification of Oedipal wishes associated with the threat of aphanisis which starts this process in both sexes.*

Homosexual women are divided into two groups, those who still are interested in men but would like to be considered as one of them, and those who are not interested in men but in women—women representing the femininity they themselves have not been able to enjoy directly. One can say that women of the first group have chosen to give up their sex but to keep the object. In this case the woman has identified with her father and desires to be loved by the father in this fashion by making him acknowledge her virility. The woman of the second group has given up the father as an object after having identified with him. But in reality her external object-relation to a woman is simply based on the fact that her partner represents her projected femininity which is satisfied by the internal object (the incorporated father, object of her identification). In the second case, the woman denies her desire for a penis as she attempts to prove that she does possess one.

Jones believes that Freud's description of a phallic stage identical for boys and girls who are both unaware of the vagina is nothing but this defense of homosexual women in an attenuated form, and, like it, essentially a *secondary* phenomenon. That this defense assumes such importance as to lead to homosexuality may result from particularly intense sadism at the oral stage.

1. *The most fundamental fear for both sexes, more than fear of castration, is the complete loss of sexuality (aphanisis). The non-fulfillment of Oedipal wishes is sufficient to produce that fear. Guilt and the superego are more of an internal defense against it than formations of external origin.*

2. *The phallic phase in girls is most probably a secondary defensive construction, rather than a true stage in their development.*

THE PHALLIC PHASE (1932)[27]

Jones points out the important theoretical differences in psychoanalytic writings during the last ten years concerning male as well as female sexuality. These divergencies, however, are concealed by the authors' wish to stress the points they have in common. Jones proposes to examine these differences in detail and therefore pivots his study on the phallic phase.

He recalls his article of 1927 in which he suggested that the phallic phase in women was *defensive* and *secondary*. ("Last year Professor Freud declared this suggestion quite untenable.") Already in 1927 Jones thought that the phallic phase in boys did not represent a natural stage in development. He refers to Karen Horney's description of its defensive character in boys ("The Dread of Women").

Jones does not doubt that there is a developmental phase in which the opposites "phallic-castrated" are essential, but he questions the interpretation of this. He divides the phallic phase as described by Freud into two other phases: the "proto-phallic," which is characterized by the theory of the monistic quality of the genital organ, thereby excluding the vagina. The little boy thinks that everyone has a penis, and the little girl that everyone has a clitoris. This belief causes no conflict at this stage. In a second, or "deutero-phallic" phase, boy and girl both believe that the world is divided not into "female" and "male," but into "phallic" and "castrated." This phase is accompanied by anxiety and conflicts in both sexes. The passage from one phase to the other is linked to the fear of castration which, according to Freud, is mobilized by the sight of the genital organs of the opposite sex.

For the boy the deutero-phallic phase is characterized by an overestimation of his penis; it is also linked to a partial withdrawal from object-relations to a more narcissistic relationship. This seems to indicate that what is happening here is a flight and not a normal phase of development. When the phallic phase persists into adulthood this is even more obvious. In adults it is associated with deep anxiety. In adults as in the little boy in the deutero-phallic stage, all interest is focused on the penis, with doubts of its size and quality and with exaggerated narcissistic compensations. At this stage the little boy is not interested in the opposite sex; all his sexual curiosity is expressed in comparing himself with other boys. The time when all the individual's attention is narcissistically absorbed by his penis is also the time when the desire for penetration (main function of the penis) does not exist. It is obvious that this desire would lead to the search for its complement, an organ to penetrate. Jones does not believe that this is a deficiency due to ignorance of the vagina; early child analyses show that the little boy has active and sadistic wishes and fantasies about penetration and expresses them clearly in his play. Jones here agrees with Karen Horney that the undiscovered vagina is a vagina denied; in fact the child has an un-conscious knowledge of the vagina and this "non-awareness" has something to do with the so-called "innocence" of young women.

Freud talks about the "horror" (*Abscheu*) that boys feel at the sight of the female genital. This horror would not arise if the fear of castration had not already been in existence for a long time. According to Jones the little boy sees in the so-called "castration" of woman what will happen to him if he continues to have feminine desires. Two infantile fantasies are combined here: in coitus one of the partners is castrated. Feminine desires lead not only to castra-tion of the penis but also create a wound (infantile theory of the vulva); according to the author this link between coitus and castra-tion is established by the boy's feminine wishes toward his father. The "horror" of the female genitals must be understood as horror of the "site where these desires are satisfied." By feminine wishes Jones means the destructive oral (biting fantasy) or anal (castra-tion of the father's penis during homosexual relations) incorpora-tive impulses. The idea that these wishes can be satisfied in the mother's vagina is in accord with the infantile conception—discov-ered by Melanie Klein—that the mother has incorporated the fa-ther's penis during intercourse.

Entering the mother's vagina means encountering the fa-ther's penis which has become threatening because of the projection of the boy's sadistic feminine wishes onto it ("feminine wishes" in this context refers to the desire to incorporate the father's penis with the aim of castration). These feminine wishes are linked with Oedipal rivalry: the boy in the Oedipal situation wants to castrate his father, and the fear of castration derives from this wish. Thus, vaginal penetration is linked with the destruction of the father's penis, and by projection or retribution, with the destruction of his own penis. Here again the fantasy of coitus equals castration.

The sight of the female genital has no direct effect upon the boy's castration complex. He does not think—even though he may rationalize his fear—that women have been castrated and therefore that an analogous future awaits him, but he thinks that his Oedipal wish to have a sexual relation with his mother and to destroy and remove the father's penis might be fulfilled. This desire is linked with the fear of retribution, and it is this fear which leads him into the deutero-phallic phase. Once again it is the Oedipus com-plex, Jones states, which gives us the key to the problem of the phallic phase.

Jones recalls that in the Freudian conception of the Oedipus complex and of the castration complex, the boy gives up his Oedipal wishes in order to save his penis. However, if the penis is involved in these wishes, as Freud claims, it surely is so with regard to its own indigenous function, that of *penetration*.

The phallic phase is, therefore, according to Jones, not a normal phase in the boy's development but a *neurotic compromise.*

As far as the girl is concerned, Jones points out once again the two opposing views about femininity and describes them briefly: the first one assumes that the girl is a little boy, prompted into femininity by the blocking of her masculinity. The second view sees the little girl as feminine from the start, as if she had been prompted into a defensive masculine attitude by the blocking of her feminine wishes.

Jones refers to Freud's criticism of Karen Horney, according to whom the girl in fear of her own femininity *regresses* to the phallic phase. Jones emphasizes that Freud uses the term *regression* here because of his conviction of the identity between clitoris and penis. But if one does not believe that penis and clitoris are identical—which is precisely Karen Horney's point—this is not a regression but a new neurotic structure. In Jones's view this cannot be established just because they are analogous in the physiological sense. *"After all,"* he says, *"the clitoris is a part of the female sexual organ."*

Clitoral masturbation can be accompanied by entirely feminine fantasies. Clinical experiences show that contrary to Freud's belief vaginal desires exist at a very early stage, and lead to much stronger anxieties than does the clitoris. Apart from these wishes directly linked to the vagina, early fantasies about all the *body orifices* are frequent and take on a typically feminine *receptive* form.

Jones thinks that the Freudian theory of a pre-Oedipal phase with an exclusive pre-Oedipal attachment, girl to the mother, even though clinically observable, does not explain the girl's early unconscious fantasies about the father and, from the beginning on, about his phallus. He mentions an idea which Freud had communicated to him personally: the first sexual theory of little girls is an oral one (fellatio). Here Jones agrees with Freud but tries to draw further consequences from this idea: first he states that this "oral" theory cannot be far away in time from the oral stage of which one has every reason to believe that the theory is a part. This would lead us to place feminine receptive wish at an early stage in the little girl's development. Jones thinks, like Melanie Klein, that the girl, disappointed by the breast, imagines an object more satisfying and "penis-like." This fantasy would become the starting point of her attachment to her father.

According to Freud the child's disappointment is due to the fact that his desires have no aim, but one could also claim quite to the contrary that the child has definite aims and that his disappointment is due to the fact that he cannot fulfill them.

In little girls these aims are very similar to those of adult women: that is, the desire to have a child is primary and object-related. *The little girl desires above all to incorporate the penis and make a child of it; this is not a substitute for the impossible desire to have a penis* for purely narcissistic reasons.

According to Jones the Oedipus complex begins when the little girl realizes that what she desires (the father's penis) belongs to her mother, who then becomes her rival. He firmly disagrees with Freud's "grave" assertion that "it is only in the male children that there occurs the fateful conjunction of love for the one parent and hatred of the other as a rival." He finds himself obliged to be *"plus royaliste que le Roi."* Jones agrees with Melanie Klein that the girl's phallic desires are associated with sadistic wishes toward the mother's body and that she fears the mother's vengeance against the inside of her own body. He mentions the frequent anxieties in women of internal illnesses (for example, cancer of the uterus). The little girl's masculine deutero-phallic attitude is, in fact, a defense against the fears connected with her Oedipal feminine wishes. The little girl, like the little boy, is afraid of being mutilated by the parent of the same sex. Thus, Jones also answers Freud's argument about the source of energy behind the masculine tendencies.

Jones concludes by suggesting that the phallic phase is a neurotic compromise between libido and anxiety rather than a true phase in the child's development. As the libidinal gratification is preserved and remains *conscious* it would even merit the name of *phallic perversion.* He ends his discourse by rendering homage to Freud for his discovery of the Oedipus complex: "I can find no reason to doubt that for girls, no less than for boys, the Oedipus situation, in reality and fantasy, is the most fateful psychic event in life . . . 'In the beginning . . . male and female created He them.' "

Freud's phallic phase is not a normal developmental phase for either sex; it is a neurotic compromise. In the case of both sexes it is related to guilty and dangerous Oedipal wishes. Both boy and girl want to castrate the parent of the same sex; the boy wants to remove the father's penis from the mother's vagina and the girl wants to steal the father's penis from the mother. Both fear castration for that reason (external castration for the boy, internal for the girl). Both sexes have a positive Oedipus complex.

EARLY FEMALE SEXUALITY (1935) [28]

"This lecture is intended to be the first of a series of exchange lectures between Vienna and London which your Vice-President, Dr. Federn, has proposed for a special purpose. For some years now it has been apparent that many analysts in London do not see eye to eye with their colleagues in Vienna on a number of important topics: among these I might instance the early development of sexuality, especially in the female. . . ." "That I should have selected the present theme to discuss with you is natural. Already at the Innsbruck Congress eight years ago I supported a view of female sexual development that did not altogether coincide with the one generally accepted, and at the Wiesbaden Congress three years ago I amplified my conclusions and also extended them to the problems of male development. Put colloquially, my essential point was that there is more femininity in the young girl than analysts generally admit, and that the masculine phase through which she may pass is more complex in its motivation than is commonly thought; this phase seemed to me a reaction to her dread of femininity as well as something primary. . . ."

Jones summarizes the main points of discussion: Innate *bisexuality* seems probable, but it is difficult to prove and *in any case it must not be brought up as an argument each time one runs into clinical difficulties.*

We agree that the mother plays a preponderant role in the child's life at least during the first year. Freud said of this period that "everything connected with this first mother-attachment has in analysis seemed to me so elusive, lost in a past so dim and shadowy, so hard to resuscitate, that it seemed as if it had undergone some specially inexorable repression." Analyses carried out in London (Melanie Klein) with very young children give us precise information about this stage of development in girls. Divergences in opinion are probably due to different assumptions about this early stage.

Contrary to Freud, *Jones believes that the little girl is from the start more feminine than masculine and more concerned with the inside of the body than the outside.* At this stage her mother represents for her not a woman she thinks of as a man, but a source of objects she needs, and wishes to appropriate for herself. The frustration at the breast and the search for a "penis-like" object which would be more satisfying, occur very early and are found again later in the disappointment with the clitoris and the penis envy that follows it.

The search for a penis following frustration at the breast does not yet mean love for the father; it is a relation to the part-object (penis) which is still concerned with the mother. *In the second half of the first year the father's personality plays an increasingly important part.* A true feminine love for him begins to appear, along with rivalry toward the mother. *In the second year one can already talk of an Oedipus complex.* It differs from the later Oedipus complex (the one of which Freud speaks) inasmuch as it is even more completely repressed and concerns the fantasy of the "combined parent."

The "sadistic-oral" and "sadistic-anal" stages which find expression in fantasied attacks upon the mother's body are extremely violent in girls, and the resultant anxiety is greater than it is in boys, since the girl fears *revenge against the inside of her body;* she has no external organ on which she might displace her fears. Also she cannot, like the boy, displace her sadism onto the father. "In a word the girl has for these reasons less opportunity to externalize her sadism."

The disagreements between the London and Vienna schools regarding later stages in development follow from these divergent opinions about the earlier stages. Everyone agrees on the importance of the oral state and on the fact that it is the prototype of femininity, even though agreement on this last point is not complete. Helene Deutsch has shown the oral nature of vaginal function. *"One can at all events hardly sustain any longer the view that the relevance of the vagina does not develop before puberty."*

Vaginal anaesthesia and cases of dyspareunia in adults, according to Jones, confirm the psychological existence of the vagina before puberty since they demonstrate an erotic *counter-cathexis,* and one cannot fight against something which is not yet in existence.

The clitoris-penis question: This is the point of greatest theoretical divergence. One side (the Viennese group) claims that the girl hates her mother because she has not given her a penis; the other side suggests that the girl wants a penis because she can thus better express her hatred toward her mother. The Viennese viewpoint is that she turns to her father because she is disappointed by her clitoris (the castration complex leads her to the Oedipus complex); the London group says that she wants a penis because of the obstacles she encounters in her love for her father. The fact that so many girls admit openly that they would like to be boys should not disguise that they are at the same time coquettish, play with dolls, etc., in short, that they are truly feminine.

The little girl's penis envy is related to her sadism toward the mother through the sadistic representation that micturition can take on in the unconscious (urethral sadism). Also, the boy can check at every moment on the appropriateness of his castration fears, whereas the girl cannot verify the integrity of her internal organs.

Jones answers Freud's objection that penis envy in women and the whole phallic phase cannot be a secondary formation since its energy would have to derive from fundamental, primary needs. He thinks with Melanie Klein that the girl's repression of her femininity is related to her hatred and fear of the mother. The girl's primary penis envy is actually the feminine desire to incorporate the father's penis, first orally, then through the vagina. The desire for a child is merely the desire to incorporate the penis and make a child of it. *The desire to have a child is not, as Freud maintained, a compensation for the lack of penis, but a basically feminine wish.* Although he considers the phallic phase to be a defensive formation, Jones is not optimistic about its dissolution, as its defensive function may prolong it interminably.

Jones and the London group think that the phallic phase is a defense against an Oedipus complex already existing, so that their views about its dissolution differ from Freud's. It is achieved:

1. When a fantasy is given up because it is exposed to reality-testing.

2. When the ego grows stronger, less defense is required with the lessening of anxiety.

3. When other defenses take over.

The little girl's resentment of the mother is not only due to the fact that she did not give her a penis, but also because she has kept the father's penis for herself. The sight of the penis is not a decisive traumatic event but the last link in a long chain of events; Jones does not believe "that if *the little girl had not experienced this trauma she would have remained masculine";* he does not accept Freud's theory that it is this experience which leads the little girl to femininity. "In short, I do not see a woman . . . as *un homme manqué."*

"I think the Viennese would reproach us for making too much of early fantasy life at the expense of external reality. And we should answer that there is not danger of any analysts neglecting external reality, whereas it is always possible for them to disregard Freud's doctrine of the importance of psychical reality."

In this article Jones discusses his views and those of the English school, comparing them with Freud's views and those of the Vienna school.

Freud's clinical articles based on female cases would give further information to those who wish to follow his thought in greater detail. The discovery of the dynamic unconscious arose chiefly through clinical experience with women. (Freud and Breuer, "Studies on Hysteria," "Dora," "A Case of Paranoia Running Counter to the Psychoanalytical Theory of the Disease". . .). His paper on "The Psychogenesis of a Case of Homosexuality in a Woman" provides an interesting exposition of the two aspects of the Oedipus complex in women, according to Freud's conception. "A Child Is Being Beaten" [29] and "The Economic Problem of Masochism" [30] throw light on Freud's ideas concerning female masochistic attitudes.

To this list should be added his 1927 article on "Fetichism" [31] and his paper "On the Transformation of Instincts as Exemplified in Anal Erotism," [32] in which Freud studies the symbolic chain "penis-child-feces"; similarly, "Analysis, Terminable and Interminable" in which the difficulties encountered in the interpretation of penis envy are discussed.

One should also include studies such as Abraham's "Manifestations of the Female Castration Complex" (1921),[33] and the papers of Carl Müller Brunschwig, Annie Reich, and Hans Sachs on female superego formation, the numerous studies of Phillis Greenacre on femininity, and all psychoanalytical studies on masochism, which form a useful basis for reflection on female problems.

The authors of this book will refer in the course of their papers to all of these works. In this Introduction our aim has been restricted to an exploration of the different theoretical approaches to woman's psychosexual development in the hope that this might provide a background against which the reader may consider the ideas of the contributors to this volume.

A Masculine Mythology of Femininity

Christian David

ô surprise fatale!
La Femme au corps divin, promettant le bonheur,
Par le haut se termine en monstre bicéphale!

—BAUDELAIRE

Thanks to Freud's discovery of infantile sexuality and the continuity between the normal and the pathological, it has become possible to derive a concrete and rigorous psychological study of sexuality from individual prehistory.

Has sexuality freed itself from this prehistory, preserved as it is by universal repression, secular prejudices, and the irreducible distortions of fantasy? I do not think so, and the hesitations, the disagreements, and the contradictions even within the most authentically psychoanalytic thought provide the evidence.

Perhaps the particular problems which female sexuality presents us will emphasize these residual difficulties. The reader may already have realized this from the general introduction to this book. One can even say, without being paradoxical, that many analytical conceptions of femininity are themselves the stronghold of fantasies and the last refuge of prejudices. Is it the same in treatment? To a lesser degree, yes: there is general agreement that ideological differences subside in clinical practice, yet one cannot deny the influence of a priori assumptions, nor the unfortunate consequences they have at times. There are few domains in which failure due to countertransference is so difficult to acknowledge or its repercussions so difficult to prevent.

There is nothing very surprising about this for sexual life is deeply rooted in the unconscious. Freud himself, in spite of the admirable achievement of his self-analysis and his personal liberation, was not exempt from prejudices or emotional reactions. At the source of the aforementioned dissensions stands Freud himself, inas-

47

much as his personality and his clinical experience determined the adoption of certain (frequently prejudiced) positions to be found in work on female psychology.

Didactic analysis, even if carried out according to accepted standards has failed to prevent psychoanalysts from making mistakes because these preconceived notions are not easily eradicated and the distortions of one's own unconscious are difficult to grasp and deal with.

If the desire to know and the spirit of discovery have their origins in infantile sexual curiosity, then all research, all reflection on sexuality would appear to involve looking back into the sources of knowledge. If, on the other hand, as Freud claims, concern over sexual difference (even more than perplexity as to the origin of children) and castration-anxiety concur to structure one's sexuality and one's total personality, then research into female sexuality is of great importance, since the female sex constitutes the *primum movens* of infantile sexual anxiety for the girl as well as for the boy. Femininity, experienced as a deficiency, an absence, a near-proof of castration, is subject to questioning much more than masculinity. The female sex is the essential enigma, only to a slightly lesser degree for the girl than for the boy. This is so not only during childhood, as is attested by all the ignorance, misapprehensions, and mistakes of so many women about their own sex and the functioning of their own genitals. The male sex also creates a certain mystery around itself, but this mystery exists for both the boy and the girl in the same way, at least until the latency period. A little boy may wonder how his penis can—or one day could—relate to the feminine sex. Whether he scotomizes the phenomenon of erection or is incapable of establishing the link between erection and the girl's sex organ, he will in any event be confronted by his own sex, by the idea of the sexual act, as though faced with indecipherable signs. In the beginning each sex is a worrisome enigma for its individual members as well as for the opposite sex. Later, certainly, the vivid experience of one's own sexual individuality will, bit by bit and in conjunction with the opposite sex, throw light on the mystery for both sexes. But if a certain amazement at man's sexual functions still exists for woman, there is an even more noticeable reaction the other way round. In fact, the dark mystery surrounding the female sex for a child is rarely completely dispelled—of course this is true not of rational understanding or scientific knowledge, but only of affective and deeply instinctual experience.

Thus, among others, there is a popular convention of mysterious "femininity," the "typically feminine" tag, a luxuriant and complex mythology continually woven around woman and her sexuality. In fact, these limits to our knowledge of the other sex (limits perhaps related to experiences of the ineffable, the impossibility of communication, whose emotional significance is well known) correlate to limits in our acknowledgment of certain sexual states in the other sex but which are also present in our own sex. Not only do boys and girls ignore their own sexuality as well as the other person's, but adult men and women also persist in not recognizing what is common to both. One might add that they ignore their bisexuality, or, if they acknowledge it, they frequently do so only in the pathological area of perversion.

Even if, at first, it seems incongruous, it may well be fruitful to approach some problems of femininity through certain observations about masculinity drawn from psychoanalytical clinical experience. Of course, one could also argue the other way around, but that would make less sense because the ideas we commonly have of sexuality in general, and female sexuality in particular, derive essentially from conceptions of male sexuality.

Furthermore, it is important to look beyond sociocultural and anthropological considerations into the nature of fundamental human bisexuality and to clarify it. This does not mean though that one should continually have recourse to bisexuality as if to a *deus ex machina* every time one comes up against theoretical or clinical difficulties.

Probably because of its existence as a psychic fact, the reality of a true sexual intersubjectivity imposes itself, so that we cannot, even according to a strictly analytical view, postulate a true autistic sexuality. There is, I believe, a possibility of communicating and even exchanging experiences, particularly sexual experiences, that enables us to understand what is unknown to us, and to share what, in the face of our differences, we thought we were excluded from. . . . But the fact is, such illumination is obscured, the prospect of communion jeopardized. Yet this failure can be attributed for the most part to the luxuriant mythology which prevents the sexes from knowing and encountering each other, especially as these fallacious images of sexuality, rooted as they are in the collective unconscious and not simply in the individual unconscious, are found secretly preserved in certain social institutions.

The dominant aspect of sexual mythology concerning women is the image of woman as a deficient man. Its importance lies in the direct repercussion it has on feminine mentality. The idealization of women, equally common and often representing a conception complementary to the preceding one, is a reaction formation due to the misapprehension of women as a castrated gender. Neurosis is always accompanied by sexual problems. Even if they appear to be absent at first they will show up in the long run. Similarly, I would argue that there are few ideas in a man's mind designed to demean woman or to idealize her which are not linked to overt or covert neurotic problems.

A phenomenological description of such ideas would be endless. One has only to think of certain significant masculine reactions to a woman's figure, her sexual organs, menstruation, defloration, childbirth, breast-feeding, and even the menopause. One person might express fear and disgust at the idea of vaginal penetration during menstruation, or regard the clitoris as a ridiculous substitute, or the rupture of the hymen as ending a purity preserved until then, or feel embarrassed in the presence of a pregnant woman, or be strangely disturbed by the prospect, and then the experience, of childbirth, or lose erotic interest in his own wife once she becomes a mother, or consider the menopause (more or less consciously) the end of all real feminine life. Another person—and in some respects it could be the same one—might idealize woman's body and glorify pregnancy and maternity in general. Yet another might be able to appreciate women only when they are clothed and only according to their degree of "sophistication," these artifices giving him some protection against his anxieties.

So far I have referred only to masculine reactions immediately linked to the structure and function of woman's sexuality. Reactions to feminine personality in general are similar. We find more or less the same subjective patterns (with the same mainly defensive but at any rate unconscious features), built upon distrust and contempt or, conversely, an illusory exaltation.

More than being the vicissitudes of a poorly resolved Oedipal conflict, I tend to believe that the persistence of an archaic oral relation, strongly marked by an ambivalence in which libidinal and aggressive features are intimately entwined, is responsible for the distorted conception of woman and her sexuality, of what she *is* and what she is *supposed to be*. This persistence of misconception looks like revenge for the radical narcissistic wounds inflicted by the mother and follows from the situation of the baby at the breast for both boys and girls. Is this revenge not the source of the "racial" discrimination which so many show toward women (a certain primitive tribe refers to women as "the race which is not entitled to speak"), as well as the root of the masochistic attitude many women have toward men?

This is not to say that the obverse is the truth—the "natural superiority of women," as some people hold. An unbiased approach to both the common and the distinguishing psychosexual character-istics of both sexes seems preferable. The differences may be smaller than one is inclined to think, but they certainly exist and one has reason, therefore, to find out what true femininity is. What, in fact, is the most satisfactory mode of sexual functioning for a particular woman, irrespective of all prejudice about its worth and away from the sterile opposition between masculine and feminine militants? However, once the relativity of notions like virility, femininity, ac-tivity, and passivity is accepted, we can more easily clarify the deter-minants of preconceived notions about feminine sexuality. Only after the main prejudices are noted and set aside can we proceed to study the subject directly and independently—as J. Chasseguet rightly proposes—and not, as is so frequently the case, on the basis of, and in response to, masculine sexuality.

This is a basic condition for correctly understanding femi-ninity. There is no doubt that the pervasive influence of masculine myths has been an obstacle to this endeavor. If their influence per-sists I would suggest that the men who created these myths either managed to make women accept them or believed they were right in considering the protestations of some women as exceptions.

In this study I wish to draw attention to the difficulties en-countered on the borders of such researches on femininity but I do not propose to investigate the subject itself. At the risk of adopting a very narrow purview, marked by relatively unusual conditions, I would like to examine a case of phobia, with numerous perverse manifestations. At the beginning of his analysis this patient held a conscious and an unconscious representation (one might say, mythology) of femininity, strongly marked by his own bisexual ten-dencies. By this I mean an attitude toward women and a passivity in sexual behavior, both significant in themselves. They gained more significance as their meaning within a hysteric structure, with its phobic and perverse symptomatology, became clearer during treat-ment, which eventually led to broad and significant changes. (Be-cause of the strong link between this patient's sexual mythology and his other problems, it is difficult to separate the investigations with which this book is more explicitly concerned from material irrele-vant to its purpose.)

Phobic problems brought Philip into analysis. In fact, he had suffered from them for many years, but they became aggravated after repatriation and the difficulties caused by subsequent changes in his way of life; so much so that eventually he sought medical help. He was first sent to a psychiatrist who started face-to-face treatment and adopted a hyperactive, directive approach; the patient terminated treatment after a few weeks. He was so anxious that he immediately consulted someone else, and this time he was sent to me.

Philip is in his forties, tall, stout, rosy-cheeked, with a round, puffy face, shifty yet inquisitive, piercing and apprehensive blue eyes, shielded by tiny, gold-rimmed glasses. His speech is rapid, even hasty, marked from time to time by a high pitch in a relatively deep voice. His facial movements are expressive and varied, his gestures frequent and demonstrative.

He explains his symptoms, history, and present situation, describing his personality, his family, friends, and acquaintances without my having to prompt him. When I speak he butts in, not out of aggression but urged more by a feverishness which does not conceal his timidity. He seems afraid of me and tries to control and avoid his apprehensive reaction to our encounter; his overtalkativeness, nevertheless, does not hide his desire to avoid and conceal his fears. This behavior is surprising in view of the fact that it is combined with exhibitionism and a strikingly theatrical pose. He sighs, utters exclamations and onomatopoetic words, coughs loudly, wriggles, and fidgets, while at other times he pretends to be well controlled.

In recalling from time to time his past and present somatic complaints (both varied and benign) he supports his explanations with evocative gestures. With an evident complacency, and with no embarrassment or modesty, he spontaneously begins to talk about his concern over some features of his sexual life—and he continued to do so throughout the analysis. Superficial anxiety mingles from the beginning with a strange kind of gloating. In short, this patently hysteric patient affords us a glimpse of a more complex personality than a superficial appraisal of his condition would have suggested.

Philip's reason for coming to analysis, about which he knew almost nothing, lay in the realization that his scope of activity was rapidly diminishing and that his anxiety occurred with increasing intensity and frequency. During the past fourteen years, complicated and perverted compromises in his sexual life apparently afforded him an unstable but sufficiently workable balance in association with phobic restrictions and a deceptive and erratic use of medication.

Only when he had to adapt to a new, more restrictive and more demanding style of existence involving him in new relationships which aroused anxiety, did a sudden breakdown occur leading him to seek help. This confirms the notion of the functional efficacy of perverse organization and behavior and illustrates the ignorance or at least indifference of perverts regarding their distorted beliefs and the consequent anomalies and restrictions of their lives.

When Philip felt a serious need for treatment he simultaneously felt an uneasiness, never experienced before, concerning the significance and value of his relations with other people. He often asked me if other people thought and acted as he did, if he was not abnormal, even monstrous. This uneasiness was obviously due to his sexual behavior and beliefs, rather than to his anxieties. In short, it is only with the intensification of neurotic suffering that a perverse attitude can be "objectivated," really questioned, so that displaced impulses and obliterated needs, having been stifled for years, can again demand attention. The smug complacency of prejudices about female sexuality seems to me to bear comparison with the blindness of certain perverts, or with the narrow-mindedness typical of some character neurotics.

Philip has a panic fear of going out alone and makes his wife escort him everywhere. Whenever, by chance, they take an unusual route, her protection is not enough and he feels overwhelmed by anxiety. In order to prevent this he repeats to himself, "I shall get over it, I shall get over it," even though this intolerable situation seems to last forever. Sometimes he wrings his hands and moans, "Mummy! Mummy!"

During analysis it appeared that his need for an auxiliary ego was linked with the need to be simultaneously protected and supervised by a maternal figure. This restraint is both hated and sought after. "I shall get over it" refers to an unconscious fantasy of the primal scene. The anxiety attack, strongly eroticized, was in effect the phobic echo of long-buried feelings of identification with the passive parent. He calls for his mother to stop the unbearable specter of intercourse as well as his own guilty participation in it.

Several years ago, when his symptoms were more sporadic and less intense, he experienced a period of depersonalization which was particularly stark and painful.

On boarding his daily train, he suddenly felt that his usual seat near the doorway was on the left instead of the right. Consequently, he immediately lost the notion of where the front and the back of the train were. This disorientation aroused such confusion in him that for a moment he felt like getting off the train and giving up his trip for that day.

This episode of depersonalization, brought about by a subjective impression of a change in the spatial orientation seems to me linked to the presence of an unconscious sexual fantasy. He realizes that the penis is neither where he thought it was nor where he had believed it was in his fantasies. The front is then confused with the back.

Frequently, in order to combat his anxiety, for example before going to sleep, Philip created the following fantasy: a woman who is not his wife comes toward him and he finds himself next to her. He stands close behind her and then penetrates her anally, a practice unknown to him in reality. He feels completely protected and his erection never fails. He becomes one with his partner. It is as though they had only one head, two arms and "nothing in front." He would like to pass into the woman by penetrating her all the way up to her shoulders. Unable to achieve that, he contents himself with a substitute for the fusion; arms and legs are bound tightly by thin strings. His partner is wearing panties, stockings, garters, and high-heeled shoes. She controls the whole situation. She goes off when it pleases her and in whatever direction she wishes. When he experiences this close union, he wants to become entirely female, but at the same time keep his penis safely inside the woman's body. This is the astonishing solution, almost hermaphroditic, to his castration anxiety.

His fears not only have to do with space but also with his body. Since his earliest youth he has been concerned over the slightest disturbance affecting his body. Any pain, however insignificant, any *malaise,* however fleeting, precipitates a spate of hypochondriacal fantasies. If he has hemorroids he immediately sees himself the victim of rectal cancer; a feeling of heaviness in the lower abdomen immediately becomes cancer of the testicles. He has only to hear of a disease to experience its symptoms shortly afterward.

I have outlined Philip's varied symptomatology without yet describing his perverse tendencies and his peculiar sexual mythology. They are closely allied and need to be considered as a unit throughout his treatment. The patient married when young and virginal and had fathered three children. In twenty years of domesticity this man from a strict moral and religious background had penetrated his wife only on rare occasions. Although penetration was not especially difficult for him and gave him no conscious anxiety, his conscious sexual fantasies led him in another direction. In his wife he had been able to find a partner who, by her extreme passivity or by complementary reactions, or both, always had complied with his requirements. These consisted essentially in persuading her to play an active and sometimes sadistic role in their sexual relations. Indeed, he could achieve real pleasure only under these conditions. During sex he insisted that his wife "possess" him by her sitting on his chest, with her back towards him and buttocks resting on his face, and then masturbate him, while he imagined (with many variations) that he was at the "mercy" of a mysterious, unknown beauty imperious and cruel and much older than himself. It did not matter to him whether his wife had any "physical" pleasure or not in this relationship, for she seemed to join in willingly and spontaneously, without complaining, and even seemed happy about it; consciously, this brought him supreme pleasure, but at a deeper level it reduced him to impotence.

He had never been unfaithful to her, not even during long periods of separation, ostensibly keeping a tacit pact between them, but in reality fearful at a preconscious level of not being able to re-create his sexual arrangements with another woman. Nevertheless, his erotic life was not limited to this sado-masochistic relationship with his wife: he had always needed to masturbate in front of photographs or illustrated magazines (chosen carefully, but always improved on by his imagination). The pictures sometimes showed particularly beautiful, "sophisticated," cold women who were not completely nude or, if nude, with the *mons pubis* hidden or without pubic hair; preferably wearing either panties or "tights" which would outline the figure and emphasize "the lack of continuity" at the base of the abdomen. At other times, the pictures were of heterosexual scenes with the woman playing a role, sadistic, directly, and manifestly. In early adolescence to increase the physical excitement of his fantasies, he had adopted the habit of hanging in midair from his suspenders while masturbating, finding particular pleasure in the sensation of clothes cutting into his flesh. At the same time he had the fantasy of being violently subdued and "crushed" by a ruthless beauty; of a torture scene disguised as a surgical operation —complete castration coincided with his orgasm.

Because these masochistic fantasies did not exhaust his sexual tension, he took delight in dressing up whenever possible in women's underwear and masturbating in front of a mirror while trying to hide his genitals by wedging the penis between his legs.

His desire to be a woman was strong and conscious. It seemed wonderful to have "nothing between the legs," to be dressed in little nylon panties fitting closely over his buttocks and, at the same time, revealing no protuberance in front. Ballerinas in tights were his favorite image of female perfection. This also contributed to his fetishistic love of high-heeled shoes, panties, stockings, and women's girdles (as long as they were light and did not remind him of the long corsets his mother used to wear). "Aren't all men like me, and don't they all wish to be like women?" he would ask in his early sessions.

The desire to be a woman, common in boys, but usually denied, can be understood in several ways. It is a compensation for "feminine castration," a replacement of the desire to possess the mother, as well as a wish to participate in women's power to attract admiration and courtship and in their ability to bear children.

In sharp contrast to these erotic needs and the explicit (and, above all, implicit) representation of the female sex and the femininity underlying it, was Philip's desire to be virile in every other respect. He manifested a vigorous and unceasing virility which one could almost call a "masculine protest." This behavior was most obvious in his home, where he could not tolerate the slightest questioning of his authority from his wife (jokingly referred to as "the half portion") or from his children. He exploded in anger if he had to wait, and one day even smashed open a wardrobe in a fit of anger caused by a brief delay. He also showed considerable intolerance when his pride was hurt, as frequently happened in his civil service office when lower-ranking colleagues overlooked his prerogatives or encroached on his fields of responsibility. He projected the maternal image onto anyone who attempted to restrain or belittle him, reacting violently, for example, by writing notes "in strong terms" in order to set things right with his superiors. He nearly always succeeded in obtaining compensation for the infringement of his rights or his offended dignity.

He was adaptable, diplomatic, and sociable in everyday life, as long as nothing gave him the feeling of being ignored or disparaged. In social gatherings he would go to some pains to get the attention of the group for himself, exerting his charms, and making everyone laugh; he was at his best when circumstances allowed him to display his amateur talents. Nothing provided him with greater joy than the applause he would receive after his interpretations of "L'Air de la calomnie" or "Toréador prends garde!" in which he displayed his full vocal range before a gathering who had begun by laughing, then became intrigued by the spectacle, and finally succumbed to his charm. According to him, this should have been his vocation: to appear in front of an audience, beguiling it in such a way as to dominate it.

Jealous as he is by nature, Philip cannot bear the favors lavished upon singers, actors, artists, and political figures when their true worth or talents do not justify them. Hypocritical praise or undue adulation makes him furious. He feels then as if he personally has been abused by the latest illusion-monger.

The triumphant exhibitionism in the narcissistic strata of his life is balanced by extreme guilt with regard to his sexual life. His polymorphous drives found no outlet other than fetishism and transvestitism which provided a kind of compromise.

The fact that his parents came from very different social backgrounds has troubled Philip since childhood and has even affected him in adult life. He has always suffered because his father, who was of peasant extraction, was looked down upon and criticized by his mother for his manners and his way of dressing and talking. The mother's attitude was no doubt aggravated by the father's physical handicap, resulting from an operation involving trepanning with various sequelae, including fainting attacks. This tragedy had limited his father to an inferior job and had forced his mother, who came from a middle-class family, to become a teacher.

"Mummy was always spick and span, very tidy in her clothing. She intimidated me, always wearing the same severe tailored suit. Dad, on the other hand, was rather sloppy and grubby-looking. Everyone liked him even if they didn't respect him. Mummy wore the pants in our home." This woman, with her masculine traits, displayed to her two sons, and to Philip in particular, a narrow solicitude and pestering authority, which corresponded more or less to the attitude she had toward her husband. He never had a say in important discussions or decisions; he was controlled and henpecked. Yet she was obviously devoted to him, too. Philip had overheard his mother say that his father was "rather too keen on it," which never ceased to surprise him. Although aware that his parents got on well together, he could not help thinking that his mother must be ungrateful and mean.

The neglected father, with his few social graces, was in the habit of spitting openly: this was one of my patient's most vivid and most disagreeable memories. Even now Philip admits that he cannot help feeling sick and that he shudders whenever he sees any one spit. During his session he often spontaneously associated phlegm with sperm.

The horror in which he held his father's sexual activities, that is, the image of his father as the possessor of a penis, was less of an "Oedipification" of pregenital needs than an identification with the penis which he felt to be threatened by the mother who had appropriated it for herself. He also felt his penis threatened deep inside his wife's vagina. This is one of the conscious reasons for shunning penetration: several times during intercourse he had had the impression that his penis was encountering the glans of another penis. Karl Abraham long ago discovered this idea in some of his patients—that women had a hollow penis which the smaller male penis could penetrate. This fantasy probably has an oral origin, through an unconscious assimilation of the penis into the breast, an idea which contributes an important part to the formation of the image of a phallic mother.

Philip cannot understand how women can desire men who have only "that miserable little thing." He dreamed: he is on the beach with his wife. There is another person, too, who represents for him Woman. He goes toward her, flirts with her, and tries not to be seen by his wife. Soon he is running along the edge of a big lagoon. Suddenly, he scrambles up a tree to make himself more interesting to the woman who is subdued and now is watching him. From the branch on which he is sitting he can see a deep puddle at the base of the tree. He is about to jump into the puddle when suddenly he sees a huge, multicolored fish chasing another, much smaller one and about to swallow it. At that moment he feels very sick. The scene changes. Now he is at a banquet. His wife is opposite him. The other woman is on his side of the table but separated from him by an unknown man who came and sat down between them.

During his childhood, Philip often imagined that he was inside his father's trousers—or in those of a teacher representing his father—with his head down and his nose between soiled buttocks. Even more than a negation of the wish to castrate the fecal penis, or an anal expression of a homosexual impulse, I believe this shows a desire to be assimilated into the paternal penis. If Philip became the father's penis, his father would no longer be castrated by the phallic mother, nor would Philip run the risk of a similar predicament.

One day during a family outing, as he got out of the car with his father for a short stop, Philip was overcome by a violent and incomprehensible emotion which made him throw himself against his father's chest while repeating between sobs, "Oh, my Daddy, my poor Daddy!" Yet nothing had upset him other than his mother's pitying attitude toward his father, as well as toward himself. Even today, when she calls him "my poor Pip!" he goes into a fury and can hardly control himself. This refers also to the fact that his younger brother had to endure more than his share of this ambiguous pity during the years of illness from the effects of polio. "My poor Daddy" signified "You who are castrated by Mummy." "My poor Pip" therefore means "You who are like your father." It is hardly surprising that thereafter Philip could not bear that expression, which implied his castration. But "My poor Daddy," a variation of his mother's expression, also implies Philip's adoption of a maternal role toward his father while allying with him by affirming the solidarity between victims of a common enemy. This is a complex, homosexual link which lends to Philip's masochistic position its characteristic tone. Philip tries through sexual submission and self-inflicted humiliation to achieve some sort of union with the father.

Here is a reconstruction of Philip's first memory of anxiety: when he was about three years old his grandmother took him for a walk and left him sitting on the low wall of a community washing-place, or perhaps a fish pond. Then she walked away for a little while. He fell into the water and remained at the bottom for several interminable seconds. He remembers the sparkling surface of the water, the sensation of his body being crushed, yet at the same time he also remembers an acute pleasure, perhaps due to his body being rubbed after the accident.

He recalls his strong emotional reactions to the discovery of the anatomical difference between the sexes—the sight of a little friend, Lisa, whom he remembers looking at him while she squatted beside a tree to urinate just a few feet away from him. Why was she not made like him?

He suffered the first unbearable humiliation by being forced to wear long, curly hair tied with a ribbon (his mother had always wanted a little girl) and ridiculous clothes quite unsuitable for his age. After school, during kindergarten, his mother brought him a banana which she compelled him to eat in front of his friends.

After kindergarten he went to a Jesuit school with an atmosphere of censorship, suspicion, false kindness, and duplicity, which seemed to foster and increase the smallest feelings of guilt. "How many times have you passed urine today?" "Haven't you two been touching each other?. . . ." During this time his mother showed great respect and a kind of attraction toward some of the priests whom she invited to her home. Philip did not enjoy the sight of those sexually ambiguous robes swirling round her. Yet he had to appear polite. Possibly Philip's religious upbringing accentuated his original ambiguity about the sexes and enabled him to "femininize" men easily. The priests' relations with his mother disturbed him, intensifying his feeling of sexual ambiguity and reviving his nauseous disgust over the primal scene.

One day he was in the school playground during recreation

period, playing with a ball in the sun. Suddenly, he felt weak and confused. He scarcely had time to go to the nearest priest and collapse "onto his robe," struck by his first fainting fit. (His father, one recalls, had suffered from these since his operation.) This first attack was the unconscious symbolic equivalent of an amorous swoon. For a long time following this incident, he was terrified by the idea of going to school alone. Each time he needed his mother's reassurance, "It will be all right." Whenever she forgot to calm him he turned back on the steps to beg her to say the magic words that would encourage and protect him.

From this same period he also remembers a strange emotion —often accompanied by micturition—prompted by the curious behavior of one teacher who enjoyed teasing him by lifting him by the arms and swinging him round, giving him the feeling of being totally at the teacher's mercy.

Anything to do with sex was kept in the dark by his family. Masturbation during adolescence made him continuously uneasy. What he observed or overheard troubled him, and he did not fully understand it. He was embarrassed when dogs were "glued together," fascinated but horrified by the castrating of pigs which went on frequently in his village. What *did* happen? These animals squealed as if being slaughtered, but soon people loosened the strong straps which had held them down on the wooden planks and the pigs limped away to squat in a corner. . . .

"Keep yourselves pure for the woman you will marry! She is no doubt alive, not far away, waiting for you. . . ." He obeyed the priests' injunction, making no advances to any woman until his engagement to a young girl as ignorant and inexperienced as he was himself.

One day he asked his fiancée to lie down on a high table and reveal her sex organs to him: she obeyed. He saw "a mass of thick hair" but could distinguish little else and was therefore no more enlightened than before. Before his wedding he occasionally indulged in sexual play with his fiancée but never entered her. On the wedding night she produced all kinds of obstacles to penetration which were not overcome until after several weeks of futile effort. Docile and initially willing, the young wife tried to help her shy partner, but most of the time she participated only to the extent of "taking pleasure in pleasing him" with the sensual pleasure she provided for him. Philip found this mixture of apathy and obligingness quite natural. It was only due to the hints, the "authorization," of a third party that complete union was achieved rather hastily and without sufficient pleasure to induce them to strive for this kind of relationship.

Several years went by. One day a second "swoon" suddenly occurred when Philip was finishing a meal with his wife and one of her friends. During the previous week he had suffered a professional failure. This new attack threw him into panic and coincided with the onset of his agoraphobic symptoms. From then on he always feared that "another swoon might come over me out of the blue" with all the catastrophic results which he could imagine.

These are the main features, the relevant parts of the picture which appeared clearly during the first phase of the analysis. I could see that the sexual attitude of this patient had been arrested at the regressive stage which marked the beginning of his adolescence and the start of his married life.

Just as Philip tended to be passive in his sexuality but fiercely to reject this passivity in other aspects of his life, so did he display a two-sided attitude toward me: most obvious was his rapid continuous talking, which allowed no interruption and which ignored my few interventions. One might say that he drowned in his flood of emotion and excess of feeling. On the other side, the less apparent part of himself, he treated me as a mysteriously threatening person (through an identification with his castrated father) whom he feared but whom he wished to touch and whose intrusion he even invited. Whatever the reality and importance of his homosexual tendencies which I observed (in dreams, for example, I appeared more or less disguised, tending to him, kissing him, giving him injections, or operating on him), I do not think that he was essentially affected by their emergence, at the level which I am concerned with here. On the contrary, I think that, in association with a precocious negative Oedipus complex—or with a dual relationship to either parent of a predominantly sado-masochistic kind—the person who aroused hatred in Philip together with strong dependence, later on linked to an ambivalent admiration, was the mother. She was mainly a phallic mother because she possessed the hallucinatory penis and, thereby, omnipotence. To characterize Philip's basic relational behavior I would describe it as the result in fantasy, of a genuine reversal of the parents' sexes: it is the father who lacks something fundamental and it is the mother who has it. Of course, this is probably so because she took it from him—but this conclusion is the result of a construction. The father was loved without being desired, the mother feared and hated but also desired and envied. Supposing the mother is regarded as masculine and the father as feminine, one could, after a fashion, speak of Philip's maintaining a genuinely passive, homosexual attitude. . . . in relation to the mother! It would be a deep-seated attitude, covered early by many layers of disguise, but, in this example, never neutralized or undone. For a demonstration of it see his sexual life and his perverse dispositions as well as his phobic symptoms.

Thus, the desire to be a woman, usually closely linked to the father, is rooted in Philip in the wish to play the passive partner to the mother-with-the-penis, in a sado-masochistic relationship. Since this unconscious fantasy developed as an attempt to deal with castration anxiety, it seems to have resulted in a particularly important libidinal investment in fantasies at the price of a decathexis of real sexual objects. Distortion seems to have started at a very early age, leading to perverse developments. Perversion may have resulted from a split between fantasy and reality at a primitive stage of sexuality rather than from a fixation to a transitory mode of satisfying a component instinct. Such a hypothesis would allow the conception of a new relationship between perversion and neurosis. It may be considered not from the point of view of its expression in actual sexual behavior, as is usually done, but from an understanding of the basic fantasies determining it. If perversion is considered as a redeployment of libidinal energy in fantasies, it would not be necessary anymore to see perversion as "the negative of neurosis." At the same time the origins of perversion would from this point of view be better understood.[1]

I see in Philip, therefore, a meaningful link between his perverse tendencies and his phobic symptoms. The connection is so complete that his conscious and unconscious representations of women and their sexuality, as well as his own feminine attitudes, inasmuch as they all are a detour of primitive libidinal energy—express in condensed form the consequence of some kind of traumatic sidetracking of psychosexual development.

I would like to point out that in referring to the mother-with-the-penis I am simplifying the undifferentiated and amalgamated image of the father and the mother. This image, as has often been pointed out, was constructed from the idea of the primal scene, whether it has really been observed or merely imagined. Furthermore, in the course of development, the early fantasies are reconstructed in relation to later experiences. Masochistic, oral, anal, or phallic fantasies formed around the image of the phallic mother, or the "father-mother," can be reconstructed around the Oedipal image of the father in a classical, passive homosexual pattern. In this light one can better understand that Philip's compulsive cough at the sight or thought of spit, as well as his fantasy of "the nose between the buttocks," are the phallic reconstruction of his early oral and anal experiences in the dyadic relation with his mother.

This is what Philip's transference, which rapidly became predominantly paternal, suggested to me: the absence of imposed restraints, of moral guidance, and active intervention in the face of persistent provocations, and the creation of conditions favorable to much-needed assertion of narcissism resulted in a decrease of distrust and fear. This coincided with a mobilization of the ideal father's characteristics, which were projected on me in the transference. Progress was fragile and precarious at the beginning, involving many ups and downs, including regressions. I was like a shelter, a sanctuary in which he could let himself go, giving up all active and aggressive pretensions. Whenever I refused him in any way, or demonstrated some kind of authority, the protective barriers would immediately break down and the shelter became a dangerous den full of mysterious threats.

Parallel to the internal progress of the treatment, I noticed, after a few months, a basic transformation in Philip's sexual and affective behavior, and simultaneously an almost total cessation of his phobic problems. Mainly, perhaps, because of identification the patient arrived one day at his session to tell me that something new and important had occurred: for the first time he had felt a desire to penetrate women and even his wife. He had satisfied this desire and had also for the first time felt intense pleasure. He had felt that he was "the master," that he had "taken her," and he was happy to experience that he had his partner "at his mercy." At the same time he felt he would like to give her pleasure and had not felt his usual disgust at the vulva. This almost schematic reversal of his usual relationship with his wife eventually caused him to alter his view of the "feminine sex," an alteration which was almost too spectacular not to seem artificial. It was not necessary, after all, to see women as inaccessible, impassive, yet deliberately pitiless, angels; nor as impure, despicable creatures rightly relegated to vile, inferior tasks. It was perhaps natural that they should, like men, seek their own pleasure, rather than only that of their partners, and if the *mons pubis,* the clitoris, the vagina and all the "odd" feminine sex organs, seemed mysterious and repulsive objects it must have been the result of his educational taboos.

He had now come to realize that in order to overcome his initial fear and horror he needed to consider this deficiency as perfection, and then identify himself with this deceptive perfection.

Now the penis and the testicles were fragile and ridiculous, and the bestiality of masculine desires had to be condemned. It was so much more harmonious to have nothing between the legs, so much more noble and pure not to know the pleasures of voluptuousness. What could be more enviable than a belly created for childbearing, breasts for suckling, a graceful body with a well-defined figure to arouse desire without feeling any oneself?

To wear only a diaphanous covering over one's sex and to walk with an imperious air, proudly perched on one's high heels, ah! what rapture! . . .

As for the periodical "indispositions," which were difficult to glorify both in themselves and in Philip's distorted view of them, he had found the unconscious expedient of taking responsibility for them by psychosomatic enactments of displaced images of menstruation (bleeding piles, epistaxis, or even momentary queasiness, "vapors"). Philip has particularly acute and disagreeable memories of finding his mother's sanitary napkins in the bathroom. The wound which he had tried to deny, was bleeding; "Not only do women not have a penis, but on top of all that they have this bleeding gash!" There was only one way to defend himself against it: by inflicting the same injury on himself and thus warding off the risk forever. This method of self-punishment, due to an obvious and active desire for castration, at the same time represents a way of actively dominating the terrifying fantasy of undergoing castration (or even of "aphanisis"), clue to an unconscious mechanism of identification with the aggressor.

More than one man, whimpering at little pains which he fears are big ones, owes his tendency to hypochondria or psychosomatic afflictions to a similar process. As for the women, many are themselves the victims of this problem because of a morbid, unconscious apprehension of the role of the menstrual cycle.

It is clear that Philip has, on the one hand, a desire to be a woman, linked with an admiration and an idealization of women which is at the basis of his perverse masochistic and fetishistic sexual experiences; on the other hand, he has a virile exhibitionism, associated with a horrified disgust and hatred of women, which permeates his everyday behavior and mentality and which in an intricate fashion also affects his phobias.

It seems, at least in this case, that the phobia functions to restrain his perverse attitude by giving vent to affects resulting from the displacement of erotic needs and perverse pregenital behavior. He has in some sense a fear of a threat which is consciously unassignable, a fear which provokes both a painful uneasiness and an exciting shudder, both related to the masochistic pleasure obtained either in fantasies of castration or in sexual relations with reversed roles.

His double sexual polarity is rarely seen in such a dissociated way as it is here, although it does not conceal the radically complementary nature of antagonistic tendencies. The polarity appears to involve a pathological partition of the whole personality, as well as a highly conflicting, ambiguous attitude of the patient toward his own femininity and a mythical conception of women's nature and role, the one largely influenced by the other. Philip's attitude toward the feminine part of himself is largely determined by his intolerance toward his mother's appearance and masculine behavior. He has not been able to tolerate the phallic mother's penis, created by himself in his imagination and referring to his own castration. This, in turn, is confirmed by the father's castration. He is "trapped" on all sides, the mother has "got him." This explains his need to divide the feminine universe in two: in one half are the women who "do not belong to it," creatures who frighten and horrify him; in the other half are the pretty, young, and desirable women, the only real women, those he calls "womanly" and to whom he is strongly attracted but with whom he can have pleasure only in fantasy. This division parallels the one which separates his psychic life and his nonsexual behavior, dominated by demands of virility, from sexual behavior, where he abdicates his virility.

Whenever Philip adopts an erotic, masochistic attitude toward an all-powerful woman, even though she may have "nothing between her legs," that woman is a phallic image. Therefore, he simultaneously identifies himself with a castrated father as well as the repressed image of a castrated woman. Whenever he adopts a positively virile attitude, particularly to women, he revives archaic fantasies of the mother-with-the-penis castration. This unconscious operation is made possible by perverse libidinal cathexis. This is because he feels the castration attested to by women's inferiority has already been achieved. Or it may also be because his aggression is aroused by the authoritarian attitude of a woman to whom he then speaks harshly in order to prove his masculine prerogatives, and this precisely because his masochism strikes an unconscious balance.

In order for Philip's sexual mythology to establish itself and flourish in this mixed psychopathological picture his wife's complicity and complementary neurotic behavior are necessary. It is this morbid, but vital, response that he is afraid he will not find in any other woman, at least not within the same context of security. Is not the masculine mythology of women's sexuality and femininity to some extent an offshoot of a corresponding feminine mythology about virility, or even femininity itself?

It is not by chance that the characteristic dispositions and sexual attitudes in this case are linked to a psychological disturbance. The vivid and specific nature of these phobic problems, as well as the spectacular and sometimes unusual aspects of these perverse tendencies emphasize the pathological etiology of masculine mythology on the substrata I have here examined. I believe, however, that even in less melodramatic examples, masculine mythology is usually linked to psychological disturbances. If such distortion often escapes our attention it is because it is common and because perverse attitudes have such strong links with the total personality.

Even though masculine mythology is widespread and deeply rooted we need not accept it. Character-neurosis easily reveals certain ideologies which are far too pronounced not to be the equivalent of symptoms or at least to serve as indications of a conflicted organization. One could sum up in this fashion: "Tell me what you think of women, express your attitude toward your own femininity, and I shall tell you who you are. . . ."

Whatever the positions and attitudes toward women are at the start of analytical treatment, one notices—if progress is made—changes not in the direction of uniform affective and conceptual attitudes (as might be supposed), but toward an independence in the norms of feeling, behavior, and thought and to a freer relationship. In this way sexual values are questioned and reshuffled. The feminine mystery no longer seems so specific or so deep; the "sex war" no longer seems to be a necessity of nature; the romantic conventions are weakened. This does not mean that henceforth all will be simple or easy in love-relations. Far from it, but the difficulty has been tracked back to its vital roots: the vicissitudes of personal development in a particular cultural, social, and family background.

These vicissitudes are either real (for example, linked with contingent traumas and conflicting identifications), or they are imaginary (belonging to fantasy determining relatively autonomous developments). This choice must be faced as Freud points out, but its very form suggests the complex genesis of our myths.

To rid sexuality of these myths does not necessarily mean, contrary to many people's beliefs, "taking the fantasy away," taking the poetry out of our conception, which as a man or as a woman we have the person we desire. If one denounces as myth certain masculine attitudes toward female sexuality, one does not challenge the prerequisites of the imagination, but, on the contrary, helps to relate them to facts drawn from experience, which moreover can be understood better by free communication with the unconscious. "Prejudices" and compensatory fantasies must not be confused with the fruitful creations which continuously enrich the relations between the sexes as well as the image man has of himself.

By emphasizing bisexuality—an orthodox psychoanalytical attitude—one can encourage such creations. Bisexuality, which Freud saw as clearly more marked in women than in men, seems to have essentially the same relevance for both. (Or perhaps there has been a swift evolution in masculine mental attitudes toward a certain kind of "femininization" related to sociological causes, which are as yet poorly understood.)

Whether this is so or not, I think one must stress the importance of one characteristic of this bisexual structure: a disposition to identify oneself both with the male and the female roles lessens sexual differences.

But this attitude of "assuming as much as possible of sexuality" does not mean that psychosexual dimorphism is not as real and as important as biological dimorphism, which is its basis. In recognizing osmosis one does not need to deny cellular individuality and differences.

As it is the differences between sexes that are so often stressed, it may be more revealing to consider the similarities, by studying their source in bisexuality. Thus, Groddeck said that we are bisexual throughout life and therefore in each man there is a woman and in each woman a man.

Would not a lucid and detailed recognition of this duality provide the principal feature of a conception of sexual life, more open, more free, and more genuine?

Outline for a Study of Narcissism in Female Sexuality

Béla Grunberger

Preliminary Remarks

The study of female sexuality is a relatively neglected area in psychoanalysis. This discipline centers on the Oedipus complex, "the nodal complex of neurosis," and its method is the study of normality by means of the pathological. The Oedipus complex applies to both sexes, but Freud was constantly in difficulties over establishing a symmetry here for both men and women. In 1931 Freud wondered whether "what we know of the Oedipus complex is only valid in the boy's development, and not in the girl's," an expression of the insecurity he felt in the face of the problem of femininity, which shows up in everything he has written on the subject. He never fails to stress the tentative nature of his subject and refers both to the unsatisfactory results and to the task that research has still to complete.[1] Freud's uncertainties about the problem of femininity were aggravated by his wish to reconcile his revolutionary studies with the scientific orientation peculiar to his time.

Freud claimed that the mother is the first sexual object for both the boy and the girl because their first sexual sensations occur during feeding and bathing, activities which stimulate the erogenous zones. This is perfectly true, but it is unlikely (we shall return to this point later) that the quality of these sensations is identical for the two sexes, even though the agent bringing them about is the same. Indeed, all of Freud's difficulties over Oedipal theory arise from this purely hypothetical symmetry. One could also wonder whether the mother's ministrations themselves might not be the source of such sensations. We might reverse the statement and assume that there is already a potential sexuality—different, from the beginning, for boys and girls—which the mother merely activates.[2]

Psychoanalytical writers are habitually cautious about the

manifestations of sexuality and accept only visible and verifiable reality (following Freud's anatomical-pathological background and the aforementioned scientific orientation). These writers deny, for example, that a little girl acknowledges the existence of her vagina until she has reached a certain age (which varies, according to the author, from eight to twelve). Clinical evidence certainly shows the importance of repressing this knowledge which we would otherwise accept. (We only have to admit some kind of primitive instinct which, after all, exists in this context in the animal world). In addition, Freud himself refers on several occasions (as E. Jones points out) to "elementary fantasies," that is, to an unconscious recognition which to some extent makes this knowledge independent of actual experience (placed by analysts at various stages in psychosexual development). On it depends the castration complex and the entire psychosexual development of the child.

I do not wish to minimize the importance of the scientific method, which depends on precise laboratory observation. This method is excellent for the study of biology, of which sexuality is a part. But we know that the study of sexuality, particularly female sexuality, goes beyond biological facts. The study of masculine sexuality accommodates itself to a relatively clear and simple system, but the study of female sexuality encounters problems for which the classical psychoanalytic method proves inadequate. Accordingly it has been given second place and is studied as an appendage of sorts to the study of male sexuality, with which it is constantly compared.

Writers on female sexuality know only too well the limits to our scientific knowledge of the subject. Yet they pay no attention to them, which leads to another difficulty: the adoption of highly subjective positions which, in the absence of a rigorous scientific discipline, often derive from unacknowledged personal problems. Thus, we try to steer a course between the Charybdis of scientific materialism and the Scylla of nonscientific or pseudoscientific subjectivity. How should we then approach the subject?

It seems, first of all, that we must give up our customary approach, based strictly on the theory of instinctual drives. The phenomena we wish to study do not fit into this rigid theory. Nevertheless, these phenomena exist and, despite nuances which are tricky to define, we must try to understand them in and by themselves as well as their relation to the instinctual system of which they are a part.

A particularly rewarding approach to the study of female sexuality can be made by taking the theory of narcissism as a starting point. Time and time again Freud noted the importance of narcissism in female sexuality and in "On Narcissism: An Introduction" even described a particular type of narcissistic woman as being basically representative of all women.[3] His students, Mrs. Lampl de Groot in particular, have also stressed the importance of female narcissism; it is presented as an undeniable fact, but has not yet been made part of the Freudian system as a whole.

An attempt will be made here to integrate the theory of narcissism into the instinct theory, although this entails modifying somewhat the Freudian system.

In an earlier publication I stressed the importance of narcissism, giving it the status of an organizing agent (in the same way that the id, the ego, and the superego are agents) and emphasizing also the dialectic interplay between narcissism and other component instincts, especially the sadistic-anal. These ideas become even more important when we consider female sexuality, where the narcissistic factor is truly basic. An approach to the study of woman's unconscious merely from an object-oriented viewpoint would soon lead to a deadlock.

Freud insisted that the narcissistic woman wants "to be loved." "To be loved" means primarily to be chosen and, above all, to be loved "for herself." She wants to be specially valued in a narcissistic way. Without doubt there are many reasons for this, including the need to free herself from conflict-producing guilt (which J. Chasseguet studies in this book and to which we shall refer later). But this is only one aspect of female narcissism. We must try to understand this peculiarity of womanhood which confronts us in this characteristic way. We must try to understand why women seek narcissistic gratification above all else, even to the detriment of their own strong sexual needs and why they offer themselves sexually in order to be loved; whereas men tend to seek sexual satisfaction primarily, giving their partners narcissistic gratification only in order to obtain their own sexual satisfaction. (Men love in order to be satisfied.) [4]

Influenced by the trend in society toward reducing the differences between the sexes, a woman may seek the same sexual freedom as men, but then will be unable to invest her love life other than narcissistically. Her body self will become increasingly important, extending from her body to her clothes and accessories to her "home": her house and the material premises of her love life.

Of course, this extension of her body self will cover her partner and her children, all marked by the *singleness* characteristic of narcissistic investments and in contrast to the fundamentally primitive tendencies of the male's polyvalence. (Here we touch on the problem of polygamy and of the interchangeability of man's "object".) As man's sexual life is focussed on immediate instinctual relief, woman's love also is located in time, but she dreams of eternity and thereby suppresses the material elements, the real instinctual derivatives, of her love.

On the whole, women's sexuality is narcissistically oriented. "Love" bears the marks of this orientation, especially because it is the central interest of her life. At least in our civilization love is the core of woman's existence, whereas it is a stage of man's life (his more or less prolonged adolescence, the narcissistic age *par excellence*), for later he is supposed to be interested in serious matters alone. Men in love are considered effeminate and bashful lovers, more or less ridiculous.

Love, as a narcissistic form of sexuality, must enrich the woman; being liked, loved, having a certain radiance or a certain influence are all narcissistically enhancing factors. What then is the basis of woman's uneasiness, her constant complaints about being a woman and about the female condition? I am referring, on the one hand, to woman's psychosexual condition (leaving aside her social status, since I believe that both factors are linked to common unconscious motivations which apply to both men and women) and, on the other, to the form the uneasiness takes in the unconscious: penis envy, masochism, feminine guilt.

1.

According to Freud, Oedipal development is identical for boy and girl up to the phallic stage, at which point the castration complex orients them differently, leading to the decline of the Oedipus complex in the boy and to the Oedipal situation itself in the girl. But up until this time they *both experienced* the mother as the sexual object. This conforms with Freud's ideas about the anaclitic origin of object relations which become sexualized through the unavoidable excitement arising from the mother's physical care of her child.

We might first question whether body care alone is sufficient to establish a satisfying sexual object (and in this context we might cite Spitz's study of hospitalism).[5] Second, the mother-child relationship effects what I have referred to in previous publications as "narcissistic confirmation." During the lengthy course of psychomotor development the child integrates his component instincts, which must be cathected narcissistically in order to lead to harmonious instinct maturation. This narcissistic cathexis (meaning, the child must recognize that his instinctual needs are his own and must accept them as such) has to be accomplished by the mother *who loves her child and all expressions of his life.* Viewed from this angle the mother as a sexual object has a different value for the little girl than she has for the boy. This has important consequences. As Freud points out, the only really satisfactory relationship is that of mother and infant son. We have every reason to believe that even the most loving, most maternal mother will be *ambivalent* toward her daughter.

Furthermore, I believe, as I said before, that sexuality is always sexuality, whether it be oral or anal, and that maternal care can only activate it. But a true sexual object can only be of the opposite sex and (unless some kind of congenital homosexuality is assumed) the mother cannot be the satisfactory sexual object for the girl that she is for the boy. Psychoanalysts often claim that women are more fixated at pregenital stages than are men. This viewpoint is questionable. Although I accept the actual Oedipal reasons which cause the child to regress to earlier stages I nevertheless agree with J. Chasseguet's opinion that if an unconscious awareness of the genital organs exists virtually from the beginning, then the pregenital stages must be, by definition, frustrating. Even pregenital satisfactions are frustrating as they are only substitutes for genital satisfactions.

The pregenital stages are much more frustrating for the girl because the maternal object is only a substitute for a *truly adequate sexual object.* I believe that this uniquely feminine situation is itself the cause of many disturbances.

Freud claims that the girl encounters difficulty in changing sexual objects, that is, in shifting from mother to father. From the point of view of narcissistic confirmation, I believe the girl does not have to change objects because, in fact, she has never had one; or rather, she had an object which was essentially frustrating. For this reason she will immediately and blindly choose her father as her narcissitic ego-ideal and libidinal object.

The girl's life, then, begins with frustration, which in turn exerts considerable influence. A child gives himself narcissistic confirmation when he is mature enough to do so, but until then the mother is the source of this confirmation. However, it seems that the little girl attempts to obtain that confirmation for herself in some way long before the boy does. Those who work with children are aware that girls mature sooner than boys. Much doll play, for example, is a way of taking over the mother's role and achieving by use of the doll (with which the girl also identifies herself) a narcissistic confirmation which otherwise is the mother's responsibility.

The mother does provide such confirmation, but often without the deep love and the narcissistic cathexis that the little girl requires. She, therefore, *attempts to give it to herself, thereby becoming essentially narcissistic* in an effort to make up for the maternal deficiency. This attempt, lacking the solid basis maternal love should give, is bound to fail, and because of this the little girl is more dependent on her love objects than is the boy. (I believe that the intellectual precociousness of the little girl is due to this particular situation.)

The girl's Oedipal development is held back in some way by this state of affairs; it can best be understood by comparing it to that of the boy. He has, we might say, a sexual object and an adequate sexual object at that. He will be able to obtain his narcissistic confirmation from it, as well as an ally in the Oedipal battle with his father. But these gains are offset by certain disadvantages. In spite of some pregenital satisfaction he will be essentially frustrated in Oedipal genital satisfaction. This happens very early, at a stage when he is too immature to cope with it, causing him an early narcissistic wound. It is difficult to compensate for this, as he will soon change his relationship to his mother into a fixation on the bad (that is, frustrating) aspect of that object, owing to the numerous frustrations and obligations of this period.

On the other hand, having experienced pregenital satisfactions at an early age, some of an authentically heterosexual quality, he will tend to "genitalize" them, thus creating certain polymorphous perverse fixations.

If we now consider the little girl, we see that her pregenital satisfaction is not authentic because its source is merely a substitute object. This leads her to despise the pregenital components of sexuality and later on fosters guilt about pregenital experiences. This affects particularly the Oedipal relationship to her father, whom she will blame for his comparative absence during the pregenital period and for the frustrations resulting from it.

Thanks to the necessary distance between her and her true love object (the father), and in spite of this blame, the girl has had time to mature, to reach the true Oedipal position, and to construct an ideal image of her father, for whom she has waited so long and whom she would like to love, especially as she despises the pregenital satisfactions provided by the mother. The frustration and lengthy wait accentuate her narcissism, compensating her somewhat and enabling her at the same time to deepen the feeling she has for her father. In general, therefore, her love will be more idealized, but nevertheless will show the defective integration of the pregenital components. This explains the peculiar survival of her manifest

Oedipal attachment, her tendency to dichotomize (that is, between an ideal Oedipal love and the pre-Oedipal attachment which is opposed to it), as well as her tendency to feel guilty about her love relationships. From the start of the Oedipal complex, the female has a slowly maturing affective intensity which is infinitely greater than that of the boy. This partly explains why incest occurs more frequently between father and daughter and is less pathological than incest between mother and son.

As we have seen, the boy, unable to fill his Oedipal desires, suffers an early narcissistic wound which he then completely represses in favor of a precocious, pregenital sexuality. This pregenital emphasis adversely affects his narcissistic image, causing him to despise his *narcissistic needs* in the same way that the woman rejects her *component instincts,* especially the anal-sadistic ones of love. The girl, nevertheless, has an advantage over the boy: she has learned to wait, and through this she has acquired an optimistic attitude toward her narcissistic wounds. But she does not yet know whether to accept them or whether to hope that some day they will be repaired and she will have a phallus, symbol of completeness. This uncertainty probably influences her attitude toward reality, but it is also the source of hypersensitivity and leads to an exacerbation of her frustrations. She seeks someone to support her and to provide the narcissistic confirmation which she did not get earlier and which she continually seeks. The tragedy of this situation is that the person who could give her this confirmation, her sexual partner, is precisely the one who, as we have just seen, has come to despise narcissistic needs in an effort to disengage himself from them by strongly cathecting the anal-sadistic instinctual components.[6]

I have already pointed out that woman has deep narcissistic needs and seeks narcissistic satisfaction even at the expense of instinctual gratification. In satisfactory instances she may manage to achieve a synthesis between these two and thus obtain a degree of narcissistic completion: that is to say, an instinctual maturity with a satisfactory narcissistic confirmation, which is symbolized in her unconscious by the phallus. The acquisition of this phallus may be linked to *identification*. (I once had a patient whose dreams centered on phallus problems: the phallus, representing perfect femininity, was also equated with the mother with whom she tried to identify. But in order for this identification to be complete she had to introject the father's phallus.) Needless to say, this identity of representation between the phallus and the penis invariably becomes a source of conflict, especially as the phallic image (phallus-penis) is always the center of women's unconscious preoccupations, whether it be the paternal penis which the mother possesses (the mother having thus achieved the image of narcissistic integrity of "contained and containing" which she denies her daughter), or the penis of the father himself which she hopes to have through Oedipal union with him.

In fact, there is a kind of equivalence between the possession of the paternal penis and a successful narcissistic cathexis. The woman who is loved thereby possesses in her unconscious a phallic equivalent.[7] She sometimes becomes this phallus herself and thus achieves a state of narcissistic autonomy by cathecting herself narcissistically: becoming beautiful, charming, and desirable. This development depends upon her narcissistic investment of herself, but often to the detriment of her object-relations and instinctual life. (Freud noticed that men are attracted to women who remind them of their own narcissistic tendencies. We might add that men see in these women a successful narcissistic integrity which they themselves have not been able to achieve because of their specific way of experiencing the castration complex.) [8]

This narcissistic cathexis may not succeed completely for reasons of conflict and women often fail to achieve a satisfactory balance between narcissism and instinctual needs. Viewed from an economic standpoint, we can understand how Freud's narcissistic woman, who puts all her libido into her narcissistic cathexis, can no longer cathect her sexual instincts and becomes frigid. (Woman's orientation is narcissistic-oral, with orality expressing an equally important part of her libido.) It is necessary to add, nevertheless, that a narcissistic cathexis can use diverse elements as its substratum and that women may achieve in many ways the narcissistic completion which they seem to need so much. Thus, one woman may fulfill her narcissistic ideal through cathecting her beauty and seductive powers, while another, lacking these qualities, may cathect them negatively and develop an "antilibidinal" superego which she will narcissistically cathect as she first cathected her ego. The possibilities for narcissistic investment are infinite, and there is even an ideal narcissistic cathexis which does not need such support as was mentioned before.

In analysis we can follow step by step the freeing of narcissistic cathexes which had been inhibited by guilt. They now provide narcissistic fulfillment through cathexis of the instincts, thus allowing the person to give pleasure to himself (to love himself). Apparent restriction of sexual life in women who have exceptionally little self-regard (for example, in nymphomania) gives way in analysis as they acquire self-regard and cease devaluing themselves in a self-destructive fashion through negative object choices.

We said that singleness is the mark of narcissism and, indeed, there is a *concentric* aspect characteristic of woman's libidinal cathexis; she is always at the center of it, but at the same time the center is the phallus which is also essentially unique.

Women are usually demanding in their object-cathexis and attempt several processes of introjection and identification at once. But as they are trying to achieve, in spite of appearances, a singleness of object their ideal tends toward a robot-image, who brings together all the elements belonging to their various models of identification designated by narcissistic cathexis. Thus, the woman's partner, unable to fill all these requirements, is bound to disappoint her. She will accept her disappointment, however, as long as she can count on the essential condition of being loved. I do not mean to say that this need for love is the essential sign of normality or maturity; I have simply tried to formulate some hypotheses which could explain this need in so many women, by tracing it back to the mother-daughter relationship, frustrating to both of them because neither is a satisfactory object for the other.

II

According to psychoanalytical theory, woman's psychosexual development goes through two different stages which are in opposition to each other: the male-clitoral stage and the female-vaginal one.

For Freud, the libido is essentially male, and the only sexual organ is the penis. Female sexuality, therefore, hardly exists, and women do not have any sexual organ except a hole, that is to say, nothing. Here it is necessary to state that this allegation is wrong, since woman does have a complete sexual organ which is fully alive and vividly represented in her body image.

Women's sexuality is probably richer than men's, although in analysis we come across only its deficiencies, inhibitions, and guilt which, in turn, testify to its force, for something which does not exist cannot be cathected negatively.

Analysts do not agree about the two stages of development which women are supposed to go through; some hold that the sensation of the vagina occurs before that of the clitoris. (This question has been debated thoroughly elsewhere, so I shall not go into it here.) We might note before continuing our presentation that woman does not have only two sexual organs. Her erogenous zones extend over a great deal of her anatomy and her body as a whole can be considered a sexual organ. One often encounters this in analysis as an unconscious phallic representation of the body self. This is not to be confused with a pathological phallic identification, in which the phallus is a symbol of completeness and not of virility. In fact women have a powerful sexuality which gives them a feeling of narcissistic integrity (symbolized by the phallus), but there is a sharp contrast between this phallic image and the clitoris. If one insists on the importance of the clitoris as a sexual organ, but at the same time attributes to it an essentially male quality, one assigns it —by that very token—only a short-lived cathexis. According to classical theory, at a certain moment the clitoris should be exchanged in some way for the vagina, which is from then on the only sexual organ or, as we have just seen, a nothing. The clitoris is supposed to give up its libidinal cathexis (Marie Bonaparte thinks it is a vestigial organ, like the pronephros of the thymus).

Most analytic writers insist on the notion that women must give up their interest in the clitoris, whereas my psychoanalytical experience leads me on the contrary to emphasize the need to integrate the drives and their cathexes rather than allowing them to disappear.

I have referred several times to the mysterious guilt which accompanies all manifestations of narcissism. If we examine the characteristics of the clitoris, the organ condemned to disappear, we realize that it is primarily narcissistic, for its only function is to provide pleasure,[9] in contrast to the penis, an organ of pleasure but also of reproduction and elimination, not to mention its dynamic unconscious meanings.

The clitoris seems to be blamed for its narcissistic qualities. It is the organ of narcissistic pleasure, that is, the pleasure one gives oneself, the solitary pleasure. The clitoris does not need another person, in contradistinction to the vagina, an organ of pleasure we might call social because it does not exist for itself but only as a receptacle.

In a sense the clitoris is the sexual organ most typical of woman. This is not because it is derived embryologically from the penis (a filiation whose meaning has already been corrected by Ernest Jones) but rather because it is invested with the same narcissistic enhancement with which woman invests her body as a whole. This narcissistic cathexis in no way negates the phallic significance of the clitoris in the unconscious.

There is a rivalry between men and women for the possession of this narcissistic integrity and wholeness symbolized by the phallus in the unconscious. The historic origins of this investment are connected with the father's penis. This brings us to the important question of "the war between the sexes," but that lies beyond the scope of the present paper. I should like to point out, however, that men sometimes blame woman for "acting as though she had one," but at the same time blame the clitoris for "acting as if it were a penis." (In societies where excision of the clitoris is practiced, it might be due to its being given a masculine significance and therefore the prerogative of man alone.)

These considerations bring us to another problem which, though different, is of great importance for our present study: that of harmony, or rather disharmony, in sexual relations. Women usually complain about their partners, and popular literature tends to justify this: man appears to behave like a lout; he is clumsy; lacking understanding of women, he cannot give them sexual satisfaction. Is there any truth in this? It certainly is an oversimplification, but is there also something to it?

It is clear that from a psychophysiological viewpoint coitus follows a different course for men than for women, that particularly woman's orgasm has a different rhythm. Elaborate graphs have been constructed to prove this. Yet it seems that these slight differences do not prevent normal lovers from finding happiness through intercourse, without needing synchronization, organized techniques, or preparation by the partners, or, more precisely, the male partner.

Each case of disharmony has its specificity; analysis usually leads to spontaneous relief and to a love life which does not require highly technical approaches. But here I must underline again that I am considering neither special cases of disturbance with their genetic, historical, or other explanations, nor normal cases which need no special attention or study. What I am examining here are *tendencies* which exist in a sufficiently large number of people for me to say that they are characteristic of women (as opposed to men); these tendencies have their origin in the woman's unconscious, thus characterizing all women, at least in our society. Even if there are women whose sexuality is uncomplicated, whose orgasms are adapted to their partner's activity, and whose sexual satisfaction is achieved without their partners losing spontaneity, their sexuality, nevertheless, is fundamentally different from men's. In other words this fundamental difference exists even between partners of a well-matched couple because it is due to a basic difference between the sexes. What exactly does this mean?

Among the tacit or overt grievances women have is that the man does not care sufficiently for her, that he does not show that he appreciates, needs, or values her. (One might add to the list "loves her," but we know from Freud that to be loved is a narcissistic desire; women need their narcissism satisfied and men seem unfit to do so.) A woman is narcissistic before all else. Narcissism's motto is "all or nothing," for perfection cannot be divided or rationed; it either exists or it does not. A woman cathects her ego. This cathexis spreads outward in a concentric manner (like the circles in water around the spot where a pebble has been thrown) with herself always in the center: her own love and love in general receive all her investment, and woman would like this center also to be invested in mirror fashion by her partner, too. Women live in, and by, love. Because they are deprived of adequate narcissistic confirmation from the beginning of their lives they project their badly integrated, unfulfilled narcissism onto their relations with their partners; in a sense their lives are the story of this projection, its partial and fleeting successes and its inevitable failures.

What is the difference in man's attitude? One could deliberately simplify or exaggerate and say that it is fundamentally different. Of course, there are narcissistic men, with the unintegrated and unfulfilled narcissism which is the prerogative of women, but such men have an important feminine component, and their sexuality has deficiences different from those of nonnarcissistic men. Men's attitude has an instinctual basis which is organized along anal-sadistic lines: things exist for him in a hierarchy of realities, delineated precisely in their relation to one another. Woman and her love are perhaps man's first object of cathexis, but they are certainly not his only one. Furthermore, the narcissistic portion in his cathexis is subordinated to the truly instinctual one. He cathects not his relationship to the ego and its object (which leads to instinctual *satisfaction*) but the instinctual satisfaction itself. That is why man is only partly engaged in love and why he is less vulnerable if his love relation fails. As his involvement is more instinctual than narcissistic, a narcissistic wound will be less deep and more likely to heal.

We can now return to the problems of sexual disharmony and, in particular, the problem of woman's preparation for the sexual act. What I shall say about this problem is merely an integration on the level of coitus of what has been said about the respective relations of men and women to narcissism.

In classical psychoanalytic theory preparation for the genital act includes partial instinctual needs and forepleasure. These instinctual needs are autoerotic, but they normally occur in coitus (see Ferenczi's theory of amphimixis). The genital event is a *cluster* of pregenital components. Coitus begins with the partners becoming sexually intimate, with the time between the beginning of the act and actual sexual intercourse depending on the perfection and promptness with which the *cluster* organizes itself. It all apparently depends on the strength of the organizing anal-sadistic component and on the energetic origins of the sexual act. In other words, the more intact and vigorous the anal-sadistic component, the faster and better will the cluster organize itself until the act occurs, bringing instinctual satisfaction and relief for both partners. (I am not, of course, considering ejaculatio praecox or severe ejaculatio retardata, signs of functional disturbance in the component in question which correspond either to superficial clitoral orgasm or total frigidity in women.)

To say that woman is mainly narcissistic means: independent of all instinctual components of the cluster. She introduces into her sexual life an additional element (narcissism), an element whose effects are numerous. Indeed, instinctual maturation is achieved through narcissistically cathected instincts and narcissisms providing a well-integrated instinctual basis for harmonious development. But in neurosis this synthesis is disturbed, producing conflict; what should be synthesized becomes a source of interference. The more narcissism grows in importance in normal object-relations, the more will object love intensify. In neurosis the process is inverted: the more narcissism, the less important become object-relations. As long as all is well, narcissism and the instincts collaborate, but when there is conflict they become antagonistic and turn against each other.

In other words, if the woman in a slightly neurotic couple invests too much in the narcissistic aspect of that relationship, less of her libido (absorbed by that aspect) will be available to be invested into the instinctual side of that relationship. Instead of facilitating synthesis of the pregenital elements, the state of her libido will block an adequate fusion of them, slowing it down and even preventing it altogether. In women, therefore, there is a narcissistic stage between the instinctual and true genital stages; this intermediate stage can serve as a link, but also as an obstacle, according to the circumstances.

In a neurotic context, narcissism tends to become "less sexual." By this I mean an isolation of the component instincts, particularly the anal-sadistic component, which I described earlier as the essential element in feminine sexual guilt (in male sexual guilt, too, but to a lesser extent).

This leads the woman to idealize sexuality and to emphasize the asexual elements of love but to despise "carnal relations" (so that even the phrase itself has a depreciatory connotation for her).

Such narcissistic opposition to the anal-sadistic component prevents complete and satisfactory sexual fulfillment.

Sometimes the clitoris is isolated from the rest of woman's sexuality. In such cases narcissism, intervening as it does between component instincts and genitality, proves more an obstacle than a link. If female sexuality must pass through a narcissistic stage (inserted each time into the sexual act) it results in a neurotic impasse: the clitoris cannot fulfill its function of inducing true sexual or vaginal pleasure.

All this is quite different when the woman is less inhibited sexually. What role does the clitoris have then? We know that genital sexuality emerges from the pregenital cluster and that the components of the cluster all play a certain role until genitality is attained. The various components are not all equally important: for example, either orality or anality may dominate. Excitation of the erogenous zones (or an equivalent function) can arouse true sexual excitation by its predominance—indeed this may be its prerogative. One might mention here the role of kissing in genital excitation, as well as that of various erogenous zones and the functions of the anal-sadistic component, including all kinds of body movement. One could speak of *elective genital induction,* especially as the genital function tends in each case to take on the pregenital character of that component, for example the oral or anal one. This must not be confused with perversion, where the pregenital component does not contribute to genitality but replaces it. Therefore, when woman's sexuality is relatively normal the chief inductors are the clitoris and narcissistic sexual excitation, which is the specific function of the clitoris. The impulse passes from its apparent source, the clitoris, to the sexual region, more instinctual and broader in its capacity of investing sexuality narcissistically and thereby supporting the cathexis of instinctual sexuality. This "sexualization" of narcissism should, probably, be called "resexualization," that is, a return to autoeroticism, integrated into the object-related instinctual ego, which at the beginning of development is identical with all eroticism. Later it leads to complete sexuality, after passing through an obligatory polymorph-perverse stage, where it might have been held up indefinitely, had there been a narcissistic perversion.

Narcissism has several forms because its roots lie buried in undifferentiated layers of psychic life which, according to Freud, could just as easily have become libido or aggression. This stratum holds within it a potential of great variability which cannot be studied in any more depth here.

Children, and sometimes adults, are often tempted to masturbate immediately when they are alone, not only because solitude permits solitary pleasures but because there is a simultaneous narcissistic sensation associated with being alone, which arouses a specifically sexual excitation in the child. It demands adequate masturbatory satisfaction unless the child employs the link to an object—a sexual relationship with someone else. And women, because of their essential narcissism, the specifically narcissistic cathexis of their bodies, their occupations, their family and friends, their "interior," are at least to some degree always in this stage of narcissistic sexual excitation, even if it does not have a truly erotic quality. Such excitation should normally be an inductor to sexual intercourse, and this is often its role. But it is not always so, and in these exceptional cases the sexual partner can achieve what the woman's own inductive, narcissistic stimulation is incapable of doing by itself.

I have said that the clitoris, as a narcissistic sexual organ, must project the narcissistic cathexis onto the vagina, the true center of the instinctual drive, but also onto the whole—internal and external—anal and perineal region. Of course, there are other possible inductors (muscular, sadistic, oral, etc.). Here I am considering only the instance of the clitoris as the dominant inductor because it is the most common one, not wishing thereby to explain bisexuality but only the narcissism which in my observation mainly attaches itself to the clitoris.

I am not concerned here with woman's purely instinctual preparation for coitus—that would lead us beyond the subject of this study. Let me therefore return to the study of the narcissistic "preparation" which, in an anatomical or physical way, consists of the excitation of the clitoral region; we have noted, however, that this is not sufficient and that narcissistic sexuality cannot be limited to it.

We know, and this was our starting point, that women feel a certain lack in narcissistic confirmation and look to men to give it to them. We also know that such confirmation must be achieved in a manner which is both erotic and endorses its subject. Each aspect strengthens the other when they are combined, and this is precisely what is missing in woman's normal development because the first object, the mother, is a homosexual one. Man provides woman with narcissistic confirmation and, in her need for recognition (that is, for being loved), this means love, since love is a narcissistic contribution. Indeed, what does it mean to "court" a woman? In order to obtain her favors, the man acts like a courtier, flattering and praising the sovereign. Does not "courting" mean to give sovereignty to women? The man who is courting tries his best to say agreeable, flattering things to the woman and takes advantage of every occasion to acknowledge her value, her uniqueness. He showers her with presents in order to demonstrate how much he appreciates the gift he hopes to receive from her, thus expressing true adoration and holding up to her a narcissistic mirror, as satisfactory as he can possibly make it. Although one cannot speak of a true sexual excitation, women on such an occasion experience the agreeable feeling of receiving the long-awaited narcissistic confirmation.

In the end, even the use of a coldly skillful technique which aims at a purely instinctual "preparation" owes much of its effectiveness to the fact that it testifies to the man's attraction and his interest in the woman. In other words it implies narcissistic confirmation. Thus, narcissistic preparation means much more than clitoral or erotic excitation and covers all the intricate relations between men and women.

The Change of Object

Catherine Luquet-Parat

The change of object is a crucial step in woman's development. It is the move in which the little girl decathects her mother as the object of love in order to cathect her father. But this definition is inadequate as it ignores many changes which occur simultaneously in the cathexis of the love object, or erogenous zones, and in the structure of the entire ego. Probably, in view of this complexity Freud spoke of a "triple change" during the little girl's Oedipus complex: change of the love object, change of the leading erogenous zone (the erotic cathexis of the clitoris yielding to that of the vagina), and change from a position of activity to one of passivity toward the love object.

In fact, if one compares the situation at the end of the pre-Oedipal period to that at the passing of the Oedipus complex, one notices that this passage through the Oedipal period did end with such a triple change. I consider it most pertinent that attitudes and emotions of the female related to the penis have also been changed considerably. It is as though there were at the time certain transformations which while undoing and eliminating the old attitudes substantiate the claim for the penis. We shall come back to this point later.

Yet no two authors agree on the details of this "triple change," neither on the coordination and possible interrelationship between the various elements, each of different origin, nor on their relationship in time, be it successive or simultaneous. Therefore, the problem is always stated ambiguously, further affecting our grasp of the complexity of this period. During the period immediately preceding the change of object the little girl manifests toward her mother, the main object of her love, both an active and a possessive attitude. She identifies herself with her father, who is at the

84

same time seen as a rival. At this stage the clitoris is the primary erogenous zone. Most authors agree on these points. Some believe that this attitude represents the most natural and spontaneous tendencies of the feminine self, while others hold that it results from defensive attitudes which conceal the naturally passive inclination of the feminine ego.

For Freud the change begins with a diminution of the active and an increase of the passive impulses; the passive tendencies are the ones which facilitate the transition to father as an object. J. Lampl de Groot believes that first the active attitude toward the mother becomes a passive attitude toward her. Only later does the child turn toward her father and, simultaneously with this second move, the aggressive needs turn into more masochistic ones. According to Marie Bonaparte there is a reversal of the clitoris-centered sadistic fantasies about the mother now become passive fantasies about the father. This transformation is possible if one calls upon the idea of the unfolding female, masochistic, passive drives. The transition from clitoral passivity to vaginal passivity represents a secondary development. According to H. Deutsch it is the active sadistic libido, following upon the little girl's castration complex experienced after discovering her lack of a penis, which is changed into masochism. This masochism becomes then the basis of female sexuality.

All these theories, focused on the instinctual drives and their biological origins and implications, ignore the significance of object relations and their fundamental role in the formation of the ego. The instinctual drives cannot exist without object relations, except at the very early stages of life. It is, therefore, important to consider briefly instinctual development up to the point discussed here, and in particular the changes from activity to passivity and from aggression to masochism.

In early life, when immaturity precludes object relations and when the infant is as yet unable to distinguish between himself and the outer world, the baby goes from moments of need, in which he actively manifests his tensions (due to hunger, cold, etc.) by cries and gestures, to moments of satisfaction, with varying proportions of active and passive components. In the first few weeks there is no apparent difference between the behavior and instinctual manifestations of either sex. However, during this very first period changes from activity to passivity do already occur. The infant may accept them easily, but when they are associated with organic illness or defaults of maternal care, such changes can be jolting and painful. They may also vary in time, quantity, and quality. The anaclitic re-

lationship and the appearance of anxiety setting the tone for the relationship will surely influence the way the child experiences situations in which he must be passive.

Aggression, which at this stage may easily be confused with
the increase of tensions requiring discharge (resulting as it does
from the failure to differentiate between the self and the outer
world), is experienced as unbearable. It is probably insufficiently
discharged by the infant's tension-releasing cries, which often end
only with exhaustion and sleep, unless a real decrease of frustration
allows a sudden return to equilibrium. It is at the end of this period that the child develops a system of important fantasies reflect-
ing the beginning of the object relations.

At the age when the child is capable of object relations, his
active and aggressive drives are blended. They are directed toward
the same object which is simultaneously gratifying and frustrating.
The active search for passive pleasure is colored by primary anxiety
because the fear of passive situations derives from the fear of the active mother. Studies on children have confirmed Melanie Klein's observation that the truly external object is used by the child to reduce the internalized object at a very early stage and, providing he
has a good relation to his real (that is, external) object, he can overcome anxieties arising from his ambivalent desires. It is with these
vicissitudes of thwarted and unsatisfied desires as well as of diverse
frustrations that the child progresses from an age at which neuro-
logical immaturity restricts an important part of his pleasures to
the condition of passivity to an age at which his motility allows him
to start conquering the world actively. This is true for girls as well
as for boys. It is easy to see that aggression of preverbal children is
sometimes diverted when they find in the outside world an obstacle
blocking the satisfaction of their active, possessive, and aggressive
drives. In such an instance the child gets angry and becomes more
aggressive. But at the same time this anger makes him suffer. His
cries denote to what extent his anger affects him directly and to
what extent it makes him regress and turn it against himself, because the anger is now turned to the internalized object as much as,
or even more than, to the real external object. The child's cry re-
leases tension and expresses aggression as well as distress.

A double strand of aggressive drives combined at an earlier
stage now progressively divides: one to the external object the other
to the internal object.

During the dyadic ambivalent phase, marking the beginning
of object relations, activity and passivity are only partly linked. The
normal child enjoys many passive pleasures and directs much of his

activity to obtaining passive ones. Frequently, the child accepts or benefits from passive pleasures only inasmuch as he wishes or seeks them. If what a parent does to him is imposed it will, even if it leads to pleasure, be experienced as dangerous, disagreeably aggressive, and, above all, ambivalent. (This is a possible source of painful passive eroticism.)

The Oedipal triangle apparent at the eighth month is important throughout development. The ambivalent internalized object (the imago) is projected onto two real objects, one which is felt to be good and the other bad. The Oedipal triangle facilitates the incorporation of the object, ridding it of projective modifications. But its main function is to help resolve the masochistic component of the two aggressive developments. One object can then be rejected as being of no use for the ego.

The triangular arrangement fails when sexual identification takes place. During the primal scene the good and the bad object become one and in this way lead to the experience that something destructive is going on. The development of the concept of the primal scene spans a long period of time and impinges upon affects related to the oral, anal, and phallic modalities. One must not forget, as Freud often emphasized, that in reality these stages do not follow one another but overlap, superimpose upon, and partly coincide with each other. Aggression can easily be discharged by means of identification with the active sadistic agent of the scene, whether this sadism be oral or anal. Yet the child's activity is, at this period, strongly marked by the affects characteristic of the anal stage now at its peak and is naturally linked to the sadistic drives. When the girl because of fantasies of the primal scene has projected an intense aggressiveness onto the breast or the penis it becomes particularly difficult and anxiety-producing for her to adopt a passive attitude toward the penis. The parents' attitude, toward the child and toward each other, is important for the identifications and the confirmation or nullification of the infantile fantasies about the primal scene viewed as sado-masochistic. In every case it seems that there is sufficient projected anxiety to make it impossible to adopt a role within the primal scene without anxiety. Probably, this is why one notices first a change in the dyadic relation with the mother; the little girl takes on the active role (penile-anal) toward her mother, simultaneously manifesting her desire to have a penis, and in this way enters the pre-Oedipal phase or that of the negative Oedipus complex. She is both active and aggressive toward her love object, the mother whom the girl would like to possess exclusively, and therefore sees her father as a rival.

According to all authors the change from active to passive positions occurs before the positive libidinal Oedipal relationship with the father is established. Lampl de Groot believes that in the relationship with her mother the little girl ceases to be active, becomes passive, and then transfers this passive relationship to her father. Other authors are less precise, merely noting that during the change of object the active tendencies are converted into passive ones. Marie Bonaparte thinks that there is a reversal of the sadistic fantasies directed against the mother, which then become passive fantasies about the father. In his article "A Child Is Being Beaten" (1920) Freud pointed out this link between masochism and passivity in the masochistic Oedipal fantasy. It seems to me that the girl turns to her father in an active, possessive, and sadistic way first. She simultaneously displaces her libidinal desire and shifts her demand for the penis from the mother to the father. In spite of the Oedipal triangle which has lead her to assert her instinctual drives (love directed toward her father and hate toward her mother), at this point in her development the little girl pursues active and possessive solutions resulting from the anal stage. The feminine passive receptivity can occur only by diverting the sadistic drives directed toward the father's penis. A great part of a woman's femininity depends on this essential process which I should like to call "masochistic feminine move."

At the beginning of this period in which she actively adopts the passive role with the object closely related to the process of identification with the aggressor, the child makes use of a mechanism that can be summarized by the following sentiment: "It is I who want him to penetrate me with his penis, even though I feel this penis to be dangerous." It seems impossible for the little girl (in the fantasy relationship which she maintains prior to the Oedipus complex) to change objects, to give up the aggressor-possessor role so normal for her development and so appropriate for the natural development of her ego, without making a concomitant return to masochism. In most women the return is accepted by the ego, although it influences to some extent the development of womanhood.

The analysis of some women shows clearly the sequence of these instinctual moves. It is of particular interest that at certain stages in the analysis of the Oedipus complex, erotic and masochistic needs make a transitory appearance, linked to the revival of well-defined historical material.

Both the analyses of little girls and the direct observation of their games, fantasies, and spontaneous creations lead to the same conclusion. One can pinpoint this, which we might call *the second step,* in the change of object in the development of girls who never had and probably will not have any prominent masochistic dispositions. The masochistic fantasies and daydreams of the second step accompanying masturbatory activities are very important. If their subject matter is repressed during latency, these fantasies frequently reappear in adolescence. They enjoin masturbation or its equivalents. They are also directly related to the revival of Oedipal images, the importance of which is aggravated by a feeling of guilt. This in turn is linked to a process of identification and its echo-like variations and is stimulated by the mother who, under the guise of protecting the adolescent, stresses the dangers of seduction.

If analysis of the pregenital origin of these masochistic fantasies is omitted, insoluble problems occur, linked to overly strong masochistic affects which have in some sense "frightened" the ego and provoked a regression, thereby obstructing the development of the entire sexual organization. One can easily see how any increase in the psychological weight of this process may imperil the whole development of the Oedipus complex. Because of this pathogenic increment, linked to earlier pregenital conflicts, the conflict the little girl experiences, when she actively and sadistically desires the father's penis, is made worse by residual conflicts with the mother (the pregenital maternal imago). The masochistic inflation which still has the same significance that it had during earlier developments, is felt as a grave danger generating insuperable anxiety. It puts a stop to further development and invokes defensive procedures.

If the wished for penetration is then imagined as something which will truly affect both the integrity of the body and that of the ego if the penis still represents exaggerated phallic power (the penis that is "too big" even while the little girl desires it, a penis disproportionate in comparison with her, the image of phallic power, overwhelming, destructive, tearing apart the primitive maternal phallus), then intercourse and penetration will be experienced as an unbearable wish unacceptable to the ego, and contradictory both to fundamental narcissistic defenses and to self-preservation. At this point regression occurs and the little girl returns defensively to an active position and, because she considers it a vital defense, to the wish for the penis: she wants the penis for herself; she wants to have it so that she will not be penetrated by it. This may also mean that she wants a child for herself, a wish which differs widely from that of being impregnated by father.

In this respect secondary feminine narcissism can be seen as a defense against the wish to be penetrated, which is too frightening. The wish to be desired represents an identification with the phallus, which stands for seduction, penetration, possession, for clinging to one's possession, and for depreciating and reducing the other person.

To prevent the masochistic wish of penetration from taking this turn the father must be considered as a sufficiently good object. But for the genital imago of the father-possessor-of-the-penis to be considered good it is essential that during the pregenital period the child be able to separate sufficiently (thanks to the Oedipal triangle) a good imago from a bad one. The good maternal imago, projected and transferred onto the father, allows the Oedipal triangle to succeed.

The difficulty some girls have in accepting their desire for masochistic penetration compares to the difficulty certain boys have in considering their fear of Oedipal castration. In both cases regression and flight are linked to the intensity of the anxiety, due in reality neither to the idea of penetration nor to castration but to the fear of disintegration which would throw either boy or girl back into a world of archaic fantasies. In clinical work it is therefore necessary to analyze the persistent pregenital conflicts which have obstructed development. Indeed, the origin of those insuperable fears which are provoked by masochistic desires can always be located in strongly sado-masochistic representations of the primal scene at its different stages.

The regressive move to which I just drew attention is often reinforced by classical Oedipal guilt toward the maternal object (the dreaded Oedipal mother becoming a pregenital sadistic mother). This guilt can sometimes create illusions inasmuch as it helps to mask the essential part of the conflict.

As for the change of erogenous zones, the misleading and over-simplified, but commonly held view is that the girl has two genital erogenous zones and that the quality of being focal or even exclusive passes from one to the other. It would, however, mean distorting reality if one were not to take into account the fact that there is a "phallic" stage for the little girl, the acme of which occurs in the pre-Oedipal period. This phallic stage immediately following what is usually called the anal stage should more rightly be called (at least in the early part of its development) the anal-phallic stage. We know that the "stages" partly overlap and merge rather than abruptly succeed each other. From the point of view of erogeneity, the anal phase is rich and complex and its repercussions will influence the femininity yet to come. For a time, both the passive anal-cloacal erogeneity and oral erogeneity run parallel until the former entirely succeeds the latter. For a time passive oral erogeneity is expressed and prolonged in passive anal-cloacal erogeneity, even while active oral erogeneity is experienced through the oral zone. Gradually, anal-cloacal activity will predominate. The anal-cloacal zone will be cathected as an organ to be taken, to be appropriated, to be actively contained, to be possessed, to be destroyed. The fecal content is experienced both as a part of the person and also as "apart" from the body, and a part of the object (in relation with the mother-object), and it is progressively identified with the father's penis. Having been identified first with the mother's phallus then with that of the father this penis is itself a modality of object relation with the mother. One can therefore say that the girl's original phallic needs now take on the form of an anal need. The recognition or, more precisely, the possibility of appreciating the differences between the sexes occurs at a particular moment in development. "Appreciating" is used because the knowledge some little girls have of the difference between the sexes takes on a specific significance only at the age when children generally discover this difference.

Not enough significance has been attached to the little girl's urethral eroticism which is linked to both clitoral and anal eroticism. Education represses anal eroticism much more than it does urethral eroticism, which naturally influences the phallic aspect of both the erotic and instinctual development of the girl.

During the change of erogenous zones, the erogeneity of the clitoris is modified and may even disappear. The modification shows in an increase in passivity at the expense of activity, as the erogeneity of the clitoris has both a passive and an active component. The actual experience of vaginal erogeneity implies both conscious sensations and a precocious yet often repressed knowledge as well as anal erogeneity by virtue of their functional and anatomical affinity. Vaginal erogeneity usually occurs later and is therefore at this stage only "potential." For the little girl it is often the mouth which is symbolically equivalent to the vagina (see E. Jones). To be more precise, the active vaginal erogeneity (vaginal-anal-cloacal) is modified by an increase in passivity at the expense of activity, and is therefore more closely related to passive and anal erogeneity (which at the preceding stage was its basis) than to the active anal one.

Although there is a parallel between object relations and erogeneity it would mean distorting them if they were considered only in terms of zones and stages, forgetting that the essential part of the developments mentioned before occurs on the level of fantasy representation of love for an object. For the same reason, words like breast, cloaca, vagina, clitoris, and penis tempt one to give too precise a meaning to these anatomical realities of the adult world. In fact, these words designate both anatomic realities and symbolic representations of certain functions, but it is the latter that is usually intended by the words. For the development and the organization of her future femininity and sexuality, it is important that the girl synthesize and elaborate the dispositions resulting from the several stages into a specifically feminine receptivity.

The masochistic move has placed the little girl in a passive love position toward her paternal object. Does this mean that there is no longer any activity? It would be more correct to say that activity, having cathected passive strivings, can prepare feminine receptivity. Receptivity therefore seems to be activity with a passive aim, which also happens to correspond to the physiology of sexual intercourse. This passivity relates to the particular form of object relationship which is also true whenever one refers to passivity.

During the change of object and the masochistic comeback sexual fantasies and object relations transform activity into passivity, or activity with a passive aim. However, some activity and some of the "move toward ego development" are also subject to a parallel transformation, this time by identifications rather than by sexualized object relations. This feminine masochistic position refers to a series of identifications with the mother, but the identifications with the father, which were so important during the anal and phallic stages, do not entirely cease.

One of the most important modifications which occurs both during and because of the change of object is the disappearance of the wish for a penis. The little girl has got over the desire to have a penis like her father in order to penetrate her mother. (The desire for a penis is a readaptation, in a more or less genital fashion, of the pregenital desire of phallic power, phallic possession, primitive phallic reassurance, and phallic participation.) With the help of the masochistic move she has developed the desire to acquire the father's penis by being penetrated by it and by having a child by the father. Through her love for and her nonconflicted identifications with her mother the little girl can experience a true Oedipal love for her father and for men in general. This is an essential point in her development. He is the different object, the possessor of the penis, while she accepts the fact that she does not have a penis. She has thus achieved, by cathexis of her own gender the possibility of making her love come true as something that complements another person. Only at this point is heterosexuality achieved. Man, the image of her father, is from then on the other person: different from yet complementary to her and, because of this, loved and desired. The genital stage, the world of genital sexuality, has thus been attained.

I have already said that the masochistic move occurs at a specific transitory moment in feminine development: Does this mean that it disappears altogether? I have already mentioned the possibility that if coupled with great anxiety, it activates mechanisms of regression and reaction formations, leaving a negative mark on development. Apart from it one can still see traces of the masochistic move in the organization of feminine object relations representing trends of perverse, erogenic masochism. I shall not follow up this aspect of feminine development, as I have tried to restrict my study to the preparation of the change of object in an ideal, normal, case. I should like to conclude by considering what seems to me another frequent remnant of this masochistic move: the feminine dependence on man, or, more precisely, the adoption of an attitude of dependence due to choice rather than to necessity. One could say that erotic dependence never really ceases for women, because of their anatomical and physiological make-up. But this search for a position of dependence often reaches beyond sexual behavior and characterizes large segments of behavior in general. Women take on a certain "role" in an eroticized adaptation to the role another person has, maintaining it according to the pleasure thereby derived from it. I believe one must distinguish this from the actual dependence with which one might easily confuse it. The latter behavior, including the taking of secondary and subordinate positions, is due to inhibitions, regression, and guilt and is based on a feeling of obligation or represents a defense rather than a preference according to pleasure. Of course there are many women with mixed etiologies of whom one cannot say a priori whether passivity is due to a free erotic choice or to a neurotic obligation.

Feminine Guilt and the Oedipus Complex

Janine Chasseguet-Smirgel

"This is in disagreement with Freud's formidable statement that the concept of the Oedipus complex is strictly applicable only to male children and 'it is only in male children that there occurs the fateful conjunction of love for the one parent and hatred of the other as rival.' [1] We seem compelled here to be *plus royaliste que le roy.* . . . I can find no reason to doubt that for girls, no less than for boys, the Oedipus situation in its reality and phantasy is the most fateful psychical event in life."

—Jones ("The Phallic Phase," 1932)

It is troubling to note that Freudian theory gives the father a central role in the boy's Oedipus complex but considerably reduces that role in the girl's. In fact, in considering Freud's article "Female Sexuality" (to which Jones replies in his article "The Phallic Phase") it is suggested that the girl's positive Oedipus complex may simply not exist. If it exists, it is usually an exact replica of her relationship to her mother. Freud says in the same article, "except for the change of her love object, the second phase had scarcely added any new feature to her erotic life" (this second phase being the positive Oedipus complex).

Freud maintains that it is not because of her love for her father nor because of her feminine desires that the little girl arrives at the positive Oedipus position but because of her masculine desires and her penis envy. She tries to get what she wants from her father, the possessor of the penis. When the Oedipal position is reached, it tends to last some time as it is essentially a "haven." ("The Dissolution of the Oedipus Complex," 1924). "She enters the Oedipus situation as though into a haven or refuge." As the little girl has no fear of castration, she has nothing to give up, and she does not need a powerful superego.

During the period preceding the change of object, if it occurs at all, the father is "scarcely very different from an irritating rival" ("Female Sexuality," 1931), but at the same time the rivalry with

94

the father in the negative Oedipus complex is not so strong and is not in any way symmetrical with the boy's Oedipal rivalry accompanying his desire to possess his mother. The little girl in her homosexual love for the mother does not identify with the father.

If we turn from the study of normal or neurotic behavior to that of psychotics, we note the importance Freud gave to the role of homosexuality in his theories of delusion formation. Desires of passive submission to the father, dangerous for the ego, play the main role in masculine delusions. One of the most important of these wishes is the desire to have a child from the father. It is surprising that Freud, when he considered this desire in the context of a little girl's normal development, did not believe it to be a primary desire arising from her femininity but, on the contrary, a secondary desire, a substitute for penis envy.

Paradoxically, the father seems to occupy a much more important place in the psychosexual development of the boy than of the girl, be it as a love object or as a rival. I would even say that Freud, if one accepts all the implications of his theory, believes the father to be much more important in general for the boy than for the girl. However, Freud, with the open, scientific mind and concern for truth which characterize genius, never considered his studies of femininity to be complete or definitive, and he encouraged his disciples to continue their exploration of "the dark continent." One need only refer to the final sentence of one of his last works on the psychology of women: "If you want to know more about femininity, enquire from your own experience of life, or turn to the poets, or wait until science can give you deeper and more coherent information" (in "Femininity," 1932).

My aim in this study is to discuss certain specifically feminine positions in the Oedipal situation which are not found in that of the male. Perhaps I shall be able to reveal a little of their deeper motivation and describe their eventual consequences. Time will prevent our studying in detail many problems of woman's psychosexual life on which this study will inevitably touch, such as penis envy, female masochism, the superego, and the resolution of the Oedipus complex in girls. I shall treat of them only inasmuch as they relate to my central theme. Because of the numerous difficulties involved in this type of study a somewhat artificial presentation becomes unavoidable. I have placed greater emphasis on the particular characteristics of the girl's relation to her father, without taking into consideration, as one should, the significant early history of this relationship; neither have I touched on the particular problems of identification so important in homosexual development, as Joyce

McDougall deals with them more fully in her article in this book. Whenever one discusses "the specificity" of certain female attitudes one should compare them to male ones. In this study such a comparison can be no more than implied.

Most psychoanalytical authors have noted that women on the road to genital and Oedipal maturity are faced with greater difficulties than men, so much so that Freud, as we know, was led to reconsider his belief in the universality of the Oedipus complex as the nucleus of the neuroses. Those authors who do not agree with Freud generally believe that the difficulties the little girl encounters in her psychosexual development are due mainly to the fears for the ego—*narcissistic anxieties* awakened by the feminine role.

For my part, I shall concern myself with aspects of the female Oedipus complex which have no counterpart in the male, and which are the source of a specific form of feminine *guilt* inherent in a specific moment in woman's psychosexual development: the change of object.

I

Object Idealization in the Girl's Relation to Her Father

The theories of Freud and those who have followed him, as well as the theories of those who oppose him (Melanie Klein and Ernest Jones in particular), all agree on one point about the girl's development: the *change of object* inherent in the Oedipal development of women is based on *frustration*.

Thus, for Freud, the girl's Oedipus complex is due to a double misapprehension, having to do first with objects, then with her own narcissism. This disappointment is caused mainly by the fact that the little girl discovers her "castration"—the mother has given her neither the love nor the penis she wanted. According to Freud, this frustrated penis envy, replaced by a desire for a penis substitute, a child, prompts the little girl to turn to her father. Melanie Klein and Ernest Jones, on the other hand, thought that "the girl is brought under the sway of her Oedipus impulses, not indirectly, through her masculine tendencies and her penis envy, but directly, as a result of her dominant feminine instinctual components" (Melanie Klein, *The Psychoanalysis of Children*, 1932). Most of all the little girl wants to incorporate a penis, not for itself but in order to have a child by it. The desire to have a child is not a substitute for the impossible desire to have a penis (Jones, "The Phallic Phase," 1932). These authors, in spite of their refusal to admit the secondary quality of the feminine Oedipus complex, believe that the little girl's Oedipal desire is activated and awakened precociously by the *frustration* caused by the maternal breast, which then becomes "bad." It is, therefore, *the bad aspect of the first object* which (in both these views opposing Freud) lies at the basis of the change of object, the little girl seeking a good object capable of procuring for her the object-oriented and narcissistic satisfactions she lacks. The second object—the father or the penis—will be *idealized* because of the disappointment with the first object.

Indeed, a belief in the existence of a good object capable of alleviating the shortcomings of the first one is vital in order for any change of object to take place. This belief is accompanied by a projection of all the good aspects of the primary object onto the secondary object, while at the same time projection onto the original primitive object is maintained (temporarily at least) of all the bad aspects of that (new) object. This splitting is the indispensable condition leading to the change of object which would otherwise have no reason to occur. It is at the base of the girl's triangular orientation, as Catherine Luquet-Parat's article in this book has emphasized. But the splitting of the maternal image implies an *idealization* of the second object, if one may so refer to the projection of qualities all of which are exclusively good.

Several authors have stressed the importance of the idealization of this second object in girls. Thus, in *Envy and Gratitude*,[2] Klein refers to the exacerbation of negative feelings toward the mother, which turn the little girl away from her: "But an idealization of the second object, the father's penis and the father, may then be more successful. This idealization derives mainly from the search for a good object."

The idealization process on which the change of object is founded weighs heavily on women's future psychosexual development. In fact it implies an *instinctual disfusion,* each object being, at the time of the change of object, either entirely negatively cathected (the mother, her breast, her phallus) or entirely positively cathected (the father and his penis). Because of this the little girl will tend to *repress and countercathect* the aggressive instincts which exist in her relation to her father in order to maintain this instinctual disfusion. As a result there arises *a specifically feminine form of guilt attached to the anal-sadistic component of sexuality,* which is radically opposed to idealization.

The conflicts the little girl experiences in her relation with her father are, of course, linked to her first experiences with the maternal object as well as the peculiarities of the second object.

If positive experiences and progressively dosed "normal frustrations" (those which are necessary for the development of a strong and harmonious ego) prevail in the girl's relation to her mother, if the father's personality offers an adequate basis for the projection of the object's good aspects onto him, and if at the same time he is solid enough, the little girl will be able to go through that change of object when prompted by these frustrations, achieving thereby a nonconflictual identification with the mother without the idealization of the second object becoming unduly important at this particular moment of her development.

The need to make permanent the idealization of the object concomitant with an instinctual disfusion is in this situation less pressing, and feminine psychosexuality can now progress under more satisfactory conditions. On the other hand, if the first attempts turn out badly, and if the second object does not offer the attributes necessary for the projection of good qualities, then character problems, perversions, and psychoses may develop.

Nevertheless, in most cases—and this seems practically inherent in woman's situation—the change of object coincides with dosages of maternal frustration at the wrong times. The father then becomes the last resort, the last chance of establishing a relation with a satisfying object. Indeed, the relation between mother and daughter is handicapped from the start; one might even say intrinsically so since, as Dr. Grunberger points out in the article on female narcissism, this state is due to the sexual identity between mother and daughter. Freud himself stressed that the only relation that could avoid "the ambivalence characterizing all human relations" is that of mother and son. Later, I shall try to show some aspects of the father-daughter relationship which may help to explain why the idealization of the second object can be induced by the paternal attitude itself.

In most cases the father-daughter relation is characterized by the persistence of instinctual disfusion; the aggressive and anal-sadistic components are countercathected and repressed, since the second object must be safeguarded. At the same time the counteridentifications with the bad aspects of the first object are maintained.

The fact that the girl encounters greater difficulties in her psychosexual development than the boy is stressed by all authors. The frequency of female frigidity shows this. The guilt toward the mother alone is not sufficient to explain it; if it were, there ought to be something in the male that corresponds to it.

When Marie Bonaparte says that the cause of frigidity is to be found in the fact that woman has less libidinal energy, while Hélène Deutsch believes it to be linked to "constitutional inhibitions," [3] or when other authors believe it to be due to bisexuality, then it seems to me that they are sidestepping the discovery and interpretation of unconscious factors which, as Jones stressed in "Early Female Sexuality," form the main part of the analyst's task.

Many writers have noted, on the other hand, that woman's tendency toward idealization of sexuality is commonplace. One has only to think of adolescents or even of mature women who live in a romantic dream à la Madame Bovary waiting for Prince Charming, for eternal love, etc. . . . (In a recent sociological study Evelyne Sullerot mentions that the publishers of romantic pulp sell sixteen million copies a year.) Thus, in *The Psychology of Women*, Hélène Deutsch notes:

> As a result of a process of sublimation, woman's sexuality is more spiritual than man's. . . .
>
> This process of sublimation enriches woman's entire erotic affective life and makes it more individually varied than man's, but it endangers her capacity for direct sexual gratification. The constitutional inhibition of woman's sexuality is all the more difficult to overcome because, as a result of sublimation, it is more complicated (and the conditions for its gratification more exacting) than the primitive desire to get rid of sexual tension that more commonly characterizes masculine sexuality.

Hélène Deutsch stresses the "spiritualized" character of female sexuality and speaks of "sublimation" when she refers to it. But if this were a true sublimation the process would not end in inhibition. On the contrary, it seems to me that this is a reaction formation based on repression and countercathexis of those instinctual components opposed by nature to idealization or to anything spiritual or sublime; in other words, the anal-sadistic component instincts.

I shall now try to show the consequences of the repression of the anal-sadistic component for woman's psychosexual development. I shall make no attempt here to reconsider the concepts of activity and passivity, let alone the death instinct, but I would still like to quote certain statements by Freud about these concepts inasmuch as they concern the subject of this paper.

Discussing sexuality in general (not simply masculine sexuality) and referring to the *Three Essays*, Freud says in *Beyond the*

Pleasure Principle: "From the very start we recognized the presence of a sadistic component in the sexual instinct . . . later, the sadistic instinct separates off, and finally, at the stage of genital primacy, it takes on, for the purposes of reproduction, the function of overpowering the sexual object to the extent necessary for carrying out the sexual act." [4]

In this passage Freud identifies sadism with destructive and death instincts, pointing out that in the sexual act these instincts are subordinated to Eros in order to secure control of the object. This instinctual control explicitly links Freud, in *Three Essays* (1905), to the anal-sadistic stage and to mobility. In the 1915 revision he adds: "It may be assumed the impulse of cruelty arises from the instinct for mastery and appears at a period of sexual life at which the genitals have not yet taken over their later role."

In *The Ego and the Id* [5] (1923), Freud repeats this idea but this time insists on the importance of instinctual disfusion:

> The sadistic component of the sexual instinct would be a classical example of a serviceable instinctual fusion . . . Making a swift generalization, we might conjecture that the essence of a regression of libido (e.g., from the genital to the sadistic-anal phase) lies in a disfusion of instincts. . . .

Freud shows, in *Inhibitions, Symptoms, Anxiety,*[6] that Eros desires contact because it strives to make the ego and the loved object one, "to abolish all spatial barriers between the Ego and the loved object"; "the aggressive object cathexis has the same aim." Here again we see that aggression, according to Freud, is put in the service of Eros, desiring close contact with the object.

In these quotations we can see a sequential chain: mastery-sadism-anality; this chain is indispensable for sexual maturity, and its effective formation is a sign of genital maturation. Does the fact that this chain also has another link, "activity," mean that female sexuality is excluded from the Freudian concept of instinctual fusion which I have just mentioned? Once more, it is beyond my purpose to consider the concepts of activity and passivity in general. I merely wish to recall that one can follow Freud's thought and its numerous variations through all his writings on female sexuality in terms of antagonistic pairs of "masculine-feminine" and "active-passive." Whenever Freud attempts to liken these pairs of concepts he feels compelled to retract what he has said. In spite of his attempt to avoid equating these terms, other authors have completely identified activity with masculinity, passivity with femininity, and have reached doubtful conclusions as a result, especially as they have taken passivity to mean inertia or inactivity.

Thus, J. Lampl de Groot, in her article "Contribution to the Problem of Femininity" (1933), equates masculinity with activity and passivity with femininity. She draws a series of conclusions to the effect that "feminine" women do not know object love, activity under any guise, nor aggression. Since activity and love undoubtedly play a role in maternity, Lampl de Groot makes her famous postulate that it is women's *masculinity* which is expressed in the experience of pregnancy; and as this masculinity is opposed to female sexuality, "good mothers are frigid wives." This is not really proved because the postulate with which the article begins is merely repeated throughout in various tautological ways. Her essay ends with the statement that *introjection,* because it activates aggression, does not exist in truly "feminine" women.

Hélène Deutsch emphasized [7] the idea of a typically feminine activity "directed inward," and the amphimixis of oral, anal, and urethral instincts connected with the vagina during coitus and orgasm. Yet in a symposium on frigidity (1961) at which she presided, she held that orgasmic climax could only occur in men, because it is a sphincter activity typical of the male.

As early as 1930 authors like Imre Hermann, Fritz Wittels, and Paul Schilder had warned against the theoretical and therapeutic dangers of identifying femininity with passivity, or even inertia. Therefore, in order to avoid ambiguity in the use of such terms as "passivity" and "activity," I shall refer instead to the anal-sadistic component, whether it is the aggressive component of incorporative impulses or the aggressiveness linked to all attempts at achievement, for these two seem to me especially charged with conflict for women.

How Incorporation Becomes Charged with Conflict

Referring in the *Three Essays* to infantile masturbation Freud states that the girl often masturbates by pressing her thighs together, whereas the boy prefers to use his hand. "The preference for the hand which is shown by boys is already evidence of the important contribution which the instinct for mastery is destined to make to masculine sexual activity." In fact I believe that Freud is also indicating the importance this same instinct will have in female sexual activity. In coitus the vagina replaces the hand and like the hand it grasps the penis; this is reflected in the fantasies and problems characteristic for female sexuality, to the point that the anal

component in the control of the vagina causes conflict. Psychoanalytical writings frequently refer to man's fear of the vagina (Freud,
"The Taboo of Virginity," 1918; [8] Karen Horney, "The Dread of
Women," 1932), but they rarely mention the other side of the problem, which is the attitude of the woman (her superego) toward her
own aggression to the penis; if the problem is mentioned, the aggression is usually attributed to penis envy, or to defense against the
penis considered dangerous because of certain projections, but the
problem is never linked to the anal-sadistic component—as though
female sexual desire contained no aggressive or sadistic elements.

In general, women's aggression toward the penis is never seen
as a source of guilt. I do not wish in any way to deny the existence
of the forms of female aggression which are frequently discussed, but
I should like to insist particularly on the problems implied in *a basically feminine wish to incorporate the paternal penis,* which invariably includes the anal-sadistic instinctual components.

One must remember that during sexual intercourse, the
woman does actually incorporate the man's penis. Although this incorporation is only partial and temporary, women desire in fantasy
to keep the penis permanently, as Freud pointed out in his article
"On Transformations of Instincts as Exemplified in Anal Erotism"
(1924).[9]

I shall illustrate the problems connected with wishes of incorporation toward the paternal penis through one case only,
though in my experience the same conflicts are to be found in all
women's analyses.

The patient whom I shall call Ann had idealized the image
of her father. In order to protect this image she split her erotic objects into two very distinct types.

The first, a substitute for the father, is represented by a man,
far older than she is, whom she loves tenderly and purely. This man
is impotent. He loves her, protects her, encourages her career. She
speaks of him in the same terms as she speaks of her father, who
would give her a warm stone in winter to prevent the chilling of
her fingers while going to school, kiss her tenderly, or sit with her
on a bench in front of the house, offering wine to the neighbors
passing by. The other man is represented by a Negro, to whom she
feels she could show her erotic impulses, which are *linked* to the
anal impulses.

During analysis, she says, "Before, black and white were separate, now they are mixed together."

Ann is in her forties, she is an opthalmologist, married and with two children, full of vitality and spirit, but paralyzed by deep conflicts which reveal themselves in strong anxieties, depersonalization, and the impulse to throw herself into the river or off a building. The theme of *engulfment* in water is frequent in her associations in the transference.

In the first session she is already very anxious and sees the green wall of my consulting room as an aquarium. *She feels she is in this aquarium herself* and says:

"I am very frightened . . . These ideas of aquaria are fetal. . . . I feel I am becoming schizophrenic."

Several times during the analysis she expressed her anxiety in the following terms:

"I am cracking up, I am *drowning*. I need a branch to save me. Will you be that branch?"

She often expressed the fear that I might become pregnant.

She also suffered from claustrophobia: fear of being alone in a room with no exit, fear of elevators. She dreams she is enclosed in a very tiny and very dark room similar to a coffin from which she cannot escape.

Ann's parents were farmers. She was, along with her sister, brought up by a severe and castrating mother. The father, much older than the mother, was "gentle and kind."

"My mother bossed him around. She was the ruler of the home. She ruled us all with a rod of iron. . . . Father was good; he forgave her everything. She took advantage of it."

Ann often recalled incidents which represented the father's castration by the mother. For example, one day her father comes back from the fair where he had been drinking a little, lies down, and goes to sleep. The mother takes advantage of this occasion by stealing his wallet and then accusing him of having lost it. The primal scene which reveals itself through Ann's association is fantasied as a sadistic act during which the mother takes the father's penis.

I cannot give the whole development of Ann's analysis, but her treatment was centered on her difficulty in identifying with her mother. This difficulty was the major obstacle to a satisfactory Oedipal development. It was as though loving her father meant becoming like the castrating mother, sadistically incorporating his penis, and keeping it within her. But her love for her father could not allow her to adopt such a role.

Very early in the analysis, Ann expressed this conflict in the form of a dream:

"This is a very frightening dream. *I was* walking with *my mother* (an attempt to identify with the mother) in the river where

I had my first impulse to throw myself into the water. We were looking for eel traps. It reminds me of the penis in the vagina (sadistic and castrating aspect of intercourse). My mother was mean to my father. This dream frightens me."

Another dream of the same night: "My mother was coming back from the river with my father's jacket on her shoulders. She had gone mad. In real life it is I who am afraid of going mad, of giving in to my impulses."

Behind her impulses of throwing herself into the river or off a building lies the unconscious fantasy of identification with the mother who castrates her father during intercourse (the mother coming back from the river with the father's jacket). She expresses her castration wishes in the transference in many ways, sometimes even in a quasi-delirious way. She feels guilty because she is sure that *by shaking hands with me* (to bid good-bye) *she has strained my wrist* (she associates this with the paternal penis).

The transference expressions of her anal-sadistic impulses directed toward the penis were predominant in her relation with me and were mixed with anxiety and guilt. One day she associated the following recollection with her feeling of cracking up and *drowning:*

"In the River Gave there are potholes, you know, and deep eddies. One day my father nearly drowned in one; he was carried away by the current but caught hold of a branch at the last minute. . . . I am afraid of elevators. The elevator could fall in its shaft, and I would fall with it. I have the image of a penis drawn in by a vagina. . . ."

I believe Ann's conflict appears clearly in these associations of her fear of the impulse to throw herself into the river or off a building. The parents' intercourse signified for Ann an aggressive incorporation of the father's penis by the mother (the father's jacket on the mother's shoulders, the eel in the trap, the father engulfed by the eddy). In order to arrive at the Oedipal phase she must identify with the castrating mother, that is to say, *engulf the father's penis* in her vagina.

Yet, behind the patient's symptoms (her phobic impulses) there is a *reverse fantasy:* she is the contents (father's penis or father) of a destructive container (mother or mother's vagina). Her own body or vagina is identified with the mother or the mother's vagina. The destructive feature of the vagina is linked with the sphincteral anal component. The first fantasy hidden behind the symptom is therefore a compromise between the fulfillment of a desire and its punishment.

Ann achieves through guilt in fantasy the genital Oedipal desire to "engulf" the father's penis (like the mother did), but she does this by *turning the aggression* against herself, her whole body identified with the paternal penis, whereas her destructive vagina, projected onto the outer world, is experienced as a cavity into which she disappears.

The contents and the container are reversed. Ann herself becomes the contents, which have disappeared into the container.

We realize that the first fantasy (the most superficial one), in which the punishment (superego) occurs, resulting in a compromise between the instinct and the defense, merely conceals another more primitive fantasy, which directly expresses the instinct: "I am the hole in which my father (his penis) is engulfed."

Her phobic symptom contains a double unconscious fantasy which is in accord with the Freudian theory of symptoms: a compromise concealing a primitive instinct.

It is important to add that one of the precipitating factors in mobilizing Ann's neurosis was her father's death just before her analysis, when she herself was pregnant. When she spoke of her father's death it was always in relation to her pregnancy. It became obvious during the analysis that the fantasy underlying this was that of the father's destruction by incorporation. Her fear that I should become pregnant, her projection of an aquarium onto the green wall of my consulting room, along with her fantasy of fetal regression, manifested the same symptomatic reversal of her fantasy: the fear of being engulfed and shut up inside me, like the fetus in its mother's womb, the fecal stool in the anus, or the penis in the vagina.

Having had a number of female patients with phobias of being engulfed by water, claustrophobia, compulsive ideas of throwing themselves into water or from a great height, vertigo, and phobias of falling, I came to realize that they all had a common meaning. In my experience they signify reversal of contents and container. The patient, by turning the aggression onto herself, experiences the sensation that she is the contents threatened by a dangerous container.

The genital level of these phobias does not mean that the ego is not severely affected; as we have seen the guilt involved in the relation with the idealized father often results from early conflicts with the primary object, since these conflicts are numerous and dangerous.

The sexual problems of these patients are of various kinds.

Sometimes the splitting of the desired objects is enough to maintain a normal sexual appearance, but sexual pleasure is often restricted to the *clitoris* only. This particular sexual problem should be related to the same incorporation-guilt that forbids the erotic cathexis of the vagina, the organ of incorporation displacing its cathexis then onto an external organ, the clitoris. The analysis of this incorporation-guilt often allows for a more or less rapid extension of the clitoris's erotic cathexis to the vagina. This happens through the liberation of anal erotic and aggressive drive components which are then invested in the vagina. In some cases active homosexual wishes carry the same meaning of defense when conflict over incorporation is the issue.

A patient suffering from dyspareunia manifested this by a lack of vaginal stricture during intercourse. This symptom, which is in some way the reverse of vaginismus, is relatively frequent, but the patients who suffer from it believe it to be due to their anatomical make-up and become conscious of its psychogenic character only when it disappears during treatment. This symptom is the one which expresses most clearly the countercathexis of the anal-sadistic instinct of control. When this component is well integrated the vagina can allow itself to close around [10] the penis. In Freudian terms, one could say that desire of the Eros to unite with the object is satisfied, due to the instinct of control subordinating itself to the former.

Guilt Concerning Feminine Achievement

A girl's guilt toward her father does not interfere merely with her sexual life but extends to her achievements in other fields if they take on an unconscious phallic significance. Inhibition related to this guilt seems to me chiefly responsible for women's place in culture and society today. Psychoanalysts have noticed that Oedipal guilt, linked to the guilt of surpassing the mother, is associated in many intellectual, professional and creative activities with a feeling of guilt toward the father, a guilt which is specifically feminine. Indeed, I found that in patients suffering from chronic headaches their guilt over surpassing their parents on an intellectual level (which is so often the origin of cephalic symptoms, as though reproducing an autocastration of the intellectual faculties) was usually linked to the father, in both male and female patients. For both sexes successful intellectual activity is the unconscious equivalent of possessing the penis. For women this means they have the father's penis and have thus dispossessed the mother, the Oedipal drama. In addition they have also *castrated the father*. Moreover, the adequate use of such a penis also involves from the unconscious point of view the fecal origin of this image, ultimately, that of retaining an anal penis, which in turn engenders guilt.

One of my patients, a young girl of fifteen and a half who had severe migraine as well as school problems, was particularly poor in spelling and always had low marks on oral tests. When she tried to think, her thoughts blurred. She felt as though she were in a fog. Her ideas would become imprecise, she grew muddled and felt stumped—in other words her ideas lost their anal component. Her headaches began while she was preparing for an examination which she kept failing. The diploma she was trying to obtain was exactly the same as the one her father had.

This inhibition concerning the intellectual field she shared with her father was analyzed in relation to her Oedipal guilt about her mother, but it was soon obvious that interpretations on these levels were insufficient to bring to light the meaning of her symptoms.

She had a dream in which she wanted to hold her hand up, as a sign that she could answer the questions in the tests, but she felt it was "forbidden"; she had another dream in which she had a snake in her hand which turned into a pen, so she took it to the police station because "the man to whom it belonged could not write without his pen"; . . . these dreams led to interpretations in relation to her guilt about castrating her father and resulted in the cessation of her school inhibitions as well as a satisfactory Oedipal evolution. Indeed, once her aggression toward the paternal penis was accepted she was able to create fantasies about an Oedipal sexual relation with the father. The last dream she brought was one in which she received an attractive pen as a present from her father and then went with him for a walk along a sunken road, while her mother, who in the dream looked like me, was away on holiday.

Ann, the patient whom I formerly discussed, thought all her problems were due to her professional promotion. "I am classless," she would say, "I am neither peasant nor bourgeois. I would have done better to have stayed working on the farm like father." With the people who praised her for her professional success she suddenly felt like "shouting, saying stupid things, acting like a mad woman." Before her analysis she had had a period of anxiety during which she could not write any prescriptions, all the formulas blurring in her mind. Having a profession meant having a penis which she had stolen from her father just as her mother had done during the primal scene.

This meaning is expressed clearly in the following dream: "I am beside an operating table. The surgeon is operating on the brain of an elderly man who could be my father. He ablates the whole frontal part of his brain away. I think to myself, 'Poor man, he is going to be abnormal.' When the surgeon has finished, he addresses the people who are there and says of me: 'She is extremely intelligent and an excellent doctor, and she has a very pretty little girl with dark hair.' "

Her associations about this dream are:

"I worked for that surgeon when I was a student. He used to congratulate me on doing my medical studies simultaneously with working as a nurse. Oh! *What a headache I've got* . . . I had another dream:

"I was at your place and I was cutting bread. A patient came in. You diagnosed him and phoned the diagnosis to someone. I admired how fast and sure you were in your diagnosis. Then you came up to me and said, 'What is the diagnosis?' I gave the same diagnosis as you had. Then I felt embarrassed because it is as though you thought I hadn't overheard your conversation on the phone and that I thought of that diagnosis myself. So for the sake of intellectual honesty I told you that I had overheard your diagnosis. I thought I would have no difficulty in telling you this dream, but on the contrary I feel embarrassed as though I had cheated you. In the dream I had the feeling I was lying, and stealing something. One day I made a girl-friend of mine steal a toy. We were little then. When I said good-bye to you last time I again had the feeling that I had sprained your wrist. I have the feeling you are fragile."

For Ann professional capability has the meaning of castrating the father, or the analyst in the paternal transference, and this castration represents an identification with the mother who steals the father's power. This is an anal castration as one can see by her feeling that she is telling lies and cheating me, analogous to her fantasy of the Primal Scene as shown in the screen memories: the mother stealing the father's money after he had come back drunk from the fair, followed by her accusation that the father had lost the money; the mother ordering him about, hiding for hours to frighten him, making him believe that she was working all the time, while in fact she did nothing. She seemed to be like Delilah, taking advantage of Samson's trusting sleep to cut off his hair.

The guilt linked with this desire to identify with the sadistic mother leads Ann to castrate herself (have headaches, fantasies in

which she "loses her mind," professional inhibitions) and to perform acts which restore what has been taken away (she gives me
back the diagnosis she has stolen, she worries about my sprained
wrist). This fantasy of possessing a phallus is so conflict-laden that
any small intervention touching on it stimulates guilt in women
who otherwise seem quite free of work inhibitions.

I had a patient who, before she came to analysis, gave lectures on a rather feminine topic—children's education. At the end
of one of her lectures, someone came up to her and said:
"All that is very well but, you know, the sight of a woman
carrying a brief case and a whole lot of files—really, that just isn't a
woman's role!" [11]
From that day on, this patient never gave another lecture!

Analytical interpretation of these conflicts brings relief to
women involved in fields they feel belong to men and which have
an obvious phallic meaning (for example, taking exams, driving a
car) as well as in those which are specifically feminine, such as pregnancy. Here again guilt toward the mother, the Oedipal rival, is
coupled with the guilt of having taken the father's penis in order to
make a child with it. This attack against the essence of the love object applied in transformation is experienced as anal guilt.
The symbolic connection "child-penis" becomes significant in
this context. Uncontrollable vomiting during pregnancy, and all the
psychosomatic difficulties linked with the problems of accepting
motherhood are often related to this guilt, as one can see in the
analytical material of pregnant women.

Creativity.—It is commonplace that women (with few exceptions) are not great creators, scientific or artistic. Man's creativity
has been attributed to a desire to compensate for the fact that he
cannot bear children (K. Horney) and thus create life. I believe
that this is indeed one of the deep motives of creative work.
Yet creating is a means of alleviating deficiencies at various
levels of instinctual maturity, and this results in attempts to achieve
narcissistic integrity—represented in the unconscious by the phallus
(Grunberger).
The phallic significance of creativity is emphasized in Phyllis
Greenacre's article dealing with women who are creative artists. She
believes that this sometimes results in inhibitions due to fear that a
phallic achievement might interfere with the fulfillment of feminine desires. I agree with the author about the phallic meaning of

creativity, but I would here again stress the part played by feminine guilt concerning possession of the penis and aggression toward the idealized father.

Women who have not idealized their fathers usually have no urge to create, because creation implies the projection of one's narcissism onto an ideal image which can be attained only through creative work.

If creative work signified only the act of parturition, then women with children would lack any desire to create, but analysis proves this to be untrue. The giving of life is not the same thing as being creative. To create is to do something other and something more than what a mother does, and it is in this respect that we see the phallic meaning of creation and its relation to penis envy.

That so many different achievements are symbolized by the possession and use of a penis results from the unconscious meaning of the phallus for both men and women. Whatever works well is represented in the unconscious by the phallus. Grunberger demonstrates in his essay on "The Phallic Image" that the phallus is the symbol of narcissistic wholeness. Why is it that valor, creativity, integrity, and power are all, on different levels, symbolized by the male sex organ? In order to attempt to answer to this question we shall consider the problems of castration and penis envy in women.

I I

The Female Castration Complex and Penis Envy

"I've got one, and you've got none!" (Gay little song sung by a three-and-a-half-year-old boy to his six-year-old sister.)

On the subject of penis envy Freud's views are opposed to those of Josine Müller, Karen Horney, Melanie Klein, and Ernest Jones. Freud holds that, until puberty, there is a *phallic sexual monism,* and therefore a total sexual identity between boys and girls up till the development of the castration complex. According to Hélène Deutsch, who agrees with Freud on these points, the little girl has no complete sexual organ from the age of four (age of the castration complex) to puberty—she has only her clitoris, which is seen as a *castrated penis.* She has no vagina as she has not yet discovered it and does not even know of it *unconsciously.*[12] We can understand easily why Freud and those who followed him in his theory on female sexuality believed *penis envy to be a primary phe-*

nomenon and fundamental to women's psychosexuality, since the little girl wants to compensate for the instinctual and narcissistic defects which mark most of her childhood.

Authors who do not agree with Freud's theory of female sexuality refuse to consider woman as *"un homme manqué"* (Jones). According to these authors the vagina is the first sexual organ to be libidinally cathected. The little girl is a woman from the start. The cathexis of the clitoris is secondary and serves a defensive function with regard to conflicts concerning genital impulses linked to the vagina: "The undiscovered vagina is a vagina denied" (Karen Horney).

These authors agree that repression of vaginal impulses is due to narcissistic anxieties concerned with attacks against the inside of the body. Therefore, the erotic cathexis is transferred to the clitoris, a safer, external sexual organ.[13] This throws a new light on the theory of penis envy.

Josine Müller believes that self-esteem is linked to the satisfaction of the impulses peculiar to one's own sex. Penis envy, therefore, is due to the narcissistic wound resulting from unsatisfied genital (vaginal) desires, which have been repressed.

For Karen Horney penis envy results from certain characteristics of the penis (its visibility, the fact that its micturition is in the form of a jet, and so on),[14] but also from a fear of the vagina which exists in both sexes. In the girl such fears are related to her Oedipal desire to be penetrated by the father's penis, which becomes fearful because she attributes to it a power of destruction.

According to Melanie Klein, *the libidinal desire for the penis* is a primary one. It is first of all an oral desire, the prototype of vaginal desire. The fulfillment of this desire is linked to the fantasy of sadistically taking the paternal penis from the mother, who has incorporated it. This results in fear of retaliation from the mother, who might try to wound or destroy the inside of the girl's body. Therefore, penis envy can be related to the following ideas in the girl's unconscious: By using the external organ she demonstrates her fears are unfounded, testing them against reality. She regards the penis as a weapon to satisfy her sadistic desires toward her mother (cleaving to her so as to tear away the penis which is hidden inside her, to drown her in a jet of corrosive urine, etc.). The guilt resulting from these fantasies may make her wish to return the penis which she has stolen from the mother, and thus restitute her by regressing to an active homosexual position for which the possession of a penis is necessary.

Ernest Jones follows Melanie Klein's theory of penis envy in his article "The Phallic Phase" (1932) centering his ideas on the primary characteristic of the "receptive" cathexes of all the orifices of a woman's body (her mouth, anus, vagina).

All these authors attribute a large part in female psychosexuality to the father and to penis envy, whereas Freud believed the Oedipus complex to be mainly masculine. Ruth Mack Brunswick thought female neuroses lack an "Oedipus complex" and J. Lampl de Groot claims that the paternal image really exists for the little girl only when once she is six, and maintains, that until that age, the relation with the father is the same as the child's relation with any other member of the household: sometimes friendly, sometimes hostile, according to her mood.

In his article on "Female Sexuality" (1931) Freud argues against the *secondary* nature of penis envy, because the woman's envy is so violent that it can only have drawn its energy from *primary* instincts.

I believe that the fact that there may be primary receptive instincts in women, be they oral, anal, or vaginal,[15] does not prevent penis envy from being primary, too. However, even if one holds that a female sexual impulse exists right from the start, that the little girl has an adequate organ of which she has some certain knowledge, in other words, that she has all the instinctual equipment, yet we learn from clinical experience that from a narcissistic point of view the girl feels painfully incomplete. I believe the cause of this feeling of incompleteness is to be found in the primary relation with the mother and will therefore be found in children of both sexes.

The Omnipotent Mother

In the article she wrote with Freud, "The Pre-Oedipal Phase of the Libido Development" (1940), Ruth Mack Brunswick insists on the powerful character of the primitive maternal imago ("She is not only active, phallic, but *omnipotent*"). She shows that *the first activity to which the child is submitted is the mother's.* The transition passage from passivity to activity is achieved by an *identification with the mother's activity.* Because of his dependence on the omnipotent mother "who is capable of everything and possesses every valuable attribute" the child obviously sustains "early narcissistic injuries from the mother" which "enormously increases the child's hostility."

I believe that a child, whether male or female, even with the best and kindest of mothers, will maintain a terrifying maternal image in his unconscious, the result of projected hostility deriving from his own impotence.[16] This powerful image, symbolic of all that is bad, does not exclude an omnipotent, protective imago (witch *and* fairy), varying according to the mother's real characteristics.

However, the child's primary powerlessness, the intrinsic characteristics of his psychophysiological condition, and the inevitable frustrations of training are such that the imago of the good, omnipotent mother never covers over that of the terrifying, omnipotent, bad mother.

It seems to me that when the little boy becomes conscious [17] that this omnipotent mother has no penis and that he, subdued so far by her omnipotence, has an organ which she has not, this forms an important factor in his narcissistic development.

Analysts have mainly stressed the horror (the *"Abscheu"*) the little boy feels when he realizes that his mother has no penis, since it means to him that she has been castrated, thus confirming his idea that such a terrifying possibility exists. This in turn may lead to fetishistic perversion and certain kinds of homosexuality. Few people take note of Freud's other statements stressing the narcissistic satisfaction felt by the little boy at the thought that he has an organ which women do not have. Thus, Freud says (in a note on exhibitionism added to the *Three Essays* in 1920): "It is a means of constantly insisting upon the integrity of the subject's own (male) genitals and it reiterates his infantile satisfaction at the absence of a penis in those of women." Elsewhere, Freud mentions the little boy's triumphant disdain for the other sex. He believes that this feeling of triumph (a note in *Group Psychology and the Analysis of the Ego*) [18] always arises from a convergence of the ego and the ego ideal. So it is indeed a narcissistic satisfaction, a triumph at last, over the omnipotent mother.

In his 1927 article on "Fetishism" Freud pointed out the ambivalent role of the fetish. It is supposed to conceal the horrifying castration while it is at the same time the means of its possible reparation. Freud says of the fetishist that "to point out that he reverses his fetish is not the whole story; in many cases he treats it in a way which is obviously equivalent to a representation of castration," and at this point Freud refers to the people who cut off braids. When considering the Chinese custom of mutilating women's feet and then venerating them, which he believes to be analogous to fetishism, Freud states: "It seems as though the Chinese male wants to thank the woman for having submitted to being castrated."

Countless clinical details relating to both sexes testify to the frequency and wealth of wishes to castrate the mother of her breast and of her phallus. If it were not for this deep satisfaction and its associated horror, the fantasy of the castrated mother would probably be less forceful.

Is it not at this point that myths begin to prevail over scientific thought? Are we not all tempted to talk as Freud did of "the castrated condition of women," or of "the necessity for women to accept their castration," or as Ruth Mack Brunswick put it, "The real quality of the representation of the castrated mother and the fantasy quality of the phallic mother," instead of putting these two representations back under the sway of the pleasure principle?

Images of woman as deficient, as containing a hole or wound, seem to me to be a denial of the imagoes of the primitive mother; this is true for both sexes, but in women identification with such an imago leads to deep guilt.

The protective imago of the good omnipotent mother and the terrifying imago of the bad omnipotent mother are both in opposition to this representation of the castrated mother.

Generous breast, fruitful womb, softness, warmth, wholeness, abundance, harvest the earth, all symbolize the mother.

Frustration, invasion, intrusion, evil, illness, death, all symbolize the mother.

In comparison with the ideal qualities attributed to the early mother-image, the fall of the "castrated" mother appears to result from a deep desire to free oneself from her domination and evil qualities.

The little boy's triumph over the omnipotent mother has many effects on his future relations with women. Bergler points out that man attempts to reverse the infantile situation experienced with the mother and live out actively what he has endured passively, thus turning her into the dependent child he had been. This idea seems to be supported by certain aspects of woman's role, often noted by other authors. One also observes in patients the narcissistic effect of a man's realization that his mother does not possess a penis.

If the little boy has not been traumatized by the omnipotent mother, if her attitude has been neither too restraining, nor too invasive, he will be sufficiently reassured by the possession of his penis to dispense with constant reiteration of the triumphant feeling he once experienced. The need to reverse the situation might be restricted to a protective attitude toward women (this is not necessarily a reaction formation; it might be a way of linking his need for mastery to his love). But if the child was a fecal part-object serving to satisfy the mother's desire for power and authority, then the child's future object-relations with women will be deeply affected.[19]

In analysis we rarely encounter male patients who show defused anal-sadistic impulses in a pure state, nor do we find mothers in *analyses* who satisfy perverse desires through their children. But many male patients present contained sexual and relational problems, linked to a need for a specific form of narcissistic gratification which we regard as being the result of regression to the phallic-narcissistic phase.

It seems that Jones's description of the deutero-phallic phase in boys (with narcissistic overestimation of the penis, withdrawal of object-libido and lack of desire to penetrate sexually and certain aspects of ejaculatio praecox noted by Abraham) are to be found in these narcissistic-phallic men who have been disturbed in their early relation with the mother. They lack confidence in the narcissistic value of the penis and constantly have to put it to the proof; theirs is the "little penis" complex, they regard a sexual relation as narcissistic reassurance rather than an object relationship of mutual value.[20]

Such men constantly doubt their triumph over women, as they doubt the fact that she has no penis, and are always fearful of finding one concealed in the vagina. This leads to ejaculation *ante portas,* in order to avoid such a dangerous encounter. The fantasy represents not only the paternal phallus but also (as Jones pointed out) the destructive anal penis of the omnipotent mother.[21]

But, in general, possessing the penis proves to be the satisfactory narcissistic answer to the little boy's primary relation with his mother.

Like the boy, the little girl, too, has been narcissistically wounded by the mother's omnipotence—maybe even more than he, for the mother does not cathect her daughter in the same way that she cathects her son. But the girl cannot free herself from this omnipotence as she has nothing with which to oppose the mother, no narcissistic virtue the mother does not also possess. She will not be able to "show her" her independence (I think this expression relates to phallic exhibitionism). So she will envy the boy his penis and say that he can "do everything." I see penis envy *not as "a virility claim" to something one wants for its own sake, but as a revolt against the person who caused the narcissistic wound: the omnipotent mother.*

Clinical experience often shows that penis envy is stronger

and more difficult to resolve when the daughter has been traumatized by a domineering mother. The narcissistic wound aroused by
the child's helplessness and by penis envy are closely related.

Realization that possession of the penis presents the possibility of healing the narcissistic wound imposed by the omnipotent
mother [22] helps to explain some of the unconscious significance of
the penis, whether it is that of a treasure of strength, integrity,
magic power, or autonomy. In the idea connected with this organ we
find condensed all the primitive ideas of power. This power becomes then the prerogative of the man, who by attracting the
mother destroyed her power. Since women lack this power they
come to envy the one who possesses the penis. Thus, woman's envy
has its source in her conflict with her mother and must seek satisfaction through aggression (that is, what she considers to be aggression) toward her love object, the father. Any achievement which
provides her with narcissistic pleasure will be felt as an encroach-
ment on the father's power, thereby leading to many inhibitions, as
already mentioned. In fact there is often an unfortunate connection
between violent penis envy and the inhibition or fear of satisfying
this envy. The connection arises because penis envy derives from
conflict with the mother, giving rise to idealization of the father,
which must be maintained thereafter.

I think that women's fear of castration can be explained by
this equation of the narcissistic wound and the lack of a penis.
Freud could see no reason for the little girl to fear castration as she
had already undergone it. This led him to alter his proposition that
all anxieties were castration fears to that in *Inhibitions, Symptoms,
Anxiety* (1936), in which he claimed that woman's fear of losing
love is the equivalent of castration anxiety.

Jones pointed out that fears of castration do exist in women
since they have as many fears about the future as men have; he also
stressed the importance of fears about the integrity of their internal
organs. In fact, the fears of both sexes are similar (fear of going
blind, being paralyzed, becoming mad, having cancer, having an accident, failing, and so on). In the unconscious, all narcissistic fears
at any level are equivalent to castration, because of the narcissistic
value given to the phallus by both sexes. Thus, women as well as
men constantly fear castration; even if they already have lost the
penis, there are still many other things with a phallic meaning
which one might lose. And men as well as women experience penis
envy because each attempt to compensate a deficiency implies a
phallic acquisition. The fear of loss or of castration centers in the

mother as it is from her the daughter wishes to escape, *at the same time that she gives herself a penis and turns to the father.*

During the change of object even though retaining the unconscious image of the phallic mother the daughter fully realizes that *the father is the only true possessor of the penis.* The change of object and the development of the Oedipal situation come about only when the imago of the phallic mother has become that of a mother who has dispossessed the father of his penis. In order to acquire the penis the girl now turns to her father *just as her mother did;* she does this with all the guilt we have discussed earlier, grappling with both her parents at the same time, and also attacking the loved object.

As Freud said, she turns to the father to acquire the penis, but her fears, owing to the temporary split between her libidinal and aggressive cathexes *at the time of the change of object,* are tied to the mother, the guilt to the father.

I believe that it is at this stage that the imago of the phallic mother *who holds in herself the paternal penis* (Melanie Klein) becomes much more important than the imago of the phallic mother who ȯn her own possesses a phallus. Even if this latter imago persist in the unconscious it is not the prevailing one. But the father's penis, the mother's property, loses its genital and positive characteristics and acquires the same intrusive, destructive, anal properties of the phallic mother's own penis, thereby being cathected in the same way as its owner.

If the imago of the phallic mother as possessor of a penis remains the more important one, then the homosexual situation threatens to establish itself permanently, but if the imago of the mother as holder of the paternal penis dominates, the triangular situation begins in outline.

In Freud's view, then, *the girl turns away from her mother in order to acquire a penis;* and by turning to the father enters the positive Oedipus phase.

If, however, *penis envy is caused by the desire to liberate oneself from the mother,* as I propose, the sequence of events is somewhat different: the girl will *simultaneously* be envious of the penis *and* turn to her father, powerfully aided by a basic feminine wish to free herself from the mother. Thus, penis envy and the erotic desire for a penis are not opposed to each other but complementary, and if symbolic satisfaction of the former is achieved this becomes a step forward toward integration of the latter.

In his article on "Manifestations of the Female Castration

Complex" (1921), Karl Abraham states that women who have professional ambitions thereby manifest their penis envy.[23] This can be demonstrated clinically,[24] but I think the desire to fulfill oneself in any field, professional or otherwise, as well as penis envy, spring from the same narcissistic wound, and is therefore an attempt at reparation. Freud in his essay on narcissism states that once the primary stage of narcissism is passed, personal achievement provides narcissistic rewards. It is important to take this into account in analytic treatment. If one interprets desire for achievement as the manifestation of "masculine demands" (as Abraham did with regard to professional activities), if women's professional desires are invariably interpreted as penis envy, there is a risk of awakening profound guilt feelings. I believe that if one accepts that penis envy is caused by a deep narcissistic wound, then one is able to bind this wound as well as open the way to a normal Oedipus conflict. Sexuality itself is often seen as men's prerogative and, in fact, from a symbolic point of view *normal female sexuality* (a vagina which functions normally) can be regarded as the possession of a phallus, due to the fact that the penis represents wholeness even in regard to orgasm. Certain analysts, basing their views on this fantasy go so far as to say that normal women never have an orgasm. This is tantamount to acquiescing to the patients' guilt, leading indeed to castration not only of the penis but also of the vagina and of the whole of femininity. Basically, penis envy is the symbolic expression of another desire. Women do not wish to become men, but want to detach themselves from the mother and become complete, autonomous *women*.

Penis Envy as a Defense and Fears for the Integrity of the Ego
I do not wish to ignore *the role of penis envy* as a feminine defense. I have insisted upon *guilt* because this aspect of female psychosexuality seems to have been more neglected than that of *the narcissistic fears for the ego's integrity*.

Many women want a penis *to avoid being penetrated,* since penetration is felt as a threat to their integrity;[25] they want to castrate this dangerous penis in order to prevent it from approaching them. But then one wonders, *which* penis?

In the preceding article, "The Change of Object," Luquet-Parat suggests that, if penetration is desired and imagined as a danger for body as well as ego integrity, that is, if the penis continues to represent exaggerated phallic power (the immense penis the little girl desires, too big in comparison with her, is the heir to the invading, destructive, annihilating phallic power of the *primitive ma-*

ternal phallus), then sexual penetration is experienced as an intolerable desire which the ego cannot accept, since it is in contradiction to self-preservation.

I agree with Dr. Luquet-Parat that this destructive penis is the equivalent of the maternal phallus of the anal phase; this, in turn, is linked for the girl with persecution and passive homosexual attitudes and provides the basis for paranoia in women. In these cases I wonder if one can truly speak of a "change of object" (since emotions concerning the paternal penis are the same as they had been for the mother's phallus). It may be more correct to say that this was already part of the positive Oedipal situation.

The "transfer" to the father of what was invested in the mother and the fact that these cathexes are equal (as the projections have simply been displaced) seem to point to the creation of a mechanism of defense aimed at escaping the dangerous relation with the phallic mother by establishing a relation with the father. But this mechanism of defense fails because the projections remain the same while the two objects are insufficiently differentiated.

It seems as if in these cases the father did not adequately support the projection of the good aspects of the object, because the primitive object itself was particularly bad. The process of idealization could not be established and thus could not allow for the true triangular situation. Castration as a defense and penis envy which prevents penetration seem to me to be linked mainly to the phallic maternal imago even though they appear to take the father as their aim. The latter does not yet have *the attributes of the paternal role* and only plays the role of a substitute for the mother, who possesses the destructive anal phallus.[26]

Fears for ego integrity are best analyzed from the angle of passive homosexuality and identifications and provide a deeper understanding of the meaning of this narcissistic defense against penetration by the penis (unconsciously, the mother's phallus), which causes so many conjugal difficulties. Women who attack and castrate their husbands have unconsciously married the bad mother, and this is often equally true for the husband. Freud noticed that many women marry mother substitutes and act ambivalently toward them.

I believe this results both from Oedipal guilt (one must not take the father from the mother, not incorporate the father's penis) and the repetition compulsion. The issue here is to master the traumatic childhood situation, to live out actively what has been passively experienced, rather than integrated, in relation to the mother. In this case the relationship is homosexual.

It does happen—and this is a proof that the husband does not represent the father in this case—that the idealized paternal imago remains untouched and identical with the ideal portrait created by the little girl.

For example, Adrienne, a young and pretty mother, who has made an important advance in the social and financial scale, has retained a genuine simplicity. She tells me that she married her husband on the spur of the moment. At the time she was "going out" with a young man whom she loved, but for some reason which she cannot explain she yielded to her present husband's proposal. He is a rather sadistic man who beats her and makes perverse demands upon her. At the same time he is very attentive to her, which gives him an eminently ambiguous position in her eyes. She is full of bitterness toward him and grievances: he deprives her of her freedom; he does not let her gad about, or hum to herself, or whistle; he demands that she wear a girdle, etc. On top of this he is unfaithful to her. It soon became obvious that this husband was an equivalent of Adrienne's mother, who used to take her things away, keep her under her control, force her to work, and never stop pestering her.

When the mother was angry at mealtimes she would throw forks at the children's heads.

From the very beginning this aspect of the mother was projected onto me, and at the outset the analysis was very difficult, especially as she had not come of her own accord but only because her husband insisted on it. Yet she found sufficient satisfaction in the treatment to keep up the analysis despite her pointedly hysterophobic character.

Thus, when she leaves at the end of her session, she feels that she has become very small, her handbag has become a satchel, she senses that I follow her everywhere: into the subway, the streets and even her bedroom. The smell of my flat follows her everywhere, too. I am always behind her, etc. (In spite of the content of her feelings, their relation and structure are not at all paranoiac, there is a true possibility of insight.)

She liked her father but it was always the mother "who wore the trousers," who took the father's pay, controlling even the smallest expenditure, shutting him out if he came home late, etc.

Adrienne made an attempt at suicide the day her grandfather had his leg amputated. Later, she visited him in the hospital, went to much trouble for him, pampered him, even wished to become a nurse. To this day, every month she goes and gives her blood at the hospital (the links between the suicide attempt, the grandfather's amputation, and the efforts to put it right only became clear late in the analysis; they came up as separate facts, because they were unconscious). This grandfather is the mother's father whom the mother treats with indifference, hardly bothering or worrying about him, unlike Adrienne. When he died, after a second amputation, Adrienne described her mother's attitude at the grandfather's deathbed (the mother had stolen his cigarettes and his money) in the following words:

"How can she think of profiting from him? . . . I can see an animal in the forest, something like a huge wild boar surrounded by hunters. They are trying to strip him of everything he has."

Her husband had then gone hunting. He had sent her some game which she could not bring herself to eat. Adrienne's attitude to her husband is quite different from her attitude to her father or grandfather. She openly attacks him, forces him to give her money, a personal car, etc., without any inhibition whatsoever. She ridicules him, thinks he looks like a clown and says so in front of him.

One day, the imago she had projected onto her husband became clear:

"In his dressing-gown he looks amazingly like my mother-in-law."

Not long before this, she had a dream in which her mother was dressed up as a priest in a robe.

She sometimes projects onto me the good image of the idealized father, the victim of the mother's castration, at other times the image of the phallic mother, with whom she wishes and fears an anal relation, experiencing once again the intrusive sphincter-training period.

"I can still feel you behind me, I am frightened. . . . I don't want to speak. I can feel you're going to interrogate me and I'm frightened. It's stupid; in fact, you never do ask questions . . . or, at least, not in that way. . . . I shall say nothing."

"The image of my husband is haunting me. I keep thinking of him, and yet he infuriates me. I don't want to make love to him. . . . I dreamed of a rat whose claws were pinching my daughter's bottom. . . ."

It seems to me obvious that the relationships to the husband and to me in the transference express a defense against a passive homosexual relation with the phallic mother, whom she attacks, whom she defies, whom she castrates in order to prevent her approach and in order to prove that there is no collusion between them; whereas her relation with her father is based on a counter-identification with the phallic mother and so on an idealization of the paternal image she is trying to restore.

The relation with the phallic husband-mother is connected with *narcissistic fears for the body ego,* whereas the relation to the father-grandfather is connected with guilt.

III

A Conflictual Outcome of Feminine Problems:
The Daughter's Identification with the Father's Penis

OEDIPUS.   This girl is my eyes, stranger, my daughter.

. . . .

ANTIGONE.   Father, we are yours.
OEDIPUS.   Where are you?
ANTIGONE.   Near you, father. (They go toward him.)
OEDIPUS.   Oh, my torches!
ISMENE.   Of your light, father.
ANTIGONE.   In suffering and in joy.
OEDIPUS.   Let death come, I shall be alone at the time of my
                     extinction, resting on these columns like a Temple.

(*Translated from Jean Gillibert's French version of Sophocles'*
Oedipus at Colonus.)

I have tried to show that the idealization of the father, a process which underlies the change of object, can result in a specific conflict for the woman in the area of sadistic-anal instinctual components, thereby rendering difficult the instinctual fusion required for normal sexuality, as well as interfering with any achievement necessary to healthy narcissistic equilibrium.[27]

We have already referred to Freud's idea, in "On Narcissism, An Introduction," [28] according to which "everything a person possesses, or achieves, every remnant of the primitive feeling of omnipotence which his experience has confirmed, helps to increase his self-regard."

But in the same work Freud also suggested another possibility for narcissistic support: the object's love for us: "In love relations not being loved lowers the self-regard, while being loved raises it." It seems that many women unconsciously choose Freud's second solution to the need for narcissistic gratifications, because they cannot freely and without guilt fulfill themselves through their personal achievements.

I do not think this choice necessarily implies an incapacity for object love. Indeed, according to Freud ("Instincts and Their Vicissitudes"),[29] "If the object becomes a source of pleasurable feelings, a motor urge is set up which seeks to bring the object closer to the ego and to incorporate it into the ego. We then speak of the 'attraction' exercised by the pleasure-giving object, and we say that we 'love' that object."

Thus, love is first of all a response to satisfaction, that is, an answer to the love which the object gives us. The two states—loving and being loved—are therefore correlative, and loving implies the desire to renew, to perpetuate the agreeable experience and the love one has received, by incorporating the object in the ego. In fact one often gives love in order to be loved by the object. Further discussion of this subject would lead us to examine the essence of love itself, but that would take us far beyond our present purpose. Here I wished to state above all that the conflictual outcome, when partly based on guilt, necessarily implies consideration for the object, and therefore love, even if the aim is at the same time to find satisfaction for narcissistic needs.

I believe this to be a very common female attitude, and one which can be interpreted as an identification with the part-object, the father's penis. I am not referring to woman's identification with an *autonomous phallus,* but to an identification with the *penis* as such, that is a complementary and totally dependent part of the object.

Identification of oneself with an autonomous phallus results in a pathological form of secondary narcissism. The ego is libidinally overcathected and shielded from external objects without which the link with reality is broken. Favreau (personal communication) stresses the importance of the narcissistic characteristics peculiar to this situation: the woman who identifies with the phallus *desires only to be desired.* She establishes herself as a phallus; this implies impenetrability and therefore withdrawal from any relation with an external erotic object. Some of these characteristics can be compared with those found in masculine narcissistic-phallic regression.

This sort of phallic identification is traceable in models ("mannequins"), ballerinas (though, of course, many other components make up a true artist's character), vamps, etc. The phallus woman resembles, more than any other woman, what Freud described as the narcissistic woman whose fascination, similar to that of a child, is linked with her *"inaccessibility"* like "the charm of certain animals *which seem not to concern themselves about us,* such as cats and the large beasts of prey" ("On Narcissism, An Introduction," 1925). Further on Freud mentions the "enigmatic nature" and the "cold and narcissistic" attitude these women have toward men. Rather than seeing in this the essence of women's object relations, I see it as an identification with an autonomous phallus. Is it not true that men admire the phallus in these women more than the women themselves?

If I have dwelt at such length on this description of woman's identification with the autonomous phallus, it is because I wish to avoid confusing it with the position I am now going to discuss—that of the paternal-penis woman. Far from being autonomous with regard to the object, she is closely dependent on it and is also its *complement.* She is the *right hand,* the assistant, the colleague, the secretary, the auxiliary, the inspiration for an employer, a lover, a husband, a father. She may also be a companion for old age, guide, or nurse. One sees the basic conflicts underlying such relationships in clinical practice.

The autonomous phallus-woman, is similar to the woman described in Conrad Stein's article "La Castration comme négation de la féminité" (*Revue française de psychanalyse,* 1961). Stein relates this problem to bisexuality and to the dialectic of "being" and "having." I think it is necessary to distinguish in metapsychology between "being" as identification with the total object one would like to "have," and "being" the other person's "thing," as an identification with the part-object. This latter position seems to be linked with the subject's reparative tendencies and results from a counter-identification with the mother's castration of the father during the primal scene. In this case the daughter remains closely dependent on the object she makes complete.

Alice is a thirty-eight-year-old woman, small, lively, and full of humor. She is the best friend of a colleague who entrusted her to me, saying that she was "the apple of his eye."

In Alice's case this expression was full of meaning. Alice came to analysis after undergoing an operation for the removal of a neoplastic tumor. The illness naturally aroused deep narcissistic fears, but even more important was the fact that the seriousness of her illness had allowed her to do something for herself for once. Her marriage situation suddenly became unbearable. She was an only child. Her mother was a severe and demanding school teacher,

her father a kind and sentimental man who grew flowers and vines in his garden and wrote naive and delicate poems. He would say to Alice when she was little, "You are the prettiest little girl in the world." Even today Alice sometimes wakes up and asks her husband if she really is "the prettiest little girl in the world."

But Alice did not recognize her love for her father. She said her father "revolted" her, she did not like his kisses, he annoyed her, she felt like pushing him down the stairs, especially when he had had a bit too much homemade wine. "At those times," said Alice, "his eyes were very very small." He was clumsy and missed the glass as he poured out the wine. Alice did not understand why she felt irritated by this father whose love could also bring her to tears.

Alice's relation with her mother was based on a mixture of fear and the desire to be held on her lap again and have body contact with her as she was when very small. Alice avoided telling her mother that she had a malignant tumor because her mother despised illness and weakness. When Alice was little she never dared complain nor tell her mother for instance that her sweater made of rough wool itched nor that her socks were too tight.

Alice's fantasy of the primal scene was a sadistic one, the mother playing the role of a castrating and sadistic person.

She studied at the National Academy of Music and married a gifted composer. Once married she gave up her career, saying that "one artist in the family is enough."

She suffered from eczema, particularly at her son's birth; she feels the need for a nonconflictual fusion with the object (the analyst in the transference; the "allergic object relation" described by Pierre Marty). At one point in the treatment she expressed the need for fusion in the following fantasy:

She is on a lake in a foam-rubber boat with an opening only big enough to let in a little air. But when she thinks of this opening she sees flies and insects coming to bother her.

It became clear that these were her aggressive instincts which she had to leave outside the world of fusion. She associated the boat with a cradle and the mother's womb. But on the level of the triangular relationship the fusion was between her and the gentle, kind father (heir to the mother upon whose lap it was so nice to sit), the mother representing her own aggressive instincts which needed to be repressed. Before and at the beginning of the analysis, Alice dreamed of empty flats; she associated them with the parcels she used to receive from her father's house, which annoyed her and which she did not want to open. Yet one day, opening a parcel from her father, she cried because she was so touched and thus expressed the pleasure she could have felt at accepting her father's love and presents. It became obvious that her rejection of her father was only a superficial defense and that her difficulties with incorporation (empty houses) were not related solely to narcissistic fears of damage.

I cannot give a detailed account of Alice's analysis, but she did express strong guilt about her anal-sadistic instinctual impulses toward the father and his penis. Thus, she dreamed she had a shrimp-child which had dried up between the pages of a book. She felt very guilty at having killed him. She associated this with her father's body. In another dream a baby put in her mother's care was dying of dehydration. After a frantic race she managed to arrive just in time to save him. She noticed her mother was feeding the baby with a bottle full of dirty water. Etc.

This guilt became increasingly obvious in the transference. For example, she thought of offering me a reproduction of a painting by Chagall which represented a rooster. She associated this with childhood fantasies in which a woman wandered the roads with a rooster on a leash. In the sessions I am about to discuss this appears as a penis which has to be restored to the father.

For some time Alice had been feeling guilty toward me, thinking she was not paying me enough money. Her husband, also in analysis, was paying a much higher fee. Alice arrives at her session at 11:30, lies down, and wonders if she is on time. Is her session at 11:20 or 11:40? She cannot remember even though she has come at the same time since the beginning of her analysis and is on time today. She continues by listing a series of things "which are not going well." The windows in her apartment are broken, and she cannot get the caretaker to send someone round to repair them (this question of windows has taken up a great deal of the analysis lately); with her husband things are not going well, she cannot stand it any longer. She fails in what she attempts. She asks me if she has arrived early or late. I say: "It seems as if one of us must give up something (ten minutes from you or ten minutes from me) and you are trying to show me that it is *you* who loses, that you are diminished by everyone in every way. "

At the next session Alice gets muddled about the time of her appointment and arrives half an hour early. After going away and coming back at the usual time she lies down and says:

"One of my eyes is running, it stings. By the way my eye always runs when I come here." Silence. "Oh! Well what do you know! But I never told you that my father had his eye put out, right in front of me when I was little. I don't remember how old I was . . . maybe eight. We used to go together in the fields and he suddenly put his foot down on some barbed wire which flew in the air and hit him in the eye. How amazing that I never told you about that. My running eye is on the same side as my father's. Now I suddenly understand why I was fascinated for so long by the Galton portrait game, in which one glues both left sides and both right sides together. Because of his eye my father has two very different profiles. When I was little I used to imagine the story of a little girl who had one dark and one light eye." Her dark eye was due to the fact that she went to school by a path sunk between two very dark walls and the light eye was due to the fact that these walls suddenly gave way to a dazzling courtyard full of bits of glass, etc. . . .

This session was one of the most important in Alice's analysis as it allowed her to understand better and experience certain aspects of her object relations through the specially symbolized details in her fantasy (her love of big, transparent, amber pearls, her worry about the windows in her flat, her hatred of symmetry, etc.). This historical event is important inasmuch as it "crystallized" a series of emotions linked to the father and his penis; the event was traumatic because Alice's aggressive fantasies had been confirmed in reality.

Her annoyance with her father, with his "small eyes" when he was drunk, with his clumsiness (Alice never associated the "small eyes" with the event of his eye being put out), were struggles against guilt: "It is not my fault my father had this accident, in fact there was no accident, he had only drunk a little and that is why he had those "small eyes." He can see perfectly well, he is only clumsy. I must not approach him, accept his love, because any contact between us is dangerous. I must reject my father, that is the only desire I have toward him." But unconsciously all Alice's object relations are dominated by the desire to *heal* her father, as an atonement for her guilty desires toward him.

Alice, who never took full advantage of her musical knowledge, is very clever with her hands and can achieve amazing things in carpentry and handiwork. She is proud of these activities, even though she deprecates herself in so many others. During her analysis, she thinks of taking up some professional activity. At the beginning of his career her husband had written some commercial songs to earn money. She had contributed the main ideas for these, so he now suggested that she write her own songs. But she says she is incapable of doing that—she could never be inspired *unless the song could be considered as his creation.*

During one session the unconscious meaning of her handicraft becomes clear. First of all she mentions her present difficulty over driving a car, a difficulty in total contrast to the facility with which she drove her father in a car, since he was incapacitated by the accident to his eye. "Daddy was very proud of me then." She associated this with her difficulty in remembering what I had told her during the previous session, yet she had fully understood what I had said. She said that if I were to repeat the beginning of what I had said, she would remember the rest of it. In other words, if I were beside her she could drive but she could not take the initiative alone: that would have meant driving for oneself, and she could not do that any more than she could write a song if it were not to become her husband's.

Then she mentioned a disagreeable woman who had annoyed her the previous day until she had suddenly learned that this woman did a lot of handicraft. "All my irritation with her vanished, she did not seem aggressive or disagreeable any more. I thought she was very sweet." In Alice's mind handicraft seemed to make the lady as *innocent* as it made Alice herself.

One of her fantasies clarified the meaning of her attitudes and activities. She was going to Lourdes to sell miraculous, pious objects, virgins with luminous eyes. She also invented medicines for sick animals. One can see that Alice's activities are aimed at *replacing the eye lost by her father*. She is entirely involved in her prothetic function. She can only create, act, live, *for* someone of whom she becomes the complementary part, the penis.

Her love for her father meant that she could not take on an identification with the mother, castrating the father during the primal scene. All activity, all means of existing which could be symbolized in the unconscious as a penis, were forbidden her. Indeed, acting for oneself, being autonomous, creating for oneself meant possessing the paternal penis and thus castrating the father. Alice has disfused her instinctual impulses, countercathected her aggression and offered herself as a replacement for the lost paternal penis, thus making the loved object complete. The position is therefore a *reaction formation*.

Alice's sexuality follows the same pattern. She seems free, but her choice of erotic objects shows that she is not. She is loved by several charming, cultivated gentlemen, much older than herself. They court her in a slightly discreet melancholic way. Alice only shows them kindness and friendship. One of them, who is married, has even decided, with his wife's agreement, to adopt her as his daughter.

Thinking about these "affairs," Alice remembers that ten

years ago, while being courted by one of these men, she went to the cafe where they usually met and encountered some young men, her "little brothers," seeing them for an obvious sexual purpose. These adventures always occurred during her father's absence from Paris. This is a classical defense against the Oedipus complex. But another fact more precisely locates the level of this defense: these gentlemen, Alice realizes, are nearly all Jewish. In fact she only gets on well with Jews. Even a badly educated man, if he is Jewish, attracts her. Perhaps it is because of their sense of humor, or their sadness, or their persecution. Sometimes, when Alice sees beggars, she is very upset. Once, with a lump in her throat, she gave one a lot of money, the notes rolled up into a ball. Then she realized he looked like her father.

These conflicts were analyzed at great length. Alice, whose dream life had been poor, as though paralyzed, suddenly began to have many dreams and started recalling all her childhood. One series of dreams is particularly important. Having recalled the erotic games of her childhood, especially her favorite one of taking people's temperatures,[30] she remembers an adolescent dream: she was looking at the stars with her mother and one constellation looked like an agitated man. She was the only one to see this in the stars and she was going to go mad because her head kept flopping onto her shoulder. She associated this with the memory of witnessing a friend's epileptic fit. She feared that she too might have those terrible convulsions.

Next, a transference dream. A faith healer noticed that she was emitting an excessively dangerous electric vibration. The next night the healer died, very probably of this vibration.

Thereafter, every night Alice dreamed of corpses. The first one was that of the kindest of her old gentlemen; he was all broken up and was about to die when Alice called for a doctor. Strangely, the dying man was taken to a sordid barn; the next night she dreamed that her husband was taken to a sinister clinic on the outskirts of Paris, with the side of his body all black. The following night she dreamed that she was crying during a session while I was explaining that the police were coming, and I showed her a man's corpse which I kept in a coffin. The police arrived and, quite unexpectedly—that was the worst punishment of all—they took away her father while she cried, and then she had to see him die in a prison cell, while she stood by powerless, seeing his abject poverty.

This dream, in which the id disguises itself as the superego in order to fulfill the desire of anally incorporating the paternal penis, was followed by a number of memories: sex play with a farmhand who had shown her his penis, games with a cousin in the hayloft, the exciting smell of the granaries and cellars where the hams were hung and the cheese and wines matured. At the same time Alice tells me that, for some incomprehensible reason, she has deliberately omitted telling me one fact: a good-looking rag-and-bone man, with dark eyes, came to empty their cellar. He made advances to her, but although she refused them she was not indifferent to them. As the price he was asking for emptying her cellar was too steep, she decided to do it herself. Once the cellar was empty, there was a huge carpet rolled up on the ground. With a great effort Alice unrolled the carpet and very cleverly managed to hang it vertically from the cellar ceiling and leave it there.

Of course I cannot discuss here all the material from this series of sessions nor give details of the transference. I shall merely recount the two dreams which followed this last session, as they show in an abbreviated form the shape of her development.

Alice is going up the staircase in my building. She meets a handsome man who flirts with her. He is my husband. He asks her when he can see her again, and Alice replies: "I come here three times a week."

The following night Alice dreams that her father and mother are sleeping in her flat. In the middle of the night Alice's mother throws the father out of her room and he goes and sits on a stool in the kitchen. Grieved because he cannot spend the whole night there, Alice offers to let him sleep with her.

As the anal-sadistic incorporative desires toward the father's penis become conscious a true Oedipal situation is able to develop. The disfused instinct begins to appear under its own disfused aspect only to merge with the cluster which makes up genital primacy.

When the sadistic-anal instincts of incorporating the paternal penis result in guilt (as discussed at the beginning of this article) they increase the possibility of the girl's identifying with the father's penis. As we have shown, there is then an inversion of content and container, the woman identifying herself with the penis in the dangerous vagina—dangerous because of the sadistic-anal component, the fecal stool in the rectum. (This inversion is the main symptom of claustrophobia; it also exists in other structures.) The girl thus becomes the father's anal penis, she is a part of him and offers herself to his handling and mastery. Mastery, possession, or domination of the father, or of his substitutes (generally masculine ones), are forbidden to her. Thus, Alice, asked to compose the music for a ballet, is very pleased and says: "The person who asked me to do it is a friend; I know his taste. There will be no problem in doing it. But I would never dare accept a job from a stranger. He might not like what I did. I would never dare impose my taste on anybody."

I would readily see this as the source of one of woman's main conflicts, that of being *relative* to men, just as nearly all of woman's cultural or social achievements are. Women are said to produce few original works; they are often the brilliant disciple of a man or of a masculine theory. They are rarely leaders of movements. This is surely the effect of a conflict specific to women.

I believe it is important, both from a clinical and from a technical point of view, to discuss this position which can be scotomized because of the countertransference it causes. (I am here thinking of my own clinical experience.) Certain patients, and this seems to be peculiar to women—for when this happens in men the conflictual aspect of it is immediately obvious—are cured of their symptoms only in order to make publicity for their analyst; they feel they are a successful product, and experience their analysis as though the future and the reputation of the analyst depended on it. (The aggression toward the object becomes self-destructive.)

Thus, one of my patients imagined she was a sandwichman advertising my name and address. This reminded her of a brand of coffee whose advertising had taken the form of men disguised as coffee packets walking through Paris.

Certain aspects of *female masochism* seem to be related to this position. One of the main aspects of the masochistic character is the role of being "the other person's thing." "I am your thing. Do whatever you want to with me," says the masochist to his partner. In other words I am your fecal stool and you can deal with me as you wish. One explanation of female masochism is to be found in its link with the guilt of incorporating the penis in a sadistic-anal way, as though women, in order to achieve this incorporation, had to pretend to offer themselves entirely, in place of the stolen penis, proposing that the partner do to her body, to her ego, to herself, what she had, in fantasy, done to his penis.

Grunberger had based his study of masochism (in both sexes) on the guilt associated with anal introjection of the paternal penis, but the mechanism he discussed is not quite the same as the one I am here describing.

The woman's superego seems also to be linked to her identification with the paternal penis. Without entering the discussion of whether her superego is stronger than man's (Melanie Klein), or weaker (Freud), or quasi-nonexistent (J. Lampl de Groot), I wish to discuss one of the aspects of the female superego described by Freud. He states that woman's superego is more impersonal than man's. This is a common observation. Women have, at least in appearance, a superego which constantly changes, taking on new aspects, giving up old ones, according to their sexual partners. One frequently says that women are easily influenced, that they have no fixed opinions, that they readily change their principles. One of my patients, the one who gave up her lectures because of a disagreeable criticism, seems to be this type of woman who judges her acts and thoughts according to the object's judgments. She seems to hear only the rules she is told of, while being ignorant of the law. But this "malleable" character of her thought is linked only to her conscious guilt. Beyond these variations, the internalized prohibitions are very strong. One of them dominates all the others, as if it were some sort of Eleventh Commandment: "You may not have your own law—your law is your object's law." It seems as though many women have internalized this commandment, making them eternally dependent.

Here again, man's conflict with the omnipotent mother and woman's conflict with the cathexis of the loved object both contribute to this situation in which woman plays the role of a part-object.[31]

Conclusion

The cases which I have chosen to discuss, despite different nosological data, all have one feature in common: the mother was sadistic and castrating, the father was good and vulnerable. Of course, many families do not have this structure. There are families where the opposite is true, where the mother is the good element and the father the sadistic one. It is interesting that in these latter cases the paternal figure becomes ambiguous and is identified once again, in woman's unconscious, with the phallic mother. Therefore, the family structure, in the cases discussed here, even though it seems exaggerated, is nevertheless an objective one inasmuch as it represents the normal unconscious structure at the time of the change of object, the bad object being projected onto the mother, the good onto the father. When reality cannot correct this unconscious image, severe problems are bound to arise. Then the Primal Scene represents a mixture of the destructive bad object and the good object which must be safeguarded, or, in other words, a terrifying fusion of the aggressive and erotic instincts. To deny the necessity of instinctual fusion in female sexuality corresponds to ignoring men's terrifying fantasies about femininity and women's guilty fantasies about their instinctual impulses, which is rather like trying to transform black Eros into a cherubic cupid.

It seems to me that one cannot base all female conflicts with the father and his penis on primitive conflicts with the mother and her breast; that would be shortcircuiting the total transformation which occurs during the change of object inherent in the path to womanhood.

Freud has shown that the little girl's Oedipus complex, caused by penis envy, is a *haven* for her inasmuch as the girl, whose castration has already been effected, has nothing more to fear from the mother. This results in *a tendency to prolong the Oedipal situation*. It is interesting that the female Oedipus complex is not resolved in the way that the male Oedipus complex is. (Parents readily say that "a son's your son till he gets a wife; a daughter's your daughter all her life.")

Is this not related to the fact that the girl, in seeking to free herself from the mother during the change of object, and in her need to safeguard the father, offers herself to him as a part-object, protected from the mother, loved by the father, and forever dependent?

It seems as if the girl who prolongs this situation feels it to be a *haven* only inasmuch as she is not taking the mother's place beside the father because she is not identifying with her and because she stays a child rather than becomes a woman. I believe that she is, at the same time, protecting herself from castration threatened by the mother by refusing to take her place. An Oedipal situation in which the girl truly identifies with the mother in order to take her place beside the father is never a comfortable one. The obstacles which the girl encounters in her love for her father and in the rivalry with her mother are frightening enough for the girl's Oedipus complex to be just what the boy's Oedipus complex was, "the crux of neuroses."

Man and woman are born of woman: before all else we are our mother's child. Yet all our desires seem designed to deny this fact, so full of conflicts and reminiscent of our primitive dependence. The myth of Genesis seems to express this desire to free ourselves from our mother: man is born of God, an idealized paternal figure, a projection of lost omnipotence. Woman is born from man's body. If this myth expresses the victory of man over his mother and over woman, who thereby becomes his own child, it also provides a certain solution for woman inasmuch as she also is her mother's daughter: she chooses to belong to man, to be created *for* him, and not for herself, to be a part of him—Adam's rib—rather than to prolong her "attachment" to her mother. I have tried to show the conflicts which oblige so many women to choose between mother and husband as the object of dependent attachment.

The Significance of Penis Envy in Women

Maria Torok

I

In every woman's analysis, there is inevitably a period in which appears a feeling of envy and covetousness for both the male sex organ and its symbolic equivalents. This penis envy may be simply episodic with some patients, but with others it can be central. The exacerbated desire to possess what women believe themselves deprived of by fate, or the mother, is an expression of a fundamental dissatisfaction which some people believe to be woman's lot. Indeed, the conviction that what they feel themselves deprived of is exactly what other people have is common to patients of both sexes and is found in all analyses. Jealousy and demand, spite and despair, inhibition and anxiety, admiration and idealization, inner void and depression: all these are among the varied symptoms of this state of deficiency. Yet it is interesting that only women relate this feeling of deficiency to the very nature of their sex: "It is because I am a woman." One must understand such a statement to mean: I do not have a penis, that accounts for my weakness, my inertia, my lack of intelligence, my dependent state or even my illnesses.

"All things considered, my predicament is common to all women, therefore I can only hold them in contempt, as I do myself." "It is they, the men, who command everything of value, all the attributes which render them worthy of being loved and admired."

Is such an extreme devaluation of one's own sex conceivable? Do its roots lie in a real biological inferiority? Freud felt finally compelled to accept the idea after he had vainly tried to remove this obstacle to treatment—the coveting of an object which is, by nature, unattainable. One would do better to go "preaching to the winds"—to quote Freud's own expression—than to wear oneself out on such a vain enterprise: making patients renounce once and for

all their infantile desire to acquire a penis. Faced with so many failures, should one not, after all, resign oneself to allowing some legitimacy to penis envy and to ascribe it to the proper nature of things:
"the biological inferiority of the feminine sex"? In considering another point of view, namely, the child's affective development,
Freud arrived at the same conclusion. When he discovered an intermediate (the phallic) stage between the anal and the genital stages,
he imagined it similar for both sexes, that is, entirely devoted to the
penis. If it is true that only one sex, the male sex, is known to the
child, one can understand the little girl's jealous spite at being deprived of it. All her theories concerning her castrated state and the
overestimation of the other sex would find their origins here—due
to a psychobiological "phallo-centrism" inherent in the phallic stage
itself; that is why woman's penis envy, as well as the efforts to make
her renounce it, can (in Freud's analytic perspective) only end in
deadlock. But, if the theory of unisexuality at the phallic stage is
constantly confirmed in the fantasies relating to this stage, it seems
that this state of affairs could be given an accurate psychoanalytical
explanation. Therefore, we must not concede our helplessness and
rely on a biological explanation.

One can understand Freud's exasperation on being told:
"What is the good of continuing the analysis if you cannot give me
that." But one also can understand the patient's despair, when
asked to *renounce* a desire which seems so dear to her. Freud would
have been the first to agree that it is not part of an analyst's function to recommend giving up any desires, whatever.

It is none the less true that in analysis, the woman's desire to
have a penis (that is to say, to be a man) reveals itself as a subterfuge, because of its envious character. A desire can be satisfied, envy
never can. Envy can bring about only more envy and destruction.
Pseudo-desire, promulgated by envy, achieves a semblance of satisfaction, as shown in the phallic attitudes of some women, who are
immersed in imitation of the other sex, or at least of the image
they have of it. The fragile structure which they build shelters only
feelings of inner void, anxiety, and frustration. The problem of
analysis is precisely to bring back into the open the authentic but
repressed desire which, disguised as envy, has remained hidden.
Here, as with other fantasies, if one took the patient's protestations
literally one would preclude analysis. A sure way of doing this
would be to legitimatize woman's penis envy through accepting an
alleged castration as her lot, for which phylogenesis would bear the
responsibility. Another way just as certain of making analysis fail

would be to attribute the desire to extra-analytical causes, such as the inferior sociocultural status of women.

For the analyst who dares face up to this impasse in treatment—namely penis envy—the first step is to clarify the nature of the conflict which produced such a desperate solution. He should not underestimate the advantages which it unfailingly provides, and he should utilize in treatment the painful contradictions in which it inevitably locks the patient.

Among post-Freudian authors, Jones and M. Klein distinguish themselves by no longer holding penis envy to be an irreducible problem. Indeed, both believe that the nature of the first relationship with the maternal breast is the determining factor. As soon as the analyst has improved this first relationship (by allaying the conflict caused by introjection of the part-object) envy in general and penis envy in particular lose their reason for existence.

In the light of what these authors say it is worthwhile emphasizing this: for the analyst the part-objects could simply be *indications* of conscious or unconscious fears or desires, in other words, reminders of those early circumstances which led the individual to establish them. For Freud the object as such and the human object as a whole are in the individual's economy *mediators* on the way to the goal of his instinctual drive: satisfaction. *Part-objects,* of course, have their real names and can be said to exist objectively in space. The fact that everyone can recognize them makes them ideal signposts for communicating and also for concealing desires. It is the analyst's job to probe beyond the objective appearance and unearth the desire it denies as it appears to fulfill it. Therefore, analysis of envied *things* like the penis or the breast (even if they be the analyst's) will exacerbate the contradictions which affect the part and whole objects instead of removing them. This results in the appearance (and at the same time concealment) of internal conflicts which are implied by the *satisfaction* of a vital desire. Fulfillment of the desire is independent of objective anatomical circumstance. It depends on the patient's capacity for satisfaction and on his conviction of the right to satisfaction; that is, on the freedom he has to establish relations to others through his body. The objective circumstances (generally not subject to modification) brought forth as objects of deficiency or as reasons for covetousness are in fact snares set up for treatment, in order to hide (and thereby maintain) the inhibitions accompanying these relationships, snares which often keep the desire covered up for life.

That is why the penis itself—considered as a thing, an objective, biological, or even sociocultural reality—must be left aside in this essay on penis envy. For the penis itself is not involved in penis envy, even if this at first seems paradoxical. This part-object turns out to be an *ad hoc* invention to camouflage a desire, like an obstacle blocking the path to a reunified self as it would emerge if the prohibition of inhibited acts were lifted. What is the purpose of this subterfuge and what does it protect the patient from? One must *understand* it before denouncing it.

However disguised, however hidden, the desire underlying penis envy cannot fail to show through. For this reason, this symptom, like all others, deserves our respect and attention. If our analytic work has reached the origins of penis envy and rendered it superfluous, it has done so only by exchanging a desire for a renunciation. Penis envy will disappear by itself the day the patient no longer has that painful feeling of deficiency which caused it.

I I

If one agrees to abandon an object-oriented view of the envied penis—and to defer all questions concerning the sociocultural legitimacy of the envy—then one can undertake a truly psychoanalytical approach. Penis envy is the symptom, not of an illness, but of a certain state of unfulfilled desire—unfulfilled because of conflicting needs. Only an inquiry which disregards the object nature of the penis reveals the general significance of penis envy, the conflict which the symptom is trying to solve and the way it attempts to do this.

Freud believes that the little girl's visual discovery of the boy's sex organ was sufficient reason for her to envy it and, concomitantly, sufficient for her to hate her mother who (in the little girl's hypothesis) is responsible for her castrated state. Penis envy comes from experience, even when it is a pretext. But one problem still remains. At what ripe moment must this experience have taken place for the envy to last an entire lifetime? People only find what they are willing to find. "The polar bear and the whale . . . each one confined to his own surroundings . . . cannot meet," says Freud. If the moment was decisive it was not because of the difference between the boy and the girl but because of the similarity: in other words, because they both have a sex. One may suppose that the little girl's discovery of the boy's sex is part of the process of discovering her own little girl's sex. The discovery of the penis must have occurred at an important moment for it to have been more than a mere incident of early childhood. When the little girl thinks: "My mother didn't give me *that,* so I hate her," she is using a convenient pretext for expressing a hatred without explaining it.

The association of penis envy with conscious or unconscious hatred toward the mother is frequently observed. But there is another clinical fact, just as noticeable which, if examined, will enable one to detect the deeper motives of this hatred. This fact, so constant in clinical experience and also so significant, could be called *penis idealization.* Many women have the fanciful idea that the male sex organ possesses supreme qualities: infinite power for good or evil, a guarantee of its possessor's security, absolute freedom, immunity against anxiety or guilt, and a promise of pleasure, love, and the fulfillment of all his wishes. *Penis envy is always envy of an idealized penis.*

> "When one has *it* (the penis)," says Ida, "one has everything, one feels protected, nothing can touch you . . . one is what one is, and the others can only follow you and admire you . . . it is absolute power. They (men) can never find themselves feeling need, or lacking love. Woman? She is incomplete, perpetually dependent, her role is of a Vestal Virgin guarding the torch. No matter how much they told me about the Virgin Mary . . . God the Father, he is a real man, 'Purity' makes me think of 'puke' . . . I have always had a certain contempt for women."
>
> "I don't know why I have this feeling," says Agnes, "as it corresponds to nothing in reality but it has always been like this for me. As though, only man was fit to fulfill himself, to have opinions, to mature, to go always further. And everything to him is so naturally easy . . . nothing, nothing can stop him . . . he is a force that can stop anything if he wants to. Me, I am getting nowhere, hesitating, there's a kind of wall in front of me. . . . I always had the feeling I wasn't finished. Like a statue waiting for the sculptor to decide at last to model its *arms.* . . ."
>
> A little girl, Yvonne, always thought that boys "could at once succeed in doing anything . . . they instantly speak all languages . . . they could go into a church and take all the candles and nobody would stop them. If ever they find something in the way, they would naturally jump over it."

These are eloquent descriptions of an *idealized* penis. It is obvious that this always means: *"the thing* whatever it is that one doesn't have oneself." Yet such a vital defect could not be a natural one, but could only be the effect of a deprivation or a renunciation.

And then the question arises: Why is she deprived of such a precious part of herself, for the benefit of an external object, supposedly inaccessible, and, on the patient's own admission, definitely nonexistent? For the moment let us merely examine the fact. It has a name: repression. For all idealization there is a corresponding repression as a counterpart. But whom does the repression benefit? The Mother, of course, as is shown by the hatred addressed to her. Indeed, though the idealized penis has no actual existence, its counterparts, depression, self-devaluation, rage, have a very real existence. No one would believe that these affective states of such intensity could be due to an *idea* one has about an object one has once encountered. When the little girl says to the Mother within her: "I hate you because of this thing you haven't given me," she is also saying, "this is a legitimate hatred as is evident from my lack of this thing. But don't worry, I consider the real living hatred within me illegitimate because of the repression you imposed upon my desire."

What is this repression? It is not by chance that the penis, absent from the girl's anatomy, was chosen for the investment of those qualities which the patient must have deprived herself of: the sex organ one does not have represents perfectly that which is inaccessible, in that the sex organ can naturally not represent needs experienced in one's own body. In short, the choice of an inaccessible object for her envy shows that the patient's desire blocked by an impassable barrier. The overinvestment of the envied thing testifies to the primordial value belonging to the abandoned desire. Women want to ignore the occasion responsible for repression: for them it is a persecutor with an anonymous face; and in order to identify it one would have to confront those obscure areas where hate and aggression are smoldering against the object one could not but love.

A complex, unconscious speech is concentrated in "penis envy," and this speech is addressed to the maternal imago. One could expound it by the following propositions:

1) "You see, it is in a *thing* and not in *myself* that I am looking for what I am deprived of."

2) "I am searching in *vain,* because this thing can never be mine. The obvious vanity of my search must be a guarantee of the definitive renunciation of those desires you disapproved in me."

3) "I shall insist on the value of this inaccessible *thing* so that you may realize the greatness of my sacrifice in letting myself be deprived of my desire."

4) "I should accuse you and, in turn, deprive you, but that is precisely what I want to avoid, deny, and ignore, because I need your love."

"In short, idealizing the penis, in order to envy it more, is reassuring you by showing you that this will never come between us, and that consequently I shall never be reunified, I shall never fulfill myself. I tell you, it would be just as impossible as changing bodies."

"Penis envy" marks this oath of fidelity.

When the little girl, in the speech to her imago, refers to the forbidden part of herself, which is the counterpart of the "penis," this can only be her own sex, condemned to repression.

An amazing statement! It seems to mean that the little girl's sex—as she experiences it—can be symbolized by the boy's penis-*thing*; in other words, by the penis regarded as an anal object. There is, in fact, some genetic link missing in the explanation of the symbolization and that is the anal relation to the Mother. The notion of "thing"—whether it be accessible or inaccessible, permitted or forbidden—clearly refers to this. It is to the Mother that the little girl is addressing her request: "That *thing*, I want it." Furthermore, the vanity of this request, in its formulation and in its meaning, implies a reassurance for the Mother; her privileges will be maintained. It is interesting that the authority, the mother's highhandedness, does not concern the "things" which belong to her as much as the very acts of mastering the sphincter; acts which she claims to command according to her whims. Because of this the child (and later, of course, the adult) has difficulty in assuming the responsibility for these acts without recourse to the imago. Such is the context for penis envy. One can now see that it is not the "thing" itself that the patient is coveting, but the acts which allow one to master "things" in general. Coveting a *thing* is precisely the same as demonstrating to the imago the renunciation of an *act*. During the anal relationship with his mother, the child surrendered his capacity for sphincter control to please his mother. This results in overwhelming aggression directed toward her. Let us assume that the following process takes place: the Mother's control of the sphincter can only be interpreted by the child as a manifestation of her interest in possessing the feces, even while they are still in the body. Consequently, *at the same time, the body's interior also comes under maternal control.* How can one free oneself from such sovereignty, other than by reversing the relation? This is when murderous fantasies—about disemboweling, evacuation of the Mother's insides, destruction of the seat and means of her control—take place.

This is why the Mother must be reassured. We now clearly understand that the covetousness attached to the inaccessible penis-thing plays this role to perfection.

But one must answer the ultimate question: What motivated this specific choice? Why was it precisely the "penis" that was chosen?

To press the question further we shall use a complementary way of examining the symptom; as well as trying to reconstruct its *retrospective* genesis, as we have done up till now, we shall consider another equally important dimension—its *prospective* one. This new explanation might in turn enlighten us further about the origins of the symptom.

By *prospective dimension* of a symptom or of the conflict which underlies it we mean the negative aspect of the symptom. This is not a solution to a problem, since it is determined by something still nonexistent or unachieved, that is, the step forward is prevented. Yet it is this prospective moment that gives repression its dynamic character. The obstructed stages of affective maturation are claiming their fulfillment. They are certainly present despite the repression that blocked them, but the prospective aspect of the symptom is not explicit in the speech to the imago. Indeed, the little girl could not, even unconsciously, address the following sentences to her imago: "I can tell you that I am coveting the penis-thing to appropriate it myself and become a boy, but I can not even feel my aborted desire to *have pleasure with* the penis as women do, and which was *intended* in my sexual destiny." But it is precisely the fact of genital failure that gives us the clue to identifying the prohibitions responsible for the repression. The very experience which should have *prepared the way for the genital stage and its accompanying identifications* is only too clearly involved, and this experience is evidently connected with that "precious part" of oneself which has been repressed.

We have already shown that this "precious part" was the complex range of acts which had become the anal Mother's privilege. Yet the little girl possessed a means by which she could have indirectly recovered what she had been deprived of, namely *identification* with the Mother, sovereign of her powers. But one notices that penis envy testifies to a total lack of identification. To conclude, we are led to consider that not only the repression of anal-pregenital conflicts underlies penis envy, but also a specific, total or partial, inhibition of masturbation, of orgasm, and of their concomitant fantasy activities. Penis envy appears now to be a disguised claim—not for the organ and the attributes of the other sex—but for one's *own desires for maturation and development by means of the encounter with oneself in conjunction with orgastic experience and sexual identification.* These seem to be the first conclusions one can draw about the general significance of "penis envy" considered as a *symptom* in the Freudian sense of this term.

III

M. Klein, E. Jones, K. Horney, and J. Müller long ago pointed out the early discovery of vaginal sensations and their repression. I myself have noticed that the encounter with the other sex was always a reminder, or occasioned the awakening, of one's own sex. Clinically, penis envy and discovery of the boy's sex are often associated with the repressed memory of orgastic experiences.

> During several sessions Martha has violent bursts of crying or laughing. Slowly, her emotions regain a meaning; when a little girl, she met some boys in the swimming pool. Since then she often repeats the same phrase: "I cannot live like *this.*"
>
> It was this phrase which came up, during her analysis, in moments of deep depression. Consciously, "this" means "being deprived of a penis." But we must also understand that, on that occasion, she "squeezed her thighs together," "rolled up a little bit of swimsuit inside" and felt a kind of "sensitive shiver." The laughter mixed with tears (mingled joy and guilt) reflected her idea: if I am made "this" way (feeling this shiver) then, "at home, will they want me?" At puberty, this same patient had such a feeling of guilt toward her mother that she kept her periods—the sign of her genital maturity—a secret from her mother for a whole year.

Her own sexuality, far from being ignored, was a constant, but latent, preoccupation; in those days, the need to please her mother was greater than orgastic pleasure. During the sessions she expressed the desire for an orgasm, through the fits of laughter, but repressed it through penis envy itself. First of all there had been "an indescribable joy," "an immense hope." Then, she does not know why, she was convinced that "something infinitely desirable exists, not in me but over there, not in my body but in an *object*, an absolutely inaccessible object." One can see the contradiction: the "sensitive shiver of infinite goodness" makes the little girl lose her feeling of *being good* for the sake of her family. The penis is then felt, as we shall see, to be the "good" sex which gives the possessor pleasure without guilt; this pleasure is not tied up with masturbatory or internalized guilt. It has all the conditions of a perfect harmony: pleasure for oneself and harmony with others. Feeling the "shiver" is aggressive, wicked to others. So all that is "good" is abandoned and an external object substituted—the idealized penis. The void thus created in the patient is filled by sadness, bitterness, jealousy. But this smoldering aggression can never be a substitute for what she has missed, the growing and voluptuous awakenings of maturity. Only analysis can arouse those feelings by loosening up machinery, as it were.

This joy of awakening maturity goes beyond immediate satisfaction. To the patient it means a sudden opening up of the future. That is when the time of great discoveries comes, the "Ah! I understand!" "So this is how I become myself, adult; I find my worth through the joy I experience in becoming *myself.*" (J. Müller points out that freedom of infantile sexuality guarantees self-esteem.) Indeed, the orgastic joys of infancy are the true means by which genital sexuality, and through it the unfolding personality, are prepared and molded. What does the patient discover while developing the ability to have an orgasm? The possibility of identifying with the parents in fantasy and of imagining herself in all the different positions of the *primal scene* according to the moment at which it is considered. *The orgasm, once achieved, has the value of confirmation: the fantasy is valid because it has brought about sensual pleasure.* One realizes that any inhibition regarding such an encounter with herself leaves the patient with a blank in place of an identification, however vital it is for her. The result is an unfulfilled body-self (some would say body-image) and, correspondingly, a world of fragmented reality.[1]

Certain dreams remind us of the importance of those openings up of the future which give orgastic experiences their meaning:

> Agnes remembers her early orgastic experiences together with emotions accompanying them. First there is a dream of "inexpressible joy," turning into depression. Beside the sea. She is waiting. An excited crowd gathers around her (this refers to the waiting for an orgasm). Behind her there is a toilet (a reminder of a masturbation scene). She is seated. Suddenly a marvelous animal, soft and silky to stroke, settles on her taut skirt. She inhales deeply, stretches out her arms and strokes it. In admiration, the whole crowd vibrates with her. Everything was "so full," "so wonderful." This moment, she says, *was a concentration of everything, all I have been, everything I shall be.* Like saying to oneself: I want to be in a lovely country, I have an immense desire for it, and I've no sooner said it than I'm there.

So, the repressed fantasy, as the dream shows, involves the incorporation of the penis in its function as the agent of instinctual drive and as the *generator of orgasm*. This same patient thought her body was unfinished and wished a sculptor would come and "make her *arms*." She could only make very limited use of her hands, tied up in masturbation's fundamental fantasy function of being a *penis for the vagina*.

Ferenczi has shown that masturbation goes with a duality in the individual: he identifies simultaneously with both partners and achieves copulation in an autistic manner. One must add that this duality, the "touching oneself," the experience of "I-myself," authenticated by the orgasm, also suggests: "As I can do it to myself, alone, I am emancipated from those who have hitherto permitted or forbidden me this pleasure according to their whim." Masturbation, literally touching oneself, and reflective fantasy free the child from maternal dependence and at the same time establish an autonomous maternal imago, that is to say, one which can find its pleasure somewhere other than with the child, a possiblity missing when the mother forbids masturbation. Such an imago is rooted in excessive or premature anal training, and would influence all similar activities. A mother who is too exacting will cause a jealous, empty, unsatisfied maternal imago. How could she manage by herself if only mastery of the child can give her satisfaction? How could she not be jealous or suspicious if the child frees herself from her while growing to maturity? The ban on masturbation has the effect of tying the child to his mother's body and interfering with his essential growth. Patients often express this situation by saying, "some part of my body (hand, penis, feces) is still in my mother, but how can I get it back? She needs it so much! It is her only pleasure."

The hand "belonging to the Mother" can only symbolize for the patient what the mother herself forbids; this hand will never represent the penis.[2] The path leading to the father is thus blocked, and the dependent relation with the Mother perpetuates itself. The little girl will experience this insoluble dilemma: identifying with a dangerously aggressive mother who needs to be completed by having or being the useless appendage of an incomplete body (namely, that of the child). The patient might repeat the two possibilities in relation to her husband. But analysis is there precisely to help her break the magic circle of "being" and "having." It will certainly not provide an appendage-penis; the "arms" Agnes has just recovered are equivalent to a complementary penis, which represents something beyond being and having, *the right to act and to be-*

come. When the envy of an appendage-penis is not any longer hiding the desire for a complementary one, then the father's approach need no longer be blocked by the feeling that she has a body which is dangerous for the penis. This also means that masturbation, and identifications, are no longer felt destructive to the Mother.

The removal of orgastic inhibition during analysis is always accompanied by a feeling of power. A woman's analysis could not possibly bring her to genital maturity without solving penis envy, which conceals the masturbatory and the anal conflicts underlying it. For example, it is impossible that penis envy could be resolved as a desire to have a child by the father. Indeed, if the child has to play the part of a converted penis-object and supply the completion lacking up till then, how can her maturity be accepted, the fulfillment of her ambitions wished for and encouraged by a mother who, without her, would lapse into bitterness and envy! Such a mother has in the girl's fantasy only one wish: to keep the child-penis (an illusory guarantee of her own completeness) eternally in the role of an appendage.

Inasmuch as penis envy represses *pregenital* anxieties, it completely blocks genital fulfillment. The path from penis envy to genital fulfillment necessarily passes through an intermediary stage: the fantasy of *having pleasure with the father's penis.* Once this fantasy is allowed, the "desire to have a child" by the father will no longer mean what one actually *has* or receives, but will mean what is a natural part of growing up.

I V

Arrested in the process of her genital fulfillment, the woman who suffers from penis envy lives with a feeling of frustration, the nature of which she cannot guess. She has only a vague idea of what genital orgastic completion is. At any rate she cannot achieve it while the repression continues.

We have seen that the symptom consists of idealizing the penis, investing it with all she has lost hope of for herself: her aim in life, genital maturity. This is what the child has to achieve because she does not have it yet. Indeed, the desire is eternal; it never goes away, but it is either without content or fixed on stereotyped images. The greatest desire of a woman who suffers from penis envy is to meet the male in full orgastic union, and to realize herself in an authentic act, but this is what she has to avoid most. Clinicians often see women trying to obtain the complementary penis, the instrument of their fulfillment, at the cost of having to struggle with a threatening jealous imago. Then envy for the idealized penis and hatred toward its possessor arise. From then on deception will prevail over love, frustration over ample gratification.

During analysis the shift to what is usually called the genital stage is always like this: I am no longer "castrated" because "I can." This means, first of all, the disinhibition of masturbatory gestures and fantasies, otherwise the analysis will not progress. If repression means that something is missing in the ego which limits one's capacities, then freeing the repression will bring a sense of power, self-esteem and, especially, *faith* in one's own possibilities and future development.

> "I don't know how I can tell you," says Olga, "what impression your words had on me. I can't get over it. . . . It is as though you had *transferred a power* to me. Yet, I was very depressed the other day. But after going out of here, I repeated to myself everything you said. And all that anxiety melted away! I have rarely cried as much as I have this week. . . . It is like a sudden light. . . . And last night I . . . no, I've never mentioned those things to anybody. Briefly, it was like *waking up*. I had some pleasure. . . . Now I want to try myself out and I keep smiling at all the men, and you know, they answer me very kindly. And, I can't get over it, people have paid me compliments!"

During the last session, we had realized how, by means of idealization, she was forbidding herself a gratification within her reach and how, in fact, this prohibition referred to the maternal interdiction against having anything to do with her father's virility. The dismissal of the prohibiting imago revealed the knot of the problem—masturbation. At a later session Olga arrives with *"one very cold hand,"* as if it did not belong to her. She mentions all the objects her mother forbade her to touch, particularly her own genitals. This "very cold" hand was nothing but a manifestation of her obedience to the forbidding maternal imago.

Recognizing that the idealization of the penis comes from the repression of masturbation is equal to liberating energy and, as we can see, easily confers new possibilities to one's own sex. These are the ones of which the child was deprived and which are now recovered, the possibility of identifying with the protagonists of the primal scene, at each of its stages, and of verifying the validity of such identifications by the orgastic pleasure obtained through them.[3,4]

To give the reader a more concrete idea of these theories it will be helpful to read a brief sequence from analytical treatment (about twenty sessions). Ida, a young woman of Hungarian origin, had sought analytical help because of numerous professional difficulties and emotional problems:

> It gave me a shock to see Jacques doing the dishes. I was ashamed as though somebody had exposed a hidden part of my body. I am incapable of doing needlework, repairing, sewing . . . I'm ashamed to have a woman's body. I am ashamed to see Jacques becoming . . . how can I put it? . . . a woman. Of course, this doesn't mean that he is . . . but why was it so worrying? *Maybe because, for you, "woman" doesn't have the usual meaning. To be a "woman," for you, means to be "without a sex."* I don't know. I am very muddled. Why did I think that with a torch (name given to the penis) one had everything, that everything was lovely? Why have I given this great power to men? Are they really like that? No, of course, they aren't like that! *At least, if they are as you describe them to be for you, I can understand your envy of the torch.* Jacques isn't like that, neither is my father, grandfather, or anybody. It was my own idea. For my mother, women were enemies. Oliver wasn't. Oliver, my brother, could be a friend. He could say to men: this is my mother, she is wonderful. She herself, she was abandoned by her own mother. She thought children were born through the navel. It is exactly as we said last year: the child didn't give her a "lower body." For me a child is all the life of "down there," it is all one has down there, all that can grow from down there. Then she had jaundice, my mother. Deep down, I must have been like her. (This is a reminder of a dream in which she gives birth to a yellow-orange child.) In fact, I must have been like an enemy for her. But I was also a friend. . . . Why did she say to me, "You will never be as beautiful, nor as delicate, nor as sensitive as Susan?" She never protected me, she has never been a support for me. I have never had anything for myself. I have never kept anything. I have always given all my things away.

It is obvious that for Ida "woman" means "castrated." Trying to castrate men is justified by the desire to acquire the unique sex, the male sex, with all its advantages. In such an interpretation one tries to acknowledge two things: (1) the idealized character of the desired penis; (2) the subjective character of this idealization.

Having recognized that she herself was the source of the meaning "woman" and "penis" had for her, and having realized that these were not absolute, unshakable meanings, Ida can now go beyond them toward their origin—"my mother." "It is because my mother lives like that in me that 'woman' must mean for me 'castrated,' without a lower body, 'monstrous,' and I must envy and idealize the penis." Uncompleted, empty, frustrated, the Mother has devalued her and castrated her in the sense of depriving her of her future fulfillment. That is why, she realizes, she can keep nothing for herself:

> Poor mummy, she feels very let down. She believes that now I shall only look after my baby. I dreamed of a snake. He came out of my breasts and could have bitten other people. The midwife told me the baby was ready to come out. Poor mummy. She telephoned today, but it was to speak to Jacques. She must be very lonely. In the children's home there were only girls. Then this kind doctor, that nice old man. I liked him a lot. He gave me injections. At school there were always boys, too. My mother never sent me to school on time. I always had to wait around before leaving and stay longer with her. She always wanted to prolong the holidays too. She didn't like school. Yet school is strength, authority, regularity, security. I like school. (Ida has serious inhibitions about continuing her university studies.)

Ida continues to understand further the significance of her relation to her mother. She can now see that if she has her baby, mummy will become "impoverished." Daughter and mother are indissolubly tied together; one complements the other's emptiness.

The equivalence between the snake-baby which bites and that nice old doctor who injects is that they are pleasure-objects for Ida, which means that they are dangerous for the Mother. Thanks to these pleasure-objects she will be able, as she knows, to free herself. This is why she thinks her mother stops her from coming into contact with that "strength," "that authority," which school represents. Ida arrives late at her sessions for the same reason. The "empty" Mother, "with no lower body," needs to keep Ida near her in order to fill up her emptiness, with Ida as a pleasure-object *for herself*. In short, whether to be autonomous and have pleasure *with* the penis or to be the appendage of the Mother—that is the dilemma. If I have pleasure, my mother becomes empty; that is unbearable for me.

I dreamed that we were asking my mother for a little dog. Not me, my husband. When I was little, I liked to keep back my pee. The old ironing lady would send me off to the bathroom when she saw me hopping from one leg to the other. That's odd, after having made love I also go straight to the bathroom. . . . People always made me believe that woman had nothing. Nothing but a hole out of which things come. They must retain nothing. That little bear makes me laugh. I bought it for the baby, but for the time being I am keeping it for myself. I am as tight as a virgin, I can't put the dutch cap on right. It bleeds, it falls into the john. I'll pay you today.

There is something to claim from the Mother: the liberty to retain the "pee" in one's body, to play and have pleasure with it. Talking about all this is a start for the dissolution of that depressing tie with the Mother. Ida must reassure her mother—she is not trying to empty her; on the contrary, she is paying her; anyway it is so tight in there that she could not retain anything even if she wanted to. "There is no question of my satisfying myself alone, there is no danger for you, you can keep me as an appendage." In this case, to be able to retain means that one can have pleasure by oneself and, thereby, become independent. We also notice that Ida's own "lower body" begins to come up in her talks.

Now, in giving birth, I had great difficulty in getting the child out. Then suddenly I thought of all the things we have said here, I called you very loudly, very loudly, and then it was over, the anxiety had dissipated. I came late because of my cooking. And you know, I've left my work. I said to myself, suddenly, "I'm a real woman." *A real woman? What is that, for you?* Oh, a few dresses, a hairdo, five minutes rest from time to time, a well-made boeuf bourguignon. But you are right, there is something odd. I saw Jacques at his desk, he was writing. I wanted to do the same. I was kind of . . . jealous. My studies . . . they are still part of my anxiety. I still have mountains to climb. (This is a reminder of a dream in which she was climbing a mountain with her mother. Down below there is an abyss, "it's terrible," it is a box filled by a crab, a huge red crab.) My mother in that kitchen . . . terrible. That day I had two mothers, that was my impression—one like the everyday one, smiling, talking, doing hundreds of things; the other, that unknown woman, that intangible woman who's absurd. (This refers to a scene in the kitchen. Her mother had one day wounded her father during an argument in the kitchen.) I remember, I dreamed there was a shop, a haberdasher's, and they sold buttons there. I wanted a sewing box.

Ida is reassuring me that I am good for her; thanks to me she was able to get her child out. No danger of her asserting herself in independence. But will I allow her another pleasure, the real one, the one precisely which the Mother forbids—study? There can be no question of it. She asserts that now she feels a "real woman" —in other words, a real, castrated person. But that is safer than freeing herself from Mother. Hurt, incomplete, the Mother would become dangerous, as in that scene in the kitchen. Besides, to renounce one's own completeness (as when Ida pretends to be a "real woman") carries the same danger: the aggression of dissatisfaction. The only way out is total inhibition. To study, to retain, like "keeping in pee" or having pleasure in intercourse, are all forbidden. The empty Mother holds on to Ida, she stops her from going away, from going toward that "strength."

> It is impossible to arrive on time. I'm always arriving late. *Like at school.* I felt you were angry the other day. Now I can handle the baby well. When my mother didn't send me to school, I wasn't pleased, I wanted to get angry, but then in the end I acquiesced. I'm worried by the idea of starting my studies again. You mentioned that mountain dream. I was with my mother. I was behind her, very frightened. It was horrible down below. *Like everything that happens "down below."* Then I was also very frightened of falling. Oh, last night, I had a dream. I am in the sand, or something clayey. It's growing hollow, I'm sinking into it more and more. I had this impression that in order to save myself I was supposed to make certain gestures, certain movements. I was supposed to let myself go and not resist . . . do some, I don't know what . . . particular gestures. On the edge of a hole—an indeterminate man, I couldn't see his face, I didn't know who he was. An indifferent person, neutral (the analyst). I had the impression he would try to save me, also that he was incapable, and that he could do nothing for me. And I sank in more and more, still trying to recall those gestures —I absolutely *had* to remember them! But, really, in the end, it wasn't as bad as all that. I believed it would save me, in spite of everything. I don't know any more, I don't know any more. It was like when I gave birth.

The memory of the "mountain dream" (she is on the summit with her mother; there is an abyss and a crab down below) reminds her now of another, more recent, dream. This time she is "down below" with a man, in the abyss itself: she now dares explore it. She goes into it (like a baby in her body). She is able now to identify herself with the penis that penetrates her. She is reassured—it was not in danger—and even experienced orgastic pleasure. To penetrate oneself, to allow oneself to be attracted "inside," as in a masturbatory duality, means already to envisage intercourse with a man, and thereby to emancipate oneself from the "summit of the mountain," from the relationship to the Mother which made the "down below" like an "abyss of crabs." The orgastic aspect of the dream will be more explicit in a following session. "It was like giving birth," when the child separates itself from the Mother. This separation occurs by means of an orgasm by intromission. At this stage Ida can give up being the doll she was for her mother and can deal with a new problem, the genital relationship:

> I have a terrific panic when Jacques holds me! I thought about your interior corridor. I have been to see the gynecologist. This time I wasn't afraid at all. I was quite at ease. When Jacques holds me I can't free myself, I stamp my feet. I can't bear it that someone wants to tie me down. Yet, when he caresses me, I like it, but I have a terrific panic. Then, I think of something else (his home town, where his mother is still living). I was ugly in my childhood. It was because I wanted to be so. I would say to myself: I shall start by will, through really hard work. I became fat with eating so much bread all the time. That pleasure was allowed. *Instead of another one, forbidden?* (Ida laughs.) Yes, I understand what you mean. In fact, you mean that I am just as afraid of you as I am of Jacques. Perhaps that is why I always arrive late.

The mother is now endowed with an "interior corridor"—her body is no longer empty. In turn, Ida can now speak of her own inside. The woman "with no lower body" no longer threatens to tie her to herself. Ida is now attempting to formulate in the transference her panic in the face of sexual intercourse:

> For my mother I was like a doll she could dress. I am ashamed at the idea of having wandered naked in my father's country. Jacques, like you, tells me that I am running away from him. Though he is very kind, I do go into fits with him. . . . I left him and went to sleep on the carpet. He

rejoined me and we both slept on the carpet in the end. I am looking at the things that are here. When I was little I couldn't stay still in my bed. I thought it was boring. I would look at the things in the room for a long, long time. . . . For my mother, yes it is very odd. . . . I was her doll. Sometimes she wanted me to be her mother. When I am with her I disappear, I cannot exist as me. She insists that I look after her, only her. She phoned me, I said that I was ill, tired, that I had metritis. When I come to think of it, my baby is a very curious thing. He could nearly fit into a basket. Babies are funny things. Now I can handle the dutch cap very well, but I am a bit frightened. I told Jacques that it was bleeding . . . *and that it was no good inside.* I had a dream last night. Oh . . . I am not going to tell you this dream. I am going to keep you in suspense, I am going to make you wait for nothing. It was at the Galeries Lafayette. We were there with Jacques to buy some curtains. We were on the fifth floor. Then suddenly, something was burning, there was fire, smoke. Jacques climbed up to the sixth floor. It was safer to go up than down. One day he really played the role of a fireman in a house on fire. A friend said to me: I am embarrassed when I make love. I made several hypotheses about why he had gone up. I had stayed on the floor below. And I fainted. It was exactly the same impression as when I was sinking into the sand in that other dream. Why did I have this dream? Sometimes Jacques puts his tongue out at me and it is horrible. (We analyze a problem related to fellatio.) It feels good to have talked about that. You are not afraid of fire.

"It was the same impression." But no longer the same symbol. If in the dream about the "abyss" Ida enters into her own inside, in the dream about the "fire," she sees the possibility of putting the man's tongue (as a penis) inside her, and she is not afraid of fire (torch: name given to the penis in her childhood), just as the analyst, representing here the paternal imago, is not afraid of Ida's "internal fire."

I am not going to stay with you, I am going to leave! By the way I have found out how to get a reduction in my rail fare. *A reduction of me. So that nothing can go from me into you. People have always told you to take nothing from daddy!* I had a dream. There was Brigitte Bardot and me; I got angry like a child, I stamped my feet on the ground: I want it, I want it! It was about a dress. I am thinking of my father on the beach. There was something in his pants, and it was because of that I wasn't allowed to play with him. *Not allowed to have a BB*[5] *in your pants either?* Oh, something happened to me. . . . I bought a bird and I brought it home. Soon after it was dead. It was terrible. Yes, at the beach I thought: in order to play with him he would have not to have that in his pants. I was told, when there was a question of my parents divorcing, that he might take me away and therefore I had to be hidden at my grandparent's home: they would protect me. That bird, that poor little bird, and I wanted to make a nice warm nest for it. *You wanted so much to nest the "bird" warmly in you. But you feel that in you it would not be comfortable. So it is better to go away rather than to come near it. Haven't you been told to keep away from Daddy? Perhaps meeting him represented some danger for you and for him?*

But the maternal interdiction manifests itself when the desire becomes explicit: "There is no question of your having a BB." So Ida "reduces" the father's penis in order to render it ineffectual. Thus, she shelters herself from the desire to take hold of it and put it into herself. The idea of danger and the idea of the forbidding Mother appear simultaneously. The interpretation turns on this development.

I went home to my mother's. I was ill. I vomited. My mother has never wanted to teach me the secrets of cooking. She hardly allowed me to chop up the onion and the parsley. Chop and cut, nothing else. Never real cooking, I mean cooking as an art. *Just as she didn't teach you the art of approaching your father.* I had a dream last night. It was like a film. And also like going to the office. Tiring yet at the same time agreeable. There was something like an arena. . . . The lion was supposed to be inside, but, in fact, he was outside. He was running all around the arena. . . . I was with a friend and I asked him to protect me. I was beside him and we were running too. The lion was running in the same direction as us. He was like a man. How odd. I turned round and saw that he was doing leaps like a dancer, he was doing the splits in the air. . . . I went and presented myself for my nomination. It is annoying to speak in front of fifty people. I did it. How much do I owe you for this month? I was in a funk when I was there, I didn't dare speak. I would like to tell you something . . . you know I have always thought that it was all dead in me, quite dead. And then, now, I felt something . . . that my vagina was sensitive. It's staggering. I felt that I could have some pleasure! Before, I was very frightened. Now "it" is coming. I can no longer be afraid. Yes. I can feel that it is going to come. That it's already there. I don't know. I never speak about it with Jacques. I have the feeling he's frightened. If we can't resolve this, he will have to go into analysis. That's odd, I am speaking to you as though you weren't there. It's a bit as though I had nothing to say. *Perhaps you think that your pleasure frightens me?* I don't know why, but I suddenly thought of daddy and mummy, and the Germans. Mummy wasn't pleased when he came to see me. She was jealous. And it was as though something could happen when daddy held me by the hand. People were hostile. Yet he was handsome. But everyone knew they were divorcing. I also thought that I could have been born from a mother and a father who were apart. . . . Then I was afraid that something would happen to mummy. That she would be unhappy. I feel happy. . . . I was terribly worried she would have some sort of attitude towards me. I imagine her angry, screaming, saying unbearable things, like she did with daddy. I would have done anything to avoid that. She had never been as happy as when I was at boarding school. But nowadays I don't know, I don't bear her a grudge anymore. Sometimes, lately, I have been full of hatred. It's diminishing now. I think I am not responsible for them. I am thinking of something silly: I have a lovely baby and you, you haven't got one. Maybe it's not true, after all I don't know. But that's how I feel and . . . I feel sorry for you. It's silly. I want to know how much I owe you? *For the baby?* (Ida laughs.) No, I didn't mean it that way. That's odd, it is as though I had pleasure in depriving you. These things are silly. . . .

Having named the obstacle, the desire for *incorporation* can now be formulated. The complex symbol of the "lion" (man-eating man) condenses the image of the penis (pleasure-object) and the gestures of man and woman in intercourse (the "leaps" and the "splits"). The desire to have an orgasm by introducing the penis shows that she is seeking integration (the lion is running after her), but that she cannot yet accept it entirely; the lion stayed "outside." The desire to have pleasure *with* the penis becomes more precise, but Ida is frightened at the idea of feeling the orgastic sensations mentioned in the previous session. They imply a break of the tie to the mother. Frustrated, hurt, would the Mother in turn hurt the daughter, as she hurt the Father? Nevertheless, the mere fact of foreseeing the possibility of orgastic pleasure allows Ida to envisage resuming her previously inhibited professional activity.

> I am becoming insomniac. I haven't slept all night. As though I had something better to do than sleep. Yet I dreamed. Beside a swimming pool there was something like a brothel. A woman was there, a prostitute, quite sympathetic, not mean at all. It was very hot. I wanted very much to have a swim. She didn't want to. Finally, she agreed. Then there were four men, it was horrible, they wanted me to be . . . like a call girl. I was terrified, we left. Then I was in the train. I said: you must help me, there are some people who want to do terrible things to me. In such circumstances I am very efficient: I spoke to a soldier, to tell him that it was his civic duty to help me. He gave me a telephone number. I seem to remember that I failed in the end. Oh! I am so tired, I can hardly distinguish things around me. How much do I owe you? My husband told me that I was intelligent. It was nice, because it was as though someone had reassured me from outside. I don't know why I think women are worth nothing. And it is always men who are in command of everything, who do everything. Oh! My finger is cut. It bled all day yesterday. I can't imagine how I came to cut it! With a knife? It bled so much! Why? How did I do this to myself? Oh, I'm tired! And also I didn't feel at all like getting ready, like dressing myself. But how much do I owe you for this month, I never know, oh what a bore! *For the moment, you think you owe me a finger for the pleasure you took in your inside.* On the beach, in my country, I was always alone. The other children had their parents, I was alone, always. *Are you sure?* Ah, not that time, you are right. . . . Oh, but in the dream, it was the same beach as the one where I saw daddy.

Because of her guilt, Ida is trying to cancel the previous progress. "You see," she says to me, "I have put nothing inside, I have done nothing, anyway women have nothing, they have no 'lower body,' you have nothing to worry about, I will still be your doll." The equivalence is between the finger and the penis. Her finger, how did she cut it? She is sure the Mother is responsible for this. Isn't it she who stopped Ida from putting her finger-penis into herself and thus stopped her from becoming independent? But as this "finger" (her pleasure-object) is kept by the Mother, inasmuch as she cuts it off, Ida already expresses, even though in a self-punishing way, her desire to break the tie of belonging to her mother.

> Last night I dreamed that daddy was dead. We were at C. . . . Really I haven't had any letters from my parents for some time. Daddy's death would explain their silence. He was in a car. Mummy was with him. As they drew up in front of the memorial to the dead, he wasn't feeling well. He had difficulty in driving. Mummy had to ask for a light from another man. That was a sign that things weren't going well. I thought to myself: he should be careful. Then he was dead. It was his heart. There was nothing sad. An emotion just similar to the one I had when my grandmother died. A strong but irrelevant emotion. In any case with no link to anything I could understand. It was more like a feeling of shame. Then, in the dream, I had to leave town. I was with my mother. I wanted to leave but she wouldn't let me. Always the same blackmailing, the same fits of hysteria . . . I thought of mummy and I said to myself: he must have suffered a lot but now no more problems. No more worries about the person who is dead. I am less and less afraid of death. I've started work again, and reading and thinking . . . that is important. Then I went to this meeting. I felt like talking at it but I didn't do it. I am still waiting for my nomination. That would give me time for my studies. My father, poor thing, he was always threatened by my mother, always in danger of being abandoned. I also dreamed that there were fires everywhere: left, right, below, above, in front, behind. Very strange.

She is making the father "die" and in doing so separating the "Mother's fire" from the Mother. But this father is also Ida who herself suffered, like him, from pressures and threats of abandonment. Ida's desire is becoming more precise: to withdraw from the Mother, but gaining autonomous erotic pleasure of the Oedipal relationship. Yet guilt regains its importance, and in the second half of the dream Ida has become once again complementary to the Mother. Nevertheless, her fear of breaking away is diminishing. She can envisage taking up her activities again and invests all the space around, that is to say, all her body, with "fire" ("fire is life").

I am late again. Yesterday we had our wedding anniversary. I gave Jacques a pipe. Last year I hardly told you about my wedding, I had to hide it from you, to steal it from you in some sense. I am very pleased. It is no longer as before, but there is still a lot to do. And I was always waiting for you to make my decisions for me. Now I decide by myself. I had a funny dream last night. At home there was a sort of political meeting. Something suspect. My husband was in the house opposite. I wanted to comb my hair and I looked for a mirror. I arrived in the bathroom and horror! I noticed . . . I saw my skull! On it there were still a few hairs . . . like a brush . . . a few bristles. The hairs on the neck had been saved, they were falling, as if burned. It was horrible, hideous. . . . I called for help: Do something fast! "Yes, they told me, it's a serious illness, you must treat it." Then I went to see my husband. . . . I told him there was great danger, a terrible catastrophe, but he wouldn't understand. . . . When I was ten I used to imagine what would happen if they were to die and I were to become an orphan. I still want to have parents. . . . I saw an old friend in my dream, and I kissed her very warmly. There are a lot of hidden things in my relations with women. I'm glad to think that fire doesn't frighten you, that means I will be able to live. I have made this discovery —people don't really live. They are extinct. My husband is a smoldering fire. I have great confidence in him. I would like to say that I am happy but I immediately become afraid of a catastrophe.

"To comb oneself," "to touch oneself," that is to say to masturbate, means to be in danger. The meaning of the dream becomes clearer later on: Ida is trying to remember a scene. Masturbation implies the desire of freeing herself through the death of her parents. The "reunion" means that by touching herself she can achieve a reunion of the self with the self, like the parents who unite in the sexual act.

I have a friend who said to me one day: You know, you're slow to start, but once you've started, you charge. I dreamed of a locomotive and a child threatened by kidnappers. The train was between the beach and the swimmers. One had to cross the rails. I'm thinking of a lion who bit the arm of the person who was stroking him. . . . I'm afraid of Jacques. I have always been very clumsy with my hands. When I sew, I prick myself; I cut my fingers. By the way how much do I

owe you? *By the way of what?* I don't know, I can never cal-
culate a debt. I would prefer you to tell me. I don't like handling money. It was my mother's privilege. She was in charge
of the cash. Money, to open the drawer, touch it . . . for me
would be like touching fire! *The torch?* (Ida laughs). That's
odd. It pleases me to think that last time, when I didn't
come, you waited for me. Perhaps you waited for me from
one minute to the next; since the whole hour is mine it's my
session. Nobody can come in my place. And that you . . .
that you thought of me. But when I will be cured . . . I
mean when everything will be going well, when I have
started my work and my studies again, what will become of
you? *My cash-box will be empty? My room will be empty?* By
the way, my husband gave your address to someone. Because
he thinks you are good and that's rare. I don't know what I
think about it. *That it will fill the gap? Comfort me?* I don't
know. It's the first time in my life that I have something
which is really my own.

If autonomy, the definition and elaboration of oneself, occurs
in the self-experience of masturbation then this contact may fall
within that store of deep guilt associated with anal characteristics.
It is the Mother's privilege to handle the "cash-box," to fill it up,
empty it. Ida is trying to restore to the Mother the power she once
usurped with her own fingers. By this act she gives herself up to the
Mother, and becomes once again the manipulated object.

Monstrous. What do you think of someone who kisses her
baby on the mouth? I thought, I must tell you immediately.
It's like when one is condemned, I mean in my dream. There
was a dried up water course with big worms in it. You were
supposed to eat them or was it that when you ate them you
died? It was at my grandparents. Impression of horror. Big,
big worms. It reminded me of that mashed meat I left in a
plastic pot; then it rotted and there were worms in it. I was
in the classical position of a woman who doesn't want to
show her fear. My husband, just as disgusted as I was, was
pretending to be courageous. At last I regained composure. I
put the little box in a big one and went and put it in the
rubbish bin. I nearly fainted. I was determined to show that
I was courageous. And then, it's silly, just think, I interpreted this dream. I don't know anything about psychoanalysis and I didn't think, it came spontaneously. Well, I interpreted. I thought that I must be frightened that during

sexual intercourse people could die. You know it does happen, the newspapers . . . , well, I don't know who, a president or someone died that way. It's silly to want to interpret one's own dreams. *Why should it be silly?* Because I don't know anything about psychoanalysis and it's your job . . . Deep down it's like with mummy. She always said to me: you're stupid, there's sawdust in your head. She was always wanting me to depend on her, to need her absolutely. That's odd, that dream with my grandparents. I feel that the kitchen is something very important. I remember my grandfather in the kitchen, when I was living with them. . . . I had been just at the height of his . . . in such a way that my face . . . these things are terrible . . . *that you could do with his penis what you had done with your baby?* Oh, it reminds me, I also dreamed I had a tiny little baby, hardly any bigger than my pen. He was in a transparent case and I was putting him into everything! In the pocket, in the drawer, up, down, by the front, by the back. It was very amusing.

Ida's guilt no longer expresses itself in the form of a simple inhibition. She is now trying to give a demonstration for the mother imago. In spite of the apparently depressing side of the dream, she can now allow herself to handle herself—and to speak about it —"to comb herself," "to give interpretations," "to put the baby into her," "to eat the worm." At the same time this is an introjection of the analyst's function, indicating an important modification of the maternal imago.

(This is about a young girl's "kidnapping" in the street.) It gives me a strange uneasiness. It makes me think of something in the kitchen. This kitchen is haunting me. I had a dream: people were dancing, I agree to dance, then the room becomes an amphitheatre, and I'm sitting down. Then the amphitheatre becomes a kitchen. A woman offers me a crab, something gelatinous, slightly disgusting for me to eat. I hesitate, then I accept. I cut a little bit off and give her back the rest. After all I prostituted myself when I lived with the nuns. I had a fit of anger last night. I said that people should have the right to be stupid after all, if they wanted to. Why did I say it? Everybody belittled my father, I was the only one to love him. In fact my mother must have been under her parent's influence . . . That woman. . . . What did she leave unsaid about my husband! . . . I dreamed that I had twins and then that my baby had a little detachable penis, one could take it off, put it back on, and handle it. Things have never been as good as they are now with my husband; and even so, I'm jealous, I'm afraid that some woman will take him away from me. *Perhaps, precisely because you are happy?* And I'm also frightened of fire in the house. I'm frightened of hurting my husband. Yes, I am frightened of hurting him. *Of being like mummy who hurt daddy in the kitchen?* You should take my husband into analysis.

A new difficulty appears here. Although she can achieve an emancipation from the Mother in fantasy by introjecting her anal power into masturbatory acts, she has difficulty in assuming this power which is then felt to be dangerous for the partner. There is a contradiction in the imago. That is why Ida undertakes only a partial introjection by sharing the crab. Yet it requires total introjection of the "crab" to remove inhibitions concerning "the dance" and "the studies" (shared orgasm and intellectual activities). The contradiction lies precisely in the fact that at the same time she also must be the violent but frustrated Mother, who although she "cuts," does not "eat" (may not give herself any pleasure). Does not the violence manifested toward the Mother show the castration of her own genital?

> I have the impression that there are hidden vibrations between people. I am looking for other people's secret. How are they? What are they doing? Oh, they will see that my shoes are badly polished, my skirt not well put on. When I was a young girl I wanted everybody to look at me, to fall in love with me. To be seen, to be looked at. That is how one becomes an actress. I read something about the Russian revolution while coming here on the bus. Yesterday, Jacques left home; he has gone on a voyage and I cut my finger with the scissors. Mummy didn't like having to treat me. You shouldn't be sick, she would say. I am thinking that I would like a cup of tea. When they went to bed at night, mummy and daddy, I often had tummy pains. I was delighted with daddy on Sundays. Jacques's mummy is ill. Perhaps she has something very serious in her uterus.

Jacques's departure on a voyage is compared with the scene in the kitchen. This time she used the scissors to "cut" Jacques from his mother, causing guilt, self-mutilation and fear of illness. Nevertheless, the Oedipal structure becomes clearer.

> I cannot swallow anything. I'm on a diet. Maybe I've got an ulcer, or something in my stomach. I must have some X rays taken. I never used to complain when I was little. Never!

Not even when you were in your little bed? Yes, after all it is true, I often cried. I had a dream last night. A mountain, in it things of great value, ancient precious stones, it was a very hard mountain, very hard. Jacques went inside it.

Ida does not want to "swallow" the nocturnal intimacy of her parents. The dream mountain (the Mother) has things of great value inside it. There is no question of Ida—this is implied but not expressed—entering it and taking them. On the contrary she seems to give Jacques back to the "mountain." We might surmise that she has secretly made her husband into an ally who will be able to take the "riches" and give them to her.

I've been to see the doctor about my stomach. That's why I didn't come here. I have a little bit of money this month. The analysis is boring me. *It bores you to have to think once and for all that you have to take away from here some "riches" for yourself. That's why you think you must be ill, weak, impoverished. And in the long run, if you are poor, I am impoverished, I am not paid.* That's true, after all I don't know what is happening to me. I'm excited and aggressive and I don't know why. Yet you know, my husband—I love him very much and all the same I am very angry with him. I don't know what I would do to him if I could. *When you are angry with yourself this is what you do: you prick yourself, you cut and hurt yourself, and you deprive yourself of intellectual nourishment and love. Maybe this is what you want to do to someone else when you are angry.* At the nuns . . . there were no mirrors at all. I was never able to see myself in a mirror. *But you did in a dream.* Ah yes, when my hair was all burnt. *Yes and you had the impression that there was something "suspect" there.* Yes, I remember well. At the nuns, I wasn't able to wash myself entirely. I mean you had to do it bit by bit. It was ridiculous. I never looked at the bottom half of myself. That's odd. When my arm hangs from the bed between the wall and the mattress and it touches the carpet, even though it's silky and soft down there, I have the impression that somebody might cut it off or bite it. Often I even take my arm back quickly. It's such a strange feeling. *What is down below is dangerous?* I remember at the nuns, that soldier, he came one day. . . . I remember him well, that German. I was doing . . . anyway I was sleeping. . . . I suppose I might have been . . . and he said to me: If you are not good, baby . . . *and if you put your hand down there* . . . No, only, if you are not good, I will cut your arm off. Then it was Christmas and I could ask for something. I asked for a little brother. I was three years old. I was sure one could ask for that. In fact I got a teddy bear but that wasn't good enough. . . . I wasn't pleased at all. A little brother is alive, one can play with him. And especially, a little brother, this could have been a proof! *Of what?* That . . . that my parents exist somewhere, that they made him, so therefore they exist. *If that was the proof you wanted a little sister would have done, but you, you wanted a little brother.* A little brother is like an extension. Yes, it has a penis and after all, I didn't know my father very well, there were hardly any men in the convent, apart from the priest, the good old doctor . . . really that teddy bear . . . a little brother would have been like an extension toward my father. After all (that's odd, why am I thinking of that?), it's shameless that I shouldn't know it, it . . . the hymen, whereabouts is it? It can't be immediately at the entrance; it's more likely to be a little higher. A little girl can put her finger to it. Oh, I always swept the staircase going from the top to the bottom. At first, I didn't think of sweeping, only of holding the broomstick in my hand. One could handle it; I think of the way children climb stairs: they put one leg on the step first of all, then the other leg rejoins the first one. I liked to handle the broom when going up the stairs. One could put it between one's legs . . . *it extends the finger, the arm, it went toward your father.* You see? I could have played with a little brother, and a little boy is something kind, well behaved, good! *It is not like "an enemy for mummy" as you explained to me one day.*

Ida draws away from the aggression contained in the desire to "empty" the Mother of her "riches." She is running away from me in order to protect me. She refuses to see what is pushing her to "deprive" me, to "cut" me, to "prick" me, to "take back" her autonomy that I am "keeping" for myself. This session shows us *in statu nascendi,* the progression which led to penis envy. We see the exacerbation of the conflict with the anal Mother. This kind of conflict usually resolves itself due to masturbatory acts and fantasies. And, indeed, in thinking of this Ida finally mentioned the memories about masturbation which led to remembering the traumatic moment that made her give it up. It was at that moment of desperation that she invented (in the utopian solution of getting a little brother) her penis envy. To have a penis like the boy meant in the little girl's mind a great number of advantages, but they all come down to one: the ability to keep a harmonious relation with the Mother. What is the magical power of the penis due to? The answer to this question has to be looked for on three different levels, which cannot always be distinguished easily. On an anal level it seems as though the penis, seen as a fecal stick, undetachable from the body, is a sign that its owner has not been dispossessed of his sphincter autonomy. He therefore has no reason either to be aggressive with the Mother (boys are "well-behaved, kind, good") or to be guilty. On the level of personality formation, the presence of the penis is important in that it frees one from masturbatory conflict (no need to put one's finger to it, as it is a permanent "finger") and, consequently, from conflict with the family: the little boy can have his pleasure, without becoming wicked. The path to the future is open. Lastly, on a prospective level (genital future) the penis is an extension toward the father and, as Ida puts it, permits her to come nearer the little girl's genital object. These are the infantile reasons underlying Ida's penis envy, an envy which has very little to do with the male genital organ itself. It expresses the repressed identificatory autoerotic fantasies directed toward the anal Mother.

> I had a strange dream last night, but I've forgotten it. Yet I remember a little. . . . That job, I wouldn't find it disagreeable at all. And after all, it would be a good discipline . . . it would force me to be neat. To do my hair, to make myself pretty. . . . I don't know. . . . I sing and then I want to grumble, like daddy. I do contradictory things. I am going to work. I'm thinking that Jacques's mother is well. On that side things are going better . . . That is odd, I think that I'm ashamed to work, to study. As though I wasn't allowed to. When I was little I couldn't work in peace. It was like a scandalous privilege. My mother often said to me, "Leave it, you'll be able to think of yourself later." And then the more I worked the more pleasure I had and the more mummy became sad, very sad. It's like a nail still stuck in me. She needed me so much, and then suddenly one day, she was happy on her own! She didn't need me! . . . Before, I was completely enslaved and she absolutely needed me, and then I thought to myself, "You will not be alone." When I was little, she left me. . . . This dependence also had a nice side to it. It was like depending on God. I could avoid having to

live all alone. Sometimes we were as good friends as two schoolgirls. But it was only on the surface . . . Then daddy, poor thing, he was totally excluded from this strange paradise. It was more like hell. Yet he was a bit frightened of us. When two women get together they become wicked. She wanted to make an ally out of me. Sometimes he was tender to us, and it makes me feel so sad. After all, I am ashamed of him, ashamed of daddy. *Ashamed of daddy, ashamed of studies* . . . daddy thinks that from now on I shall write to him and not to mummy. It upsets me. I wonder why?

Remembering the scene with the soldier allows Ida to foresee the possibility of an identification with the father. And we notice a new difficulty. The identification must fail because of the father's weakness, like the daughter he is dominated by the Mother.

I'm worn out. I went yesterday for that job . . . I'm delighted. So, because of that I bought some hairpins, lipstick, etc. It amuses me. I'm going to be late in paying you . . . at the beginning, when I couldn't pay you, it was unbearable. Now I say to myself—"After all, you can wait a bit." See? You just shouldn't have chosen that profession. You earn your money at other people's expense. It's scandalous to have a career like that! *The other day you told me that working, studying, were like a privilege, a "scandalous" pleasure. One could say that you are now doing to me what your mother did to you—you are reproaching me for my pleasures, my work, my career, the fact that I earn money.* . . . (Ida laughs.) Yes, it's as though I bear you a grudge like with. . . . Then that dream . . . that nightmare. . . . I was at home with Jacques. I had to hide him. There was something illegal. We were pursued by the authorities, a dramatic story. Some soldiers were supposed to come and fetch him. At first he was in the room next door. The chief commissioner came personally. He explained to me that I had to hide him under the blanket in the bed; that way no one would find him. That's funny, the superior authority of those same soldiers was explaining to me how to escape his own authority. But Jacques was taking the whole thing too lightly. He kept moving, going out. I thought: they are going to knock, they are going to come in, but he wouldn't stay still, he was moving all the time. As though there had been a baby there. . . . I was on the lookout. They could come back a second time. Somebody knocks on the door. I tell Jacques to stay still, but it's no use, he gets up and goes to open the door. Then it is an old lady who comes in. "Oh! You're there!" she says, "Hello!" And then she left and I saw her speak with some soldiers. I thought, we have been betrayed. . . . I was afraid they would take him from me and kill him. Last night . . . We made love . . . me, as usual, . . . But this time I wanted to go on. I was feeling very sensual. (But an external event interrupted.) I felt kind of amputated. It's odd, with daddy, as though mysterious, curious things could happen. . . . I was not supposed to be with him. After all, everyday life is full of mysteries. That German soldier . . . loaded with rifles and tommyguns. He said to me, "Hello baby!" and I said, "Hello Andrew!" *Hello! Like the old lady in the dream, the soldier's associate?* Yes, exactly. And then, in the dream I thought, "My God, she saw what she wasn't meant to see. It is treacherous. . . . Those Germans, perhaps they were looking for the Maquis, or something else that would have been hidden well within me. I mean in the bed. There were my arms and perhaps hands at the end. (Ida laughs.) It is funny to say that. After all, hands are always at the end. *Perhaps when they feel threatened they feel somehow detached from the end.* In the boarding school you know that's exactly the style of the nuns. One doesn't sleep with one's hands under the sheets. It's odd, sometimes I don't dare look at people in the street, observe them or see exactly how they are. Before, even when I spoke to them, I didn't dare look at them. . . . I was thinking about the mother superior. She was a witch. Everybody knew that she stole fruit. And then, I wonder why she slept in a big bed? We had our little beds, our little blankets. . . .

Ida continues, using the same words as her mother, to negate her ambitions and achievements. Yet the dream shows the modification of the imago's demands: this time it is a superior authority who shows her how to escape its hold, allowing her to relive the "scene with the soldier" and to keep the pleasure-object under her blanket (hand, penis, husband). The external event which interrupted coitus is interpreted by Ida according to her guilt: "I felt kind of amputated." One might add that this castration does not concern the orgasm but the acts and the pleasure involved in it. The pleasure-objects under her blanket appear "stolen" or at least related to an aggressive act (she is persecuted). As the persecution lessens ("the hands are still at the end"), Ida acquires the right to dispose of the pleasure-object. Concomitantly, penis envy, having lost its purpose, will disappear.

Ida's analysis continues but from now on several problems are on the way to solution. She has a growing feeling of confidence in herself and is beginning to feel equal to a professional field.

V

To conclude our study, we might formulate a question avoided until now in this essay: Why is the feeling of castration and its corollary, penis envy, the universal lot of womanhood? Why do women so often renounce creative activity, their means of making the world? Why do they agree to shut themselves up in "women's quarters," to "be quiet in church," in short, to prefer a dependent state? The question is far from simple and would require research into various sectors and a documentation I do not yet have. Yet, we can study the problem from a psychoanalytical point of view, and try to formulate hypothesis from the material we have.

From a psychoanalytical viewpoint an institution is not established and does not survive unless it resolves some particular interpersonal problem. In principle, an institutional solution must have advantages for both men and women over the situation that preceded it. We should make explicit what advantages each has in the institutional inequality of the sexes, at least in the domain accessible to psychoanalysis—that is to say in affective life.

We are right when we suppose that this age-old inequality requires woman's complicity, in spite of her apparent protest shown by penis envy. Men and women must be exposed to specific, complementary affective conflicts to have established a *modus vivendi* which could last through many civilizations.

As for the woman, consider the following: at the end of the anal stage the little girl should be able to achieve in masturbatory fantasy simultaneously both parents envisaged in terms of their genital functioning. But there are two obstacles: first, the one originating in the anal period; namely, that autonomy in masturbatory satisfaction necessarily means a sadistic dispossession of the Mother and her prerogatives; second, the Oedipal obstacle, according to which the fantasy-achievement of the primal scene, by identification with both parents, also implies supplanting the Mother. As long as these obstacles are not overcome—and usually they are not —something will be missing in the identification with: (1) the father, who can give pleasure with his penis; (2) with the Mother, who can receive pleasure from the father. This fundamental deficiency is in conjunction with a particular maternal imago: that of an exacting, jealous, and castrated Mother, and an envied, depreciated, and at the same time overvalued Father. The only way out of this impasse to identification is the establishment of an inaccessible phallic ideal (mythical image of an idealized Father), which is a reassurance to the Mother that she can keep her prerogatives, and also the nostalgic wish to make up for the deficiency fatal to genital fulfillment: the identification with the Father. When women holding such imagoes have to deal with married life, they suddenly find themselves confronted with their latent genital desires, even though their affective life is immature for want of heterosexual identification, as they are still dominated by problems of the anal stage. Thus, the fleeting Oedipal hopes will soon give way to a repetition, this time with the husbands, of the anal relationship to the Mother, a relation which is then confirmed by penis envy. The advantage of this situation consists in avoiding a frontal attack on the maternal imago and also in avoiding the feeling of deep anxiety at the idea of detaching oneself from her domination and superiority.

The little girl's drama, particularly in relationship to the Mother, is made concrete in the following situation: when, in order to disengage herself from the anal Mother, she tried to use the Father as a prop, she found herself confronted with the heterosexual object which belongs to the Mother and, consequently, in opposition to her over matters of interest. Simultaneously attacked from both sides, the Mother continuously appears as very dangerous: threatened with total destruction, she might, in turn, threaten to destroy totally. The superimposition in the same object of both mastery and rivalry blocks the way out of the anal stage and forces the girl to renounce her desires. She will then make herself into an anal appendage (the "cork," the "doll") of the Mother, and later into the "phallus" of her husband. It certainly seems that this is a universal difficulty in woman's development, a difficulty which more or less explains why such a condition of dependence toward man, the heir of the anal Mother imago, is accepted. That is the price for some of the disguised genital achievements which, in some instances, women allow themselves.

At first one sees easily the advantages which man acquires for himself from this disposition to dependence created by feminine guilt. Yet, on examining the question more closely, it is not obvious a priori that men should naturally want such a relationship of mastery. The falsity, the ambivalence, and the refusal of identifications it conceals should appear to him as so many snags on which his own full and authentic achievement comes to grief. And yet . . . who could doubt that in order to achieve his own interests in superiority man is almost universally the accomplice of woman's state of dependence and that he thrives in elevating all this into religious, metaphysical, or anthropological principles. What interest has he in giving in to his need to dominate the being through whom he could understand himself and who could understand him? To discover oneself through the other sex would be a genuine fulfillment of one's humanity, yet this is exactly what escapes most of us.

Having seen the woman's problems, let us now try to see which specific problems are in the way of man's fulfillment. When the little boy is about to free himself from the anal Mother, he can identify with the Father, possessor of the "phallus." In this way he frees himself from maternal domination; the phallic Father is his ally and the Mother is not yet his genital object. Thus, he will have to cope with two periods of anxiety in his development: (1) the liquidation of his anal relationship to the Mother by a particularly dangerous identificatory incorporation (dangerous because of the rejection of her domination as well as the inverse Oedipal exclusion of the Mother) and (2) the Oedipal moment itself, which implies an identification with the genital rival as well as his elimination. This double failure in the boy's identification is, as we see, quite symmetrical to the failure we noticed in the little girl. In the case of the boy, too, an impossible desire is crystallized into an envy, paralleling that of the girl, of the same illusory object, the "penis." It is obvious that these envies are beyond any real genital differentiation and refer to the nonintegrated anal relationship. If at this stage a difference appears between the two sexes it is about the possession or nonpossession (one is just as illusory as the other) of the penis-thing and its varied symbolic significance. From then on, phallic deception leads the way for the institutionalized relation between the sexes. The whole problem of the failure in identification will by fetishistic means be concealed behind active or passive fascination. The possession of the "fetish" is intended to arouse envy, and envy in turn is intended to confirm the value of the fetish for the man. We can now understand the meaning of the fact that men encourage "penis envy" in the other sex and try to make it part of their social institutions. Once it is conceded that the exclusive possessor of the fetish is man, is not this so-called privilege, sustained by covetousness alone, nothing but a variant of envy, projected on to woman? The penis-emblem allows the man to be enviable and thus, logically, avoid living a life of envy. Man cannot be other than envious as long as he needs to objectify as well as hide in a fetish what is missing in his genital fulfillment. Thanks to this subterfuge he will continue to ignore his dangerous desire to take the

Mother's part in the anally conceived Primal Scene. The woman, envious and guilty, is the ideal support for the projection of this desire. She can thus become man's unacknowledged "feminine part," which he must then master and control. That is why man will be driven to prefer a mutilated, dependent, and envious woman to a partner, successful in her creative fullness.

The biblical myth of the first couple gives us an eloquent articulation of these problems. Eve, split off from Adam's self, represents what he refuses to allow himself. To her is also attributed the original sin for which he thus completely avoids responsibility. Eve shall transgress the divine interdiction, she shall "castrate" the heavenly Father. Thus, she must bow beneath the weight of this double guilt: her own and that which man has projected on her. She is doomed to double servitude: toward God (the castrated Father) and toward her husband (the Mother who must not be castrated). She will live in enmity with the Serpent. Such is the divine decree which lays the basis for "penis envy." Part of Adam's body, Eve is at the same time his chattel (his servant) and his attribute. Object of his projections, controlled and enslaved, she is compelled to live in submissiveness—not with a real partner of the opposite sex—but with a tyrannical representative of the anal mother image.

This, briefly, is our psychoanalytical hypothesis concerning the affective aspects of the institution which postulates female dependence and passivity and imposes on woman the envy of an emblem which serves to conceal her desires. This hypothesis has at least one advantage over various cultural and philosophical concepts: it is drawn from clinical experience and is of therapeutic value. Indeed, we believe that on an individual level, the solution to penis envy is the job of the analyst—on condition that he himself be free from this phallo-centric prejudice, old as humanity itself.

Homosexuality in Women

Joyce McDougall

Bisexuality! I am sure you are right about it. I am accustoming myself to regarding every sexual act as an event between four individuals.

Freud to Fliess, 1889

Clinical studies of overt homosexuality are rendered difficult by the fact that only when the delicate balance achieved by manifest homosexuality is threatened or lost will homosexuals of either sex turn to a psychiatrist or analyst for help. I have been fortunate enough to have had in analysis four homosexual women and three others who, while not exclusively homosexual, were dominated by conscious homosexual wishes. My thanks are due to these cases for the clinical material which furnished the basis for this paper. These patients enabled me to recognize a specific form of Oedipal constellation and to appreciate the significance of overt homosexuality in maintaining psychic equilibrium and ego identity in spite of the evident disturbance in sexual identity.

Before studying the clinical findings for the light they may shed on the psychic structure and its instinctual economy, it is important to delimit our area of research from a theoretical and a clinical point of view. First, psychoanalytic theory considers the homosexual component of the libido to be an integral part of every human being's psychic structure, so it is well to define what we mean by "homosexual libido" and to ask in what manner this component is cathected and integrated into the adult personality in people who are not homosexual. Second, since clinical categories notoriously overlap (particularly with regard to homosexual elements where there is constant reference to conscious, unconscious, and latent homosexual aspects in the classical neurotic and psychotic structures), it is necessary to differentiate between commonly disguised expressions of homosexuality and its overt expression in sexual relations. Where do "normal-neurotic" and "psychotic" leave off and where does "perverse" begin? Does the term "latent homosexual" really mean anything? What place do we accord homosexual and perverse fantasy in daydreams and masturbation? What relationship might be found to exist between the overt homosexual woman and the "masculine woman" who feels at home among men and abhors the company of other women?

It seems evident that the homosexual component of the libido implies two distinct aims, depending on the object; in the little girl one of these instinctual aims corresponds to a desire for total *possession of the mother* in a world without men; while the other represents *a desire to be the father* and, therefore, masculine. Expanding this we might say that in every small girl's relation to her mother (both the real mother and her internal representation) her homosexual attachment will express itself in positive feelings toward the mother as a sexual object and in defenses against these wishes. In relation to the real and internalized father, homosexual libido is expressed in a desire to be like, or *be,* the father—which may or may not include identification with him in his sexual role. However, to say that the little girl must make either an object-choice or an identification oversimplifies the problem. It goes without saying that she must achieve various identifications with her mother if she is to function harmoniously as an adult woman; but her equally essential identifications with her father raise a number of important questions for the understanding of female sexuality and ego identity. For example, is she trying to become her father in order to be an object of desire and love for the mother? Or, on the contrary, is she trying to camouflage her Oedipal wishes by saying in effect: "See, I don't want to take daddy from my mother. I don't even want to be a girl!" To say that the little girl wants a penis still leaves open the question of why she wants one. What significance has she given to her father's possession of the penis? Does it represent a purely narcissistic enhancement to be desired as such? Or does it stand for the object of the mother's desire? Or a symbol of power? Or protection? The two latter meanings arise frequently from the period of pregenital conflicts before the Oedipal significance of sexual differences is acknowledged; that is, the father (or his penis) comes to represent a protection from the all-controlling "anal" mother or from being engulfed by a devouring "oral" mother, protection therefore against the primitive anxieties associated with these images. Any or all of these fantasies may play a dynamic role in the structure of the unconscious. Then again, fragmented "penis identifications" are also common, for example, the wish to fulfill the role of a penis for the mother. This may be conceived of as a way of repairing her, of tying oneself up to her, of remaining the constant object of her desire and preoccupation, etc.

We clearly cannot advance too far on the basis of fantasy alone. Certain reality experiences leave their imprint. Children, caught in the nets of their parents' unconscious desires, weave their fantasies out of an amalgam of primitive instinctual drives organized around what they have decoded of their parents' wishes and around what they believe they represent to their parents. Of such stuff is ego identity made.

Before trying to understand why certain women create a homosexual identity, we might first of all attempt to see how homosexual libido (in its double aspect) is integrated in women who do not become overtly homosexual.

To my mind, this complex instinctual component finds three main expressions in the adult woman. First, it enriches and makes possible sublimated object relations with friends of her own sex. Second, although it is only in her relation to a man that a woman feels herself to be sexually a woman and complementary to her mate, nevertheless her ability to identify with him in the sex act enriches her love life in all its aspects. (The same is, of course, true for the man.) Freud's statement, quoted at the beginning of this paper, already suggests this double identification. Thus, her ability to identify sexually with the father eventually contributes an important element to her feeling of feminine identity. Finally, much homosexual libido is expressed in her various ego activities, particularly in creative and professional work and in the activity of motherhood. Her normal homosexual demands on both parents find manifold sublimated satisfactions when she herself becomes a parent; as regards work capacity, unconscious identification with the opposite sex allows both sexes to bring forth—parthenogenetically, so to speak—their self-created brain children. Failure to accept the important homosexual element contributes to tenacious work problems in both sexes.

If, as suggested here, homosexual libido in women is normally absorbed in object relations of a sublimated kind, in the narcissistic self-image, and in sublimated activities, what then is the situation with regard to the overt homosexual? We might surmise that she on the contrary has met with severe impediments to the harmonious integration of her homosexual drives. In this paper an attempt will be made, through the medium of clinical examples, to examine the nature of these impediments and the extent to which they are reflected in her inner object world, thus affecting ego identity and ego functions. We may then be able to appreciate the dynamic and economic significance of the homosexual structure and object-relations in maintaining an equilibrium in the face of severe internal conflict for which it is an attempted solution.

The question of the limits to what is called "homosexuality" still remains to be defined. To begin with, even in all cases of *overt* homosexuality we are not necessarily dealing with the same clinical picture. That many homosexual women do not feel disturbed in such a way as to lead them to seek psychoanalytic help is in itself indicative. Although the capacity for heterosexual love is obviously impaired in the homosexual, there may be relatively unhampered capacity for social relations and for creativity, and such people are less likely to seek therapeutic aid. Others, however, find that all aspects of their lives are unfulfilling or arouse anxiety. For these women the self-image and feeling of identity are sometimes so damaged that they give rise to severe depression with suicidal ideas, or to outbursts of overwhelming anxiety, or again to episodic breakdowns in reality-testing with consequent difficulty in maintaining social relations.

Sometimes homosexual wishes themselves become the focus for conflict and anxiety and as such may motivate a decision to seek analytic help in order to understand and combat the homosexual fantasies. The question of "perverse" masturbation fantasy can be raised here. It seems to me that this is a typical expression of the *neurotic* structure, whereas in overtly perverse people sexual fantasy tends to be rigid and impoverished. One is tempted to posit in the latter an internal prohibition against fantasy which adds to the need to enact it in reality. When patients come to analysis because they are *troubled* by homosexual thoughts we are dealing more often than not with a neurotic structure in which these wishes, though warded off and repressed in the past, have surged back into consciousness, bringing guilt and panic in their wake. The woman who is overtly and exclusively homosexual on the contrary rarely feels strong guilt about her sex life. Although often sensitive to social censure of her proclivities, she usually believes that homosexual relations are an essential part of her life, which she tends to idealize rather than condemn. If she seeks the help of an analyst it is more often because of neurotic difficulties and suffering, which, indeed, are frequently mobilized by a breakdown in her homosexual relationship. Otherwise, she often defers seeking help for fear that her homosexual relations may be endangered.

This paper is not concerned with that large group of women who have created elaborate defenses against homosexual wishes as part of a neurotic picture, nor with that smaller group in which excessive guilt and anxiety over homosexual desires in a fragile structure leads to psychotic projection and paranoia. While the homosexual element is an essential pillar of these patients' psychic structure, it seems misleading to describe them as "latent homosexuals"; the term might in a greater or lesser degree apply to anybody.

There are, however, two broad clinical patterns which are related, though in different ways, to that of the overt homosexual. The first is that of the strikingly "mannish" woman who takes pains to display little femininity in manner and dress and shows a marked preference for the company of men. Such women are frequently referred to as homosexual in spite of the fact that they have no sexual desires toward women. Indeed, they distrust women, deprecate femininity, and often claim that in character they are more like men than women. Men are felt to possess superior intelligence, superior ethical values, superior courage, and so on. In being "masculine" they feel that they, too, share these interests and ideals. With few exceptions the patients of this type whom I have in mind were married and had children. Sexual relations, however, were invariably associated with disagreeable sensations ranging from suffocation to vaginismus, and with feelings of panic or disgust—such symptoms frequently being a leading motive for seeking therapeutic help. Their "virile" personality on the other hand was felt to be ego-syntonic and not regarded as a symptom. None of these patients had any conscious homosexual fantasy, and apart from banal childhood games, reported no history of homosexual experiences. When submitted to analytic scrutiny, the differences between the women of "masculine" character and the overtly homosexual women are more striking than their similarities. It does not seem justified to include them under one single clinical heading as some analytic writers have done, even though we might expect them to have certain features in common.

The second group to which I referred has more in common with the homosexual from the point of view of psychic and economic structure. This is due to the fact that the troubled identifications and inner turmoil which seek expression through homosexuality might equally well express themselves *in other forms of behavior*. I have found certain cases of kleptomania and of alcoholism to reveal a psychic structure and parental imagoes almost identical with those of the homosexual women. My interest was first drawn to the unconscious meaning of homosexual desire when I had in analysis, within a relatively short period of time, three kleptomaniac patients. All were strikingly preoccupied with homosexual wishes, though none had had any actual homosexual experiences. Their relations with other women were highly eroticized and aroused a mixture of excitement and anxiety. Although kleptomania is not invariably a psychic equivalent to sexual deviation, in the cases I have in mind the erotic element underlying the stealing was evident in various ways. One young woman, for example, described her "bouts" of shoplifting in terms more appropriate to sexuality than to compulsion. She explained: "I try to fight the urge to steal. Days go by and then little by little I find I am thinking of nothing else. It's like an unbearable tension. Finally, I give in and the feeling is just like deep relief. It's so exciting and then it's over with, and I can sleep calmly until the next time." Her pleasure was intensified if she could induce a girl friend to join her in the shoplifting expeditions. The whole cycle of events carried a scarcely disguised orgastic meaning for this patient. (It is interesting to note that similar descriptions are often applied to creative work also. Here sublimation rather than perversion has been achieved as a solution to conflictual desire through the medium of fantasy elaboration. The work has been successfully desexualized and the aggressive elements integrated in the creation itself and in the implied competitiveness. In sexual deviation and other symptomatic behavior, such as kleptomania, the aggressive as well as the erotic elements are poorly integrated.) The unconscious links between the compulsion to steal and homosexual desire will be discussed more fully in the section on overt homosexuality.

Masculinity and Homosexuality

As already indicated, a manifest desire *to be a man* and an *overt sexual desire for women* do not necessarily stem from a common unconscious structure. While both desires clearly imply a disturbance in the feeling of sexual identity, there is a considerable difference between the "masculine" woman, who regards her *ego ideals and her identity* as basically male (accompanied by a disparaging attitude to women), and the homosexual one, who has made *a masculine type of object-choice* in seeking love relations with a woman (accompanied by a disparaging attitude to men). What factors have hindered the harmonious integration of the ambivalent Oedipal attachments and the potential conflicts of the pre-Oedipal phases to such an extent as to distort the feeling of sexual identity? And what are the common features and the differences between the two groups?

To begin with it becomes clinically evident that both groups repudiate any identification with the *genital* mother, particularly in her role as sexual partner to the man and to a lesser extent in her capacity to bear children. The homosexual woman does not seek to attract men sexually and usually does not believe she could even should she desire it. At the same time she is afraid of men and constantly fears sexual attack. The masculine woman, although not afraid of men, is usually distressed and angry at the idea that she might be an object of sexual desire for them, and she frequently acts as though insulted if sexual approaches are made to her. Her sexual relations with lover or husband are not infrequently accompanied by mental and physical pain—a fact which she usually endeavors to hide.

Apart from the question of sexual relations, bitterness toward men (conscious in one group and unconscious in the other) affects work capacities in both and can affect the maintenance of satisfactory social relations with men. Homosexual women often seek to exclude men altogether from their lives, thus imposing rigid limits on their activity. Masculine women, although socially at ease and consciously identified with men, are frequently frightened by intense rivalry feelings which they attempt to stifle, and they become inhibited to a pathological degree from creating or working at anything successfully.

Thus, women of both categories complain of feelings of inadequacy, of insecurity, and of confusion about what they want from life. All are liable to periods of depression or anxiety. Although their difficulties are determined in part by a common failure to identify with the genital mother, to understand their divergence it is necessary to discuss the sharp differences in the parental imagoes in the two groups of women. The virile woman has to some extent eliminated the mother image, and with her all other women, as objects of libidinal value. By contrast the homosexual constantly seeks other women for tender and eroticized relations, which have in addition the quality of a mother-child relationship.

With regard to the paternal image we find the situation reversed. The homosexual girl appears to have eliminated the father and all other men as possible objects of libidinal investment. The masculine girl constantly seeks relations with men, but on a nongenital basis. She accepts the sexual relationship with conflict and misgiving.

The following quotations, from a woman of each group, epitomize their respective positions when they seek to justify them consciously. One of my "masculine" patients, a physicist, married, with children, says: "It's just too bad being a woman. Women don't like other women and men can't stand them either! To be born a woman is to be condemned in advance." Her position closely resembles that of a Paris journalist well known for his misogynist views, who in a radio interview, to the question: "It appears, Monsieur, that you do not like women at all?" replied, "Who does?"

In contrast, a patient whose relationships were exclusively homosexual often proclaimed: "What could one possibly hope for from a man? Only women are capable of disinterested love or of understanding the pain of another human being."

Clearly, the two patients quoted here are both endeavoring to maintain a precarious sense of integrity and identity, but the complex series of identifications by which they have attempted to solve their conflicts are different. Each runs the risk of failure, with consequent pain and disillusionment, in the field of sexual as well as of sublimatory activities. A secure feeling of sexual and personal identity can be achieved only through adequate identification with *both* parents. This allows the integration of primitive omnipotence and primitive instinctual drives toward both parents and is a necessary prerequisite to the renunciation of incestuous wishes and to the establishment of secondary identification—in other words to the resolution of the Oedipal conflict. Lacking such basic identifications the possibility of maintaining ego identity through adequate social and sexual relations is constantly threatened and likely to lead to neurotic illness or to perverse "solutions" of the Oedipal situation. It is within the scope of psychoanalysis to provide conditions in which such integration, blocked since early childhood, may once again become possible.

The Masculine Woman
Since this paper is primarily concerned with overt homosexuality this section dealing with character-patterns of virility will be somewhat schematic in the interest of brevity.

> Mrs. E., nuclear physicist by profession, married, with two children, remarked in her first interview: "My husband and I are practically identical. Students at the same university, the same degrees, same interests. In many ways we are an ideal couple. I enjoy men's company and always feel at home with them. Get on better with our male friends than my husband does! But I don't like women much. Can't get on with them. . . . My only worry is that I don't enjoy sexual relations. Every time we have sex I'm afraid my husband will find me out. . . . Neither of us wanted children for years. . . . Since

the birth of my first child sexual relations have become intolerable to me. The other day my little boy accidentally touched my genitals. I was so overwhelmed with fury that I struck him. That's exactly how I feel when my husband touches me."

Another woman with a similar psychic pattern also came to analysis after the birth of her second child. She had suffered from intermittent vaginismus for years. She was now afraid that her ever-increasing dislike of sexual relations would cause a serious rift in the marriage. Unlike Mrs. E. she had always wanted children, but from early adolescence had daydreamed of having them without having sexual relations with a man. Nevertheless, she daydreamed also of having "real" relations with men, which meant to her, working, camping, or fighting, and being their nonsexual companion. "The idea of being a simple 'femmelette' fills me with horror. Women bore me to tears. I prefer masculine conversation. If I am forced to be in the company of women I start to get anxious and fed up. Somehow I feel that men, too, prefer women like me."

Both women idealized their fathers and modeled themselves closely upon them. Their attitude to their mothers revealed thinly veiled hatred which rapidly reached conscious expression in the analysis. The intriguing question was why the idealized father could not be accepted as a valued love object in such a way as to lead to the young woman's enhancement of herself as a woman. It was clear that the father had played an important role in superego formation and that there was considerable identification also with his social, ethical, and intellectual ideals, although the ethical values showed a certain rigidity, along the lines of "sphincter morality." The firm alliance of the superego with the ego structure played an important part in the repression of instinctual wishes, while at the same time permitting close relations with the masculine world. The libidinal drives seemed to find expression only in sublimations. At the same time, however, these were frequently vitiated since they represented a wish to castrate and thus were forbidden.

It was only after many months of slow progress in analysis that these patients could reveal the image underlying the belief that they were different from all other women. In their deeper fantasy they were *castrated men*. To be a woman meant to be nothing, to have nothing, to create nothing. Activity was the privilege of the male, and he alone merited admiration and love. The fact that men displayed sexual interest in women was simply disavowed. (Although a similar denigration of women may be expressed by many neurotic women, their feeling is not usually countered by their claiming that they are really men themselves in these respects.)

As we have seen, although the internalized father played an important role in the psychic structure he had never been accepted as an object of sexual desire. Much later it was possible to reconstruct fantasies and memories which revealed the father as so dangerously seductive that he had to be excluded as a love object and in one sense perpetually kept outside the self. Therefore, a semblance of his presence was forever necessary. All men became the ideal nonsexual father, with whom the girl could have close and even affectionate contact. But this was achieved only to the detriment of her erotic life and feeling of identity.

Further insight into the castrated image these women had unconsciously formed of themselves came through the emerging portrait of the pre-Oedipal mother image. In relation to her the idealized phallic picture of the father began to change into an impotent and castratable one.

Anamnestic details were used in support of the idea that the mother had somehow forced the father into a passive and emasculated role. (In one case the mother had died when the patient was only six, following which she was replaced by a hated stepmother. In another, the mother was reported to have been continually unfaithful to the father, which he appeared to have condoned complacently.) Consciously despised because of her castrating ways, the mother was in addition condemned because of her interest in sexual relations. There was a deep belief that she was much more powerful (more phallic, in the unconscious) than the father. *Thus, the castrated self-image was not an identification with a penis-less mother* (which would have given rise to a much more common feminine character pattern) but with a father felt to have many ideal qualities yet nevertheless seen as castrated. The dominating maternal imago did not lead to any desire for identification. Instead, there was considerable fear of identifying with such a "castrating" mother.

The patient who suffered from vaginismus made an important self-discovery of her vagina as a potentially castrating organ. During a medical consultation she was asked by the doctor to remove a contraceptive ring for which she was being fitted. With some trepidation she inserted her finger into her vagina, for the first time in her conscious memory, and reported that she nearly "fainted with fright because 'something' bit her finger." Another patient had a dream in which she inserted her hand into her vagina and a finger was bitten off. Once the oral and anal cathexes of the vagina could be understood it became easier to see why this "pre-genital" vagina had been projected entirely onto the mother along with all sexual desire, and why the young woman from then on re-fused to acknowledge any vaginal sensation or desire in herself for fear of castrating her partner. The mother, object of early venera-tion, was demoted in consequence.

When the genital desires of the Oedipal period began to come to light they were felt to entail abandonment by the powerful and once loved mother. Now the devalued and abandoning mother was projected onto all women who therefore were disparaged and abandoned in advance by the patient. These patients found it rela-tively acceptable to understand their denigration of women in terms of penis envy and the female castration complex. This under-standing served as an alibi against the much deeper *fear of women.* The terror of ever being in rivalry with a woman was more vigor-ously blocked from consciousness than the desire to rival men.

The meaning of the intense disdain of these women for other women who are seductive in manner and dress now becomes ob-vious, as it does for the conviction that men do not like "feminine" women. How could they when "femininity" can only be an invita-tion to be castrated! Instead, these women felt they offered some-thing of greater value, something safe and nonfeminine. They were quite unaware that their own behavior was castrating, since they re-fused men any sexual role toward them. Their love for their men had to be nongenital.

The fact that these women tend to choose partners who un-consciously need women with such problems further complicates the picture in most cases and confirms the woman at the same time in her particular idea of female sexuality. Thus, my patients had chosen partners who also thought of women as castrated men, who were frightened of "feminine" women, and who wanted their wives to be pals rather than people different from and complementary to themselves. In any case the total picture for these women resulted in continual frustration and inability to understand why relations with both sexes were so drastically unsatisfactory. Added to the frus-trations of the sexual situation was a risk attached to all sublimated activity, since it was considered not truly their own. Compulsion to fail at whatever they undertook or to accomplish it at the price of feeling depressed and guilty was common. This contained a mea-sure of reparative guilt to ward off castration wishes toward the father, but in sexual and other spheres the feeling of having something valuable to offer and exchange was unconsciously vitiated by the fractured sense of feminine identity. It was equally difficult for these patients to identify with the needs of others, no matter what sex, though more with those of their love objects, since a genital relationship of mutuality was excluded in advance. The idealized picture of the "pal" marriage usually revealed itself to be empty and strained.

The Homosexual Woman

For the sake of clarity I shall discuss the relationship of the homosexual women to each parent separately. The artificiality of such a procedure is obvious, however, since the importance of these relationships and the series of identifications to which they gave rise draw their dynamic significance from the *relation between the parents*. Whether that relationship is perceived as loving or rejecting, as mutually enhancing or mutually destructive, the child is faced with the fact that his parents share a privileged relation from which he is excluded. The homosexual in particular (and the same is true for all people whose sexuality is predominantly perverse) deals with primal scene disavowal fantasies by rendering them null and void, through disavowal or negation. He is then free to reconstruct the sexual relation using aims and objects other than genital ones.

The Father-Image

As we shall see the father is neither idealized nor desired. If he is not totally absent from the analytic discourse he is thoroughly detested. He is described in terms of disgust, noisiness, brutality, and lack of refinement which give an anal-sadistic quality to the portrait. Furthermore, his phallic capacities seem to be contested, for he is presented as ineffectual and impotent in most respects. The once-phallic father has regressed to being an anal-sadistic one.

One striking feature of the clinical material is the fate of this image which was once introjected into the daughter's world of internal objects. We shall see that it has formed the basis of a pathological identification in the ego. In her self-appraisal the daughter shows how closely identified she is, unconsciously, with this anal-erotic and sadistic imago. This powerfully cathected and destructive introject leads to important modifications in the ego (on the depressive mode as described by Freud in *Mourning and Melancholia*, where object-loss is compensated by introjection). This is now a narcissistically important part of the homosexual patient's ego, still bearing the stamp of its original ambivalent quality. The superego becomes at the same time sadistic to the subject (again following the depressive model), but some of this persecutory guilt is reprojected onto the father and subsequently onto all other men, who become in consequence potential persecutors, giving rise in some instances to delusional fears. Other important factors contributing to this pathological outcome of the father-daughter relationship will be discussed when we consider the daughter's relationship to her mother.

> Olivia, a pretty young woman in her twenties, of French-Italian parentage, who in the first years of her analysis lived with an older woman to whom she described herself as "married," came to her session one day looking physically ill and brandishing a letter from her father. "I have to go back to Florence for the holidays! It makes me sick. I couldn't sleep all night. Thought I was going to vomit. . . . I can't bear the sound of my father with his horrible throat noises and coughing. He only does it to drive me mad. I can't stand looking at him. He makes little twitching movements with his face. Disgusting." In earlier sessions she had recalled that his beard used to scratch her when she was little. As far as she knew she had always hated him and believed he hated her, too. She continued: "I'm so afraid I shall have an 'attack' when I get back to Florence. My father hates me more than ever when I'm ill and can't go out." Olivia here referred to a severe vomiting phobia which had crippled most of her social relations and was one of her principal reasons for coming to analysis. (An intense preoccupation with vomiting existed in three of my patients.) Olivia's unconscious fantasy about vomiting apparently continued to press for expression. She went on to say: "I'm sure my father is responsible for my attacks. He tries to make me ill. You probably don't believe it, but I know he would like to kill me." She had referred on many occasions to her belief that her father desired her death, and for a certain time she had even convinced herself that he was actively plotting to eradicate her. In her third year of analysis she was able to amend this belief to: "My father is not aware of it, but *unconsciously* he would like to kill me."
>
> Another patient, Karen, a talented French actress, came to analysis because of severe anxiety attacks which stultify her work when she is in front of an audience. (At a later stage she was able to give a phobic content to these panic attacks

saying that it was as though she might suddenly defecate or
vomit on stage.) "When I think of my father I hear him
clearing his throat of mucus, blowing his nose, making horrible noises which seemed to spread over the dinner table
and envelope us all (herself and her sisters). I used to think
I would faint when he spoke to me, as though he were going
to spit at me. I'd like to tear his guts out, filthy pig! Makes
you want to vomit. He couldn't even eat without making a
noise." On another occasion she said: "As a child I was always afraid of losing control of myself. I used to faint a lot.
. . . Every morning before going to school I would pray
'Please God don't let me vomit today.'" At other times she
described a frightening fantasy which had persisted for
some twenty years in which she imagined her father creeping
up behind her to cut off her head. "I think he must have
threatened to kill me when I was little. I would jump whenever he came up behind me. Always kept my distance.
Would never sit beside him in the car and so on."

Or again Eva, young American student: "I can't describe
the terrible look on my father's face. Even though I've done
nothing I'm always afraid he will shout at me. My heart
races as though he's going to kill me. . . . I have lost a pearl
out of a brooch my parents gave me. I'm sick at the thought
of what will happen if my father finds out. . . . He is brutal and
disgusting. And so rude at the table. When he's there I'm
paralyzed with fright and can't eat or talk."

These three examples, typical in all respects, will suffice. (At
the risk of emphasizing the obvious, I shall nevertheless remark at
this point that these caricatures of the fathers did not correspond to
anything that would be recognized by anybody other than the
daughters themselves.) We see that the paternal imago is strong
and dangerous. Physical closeness to the father gives rise to feelings
of disgust. This enables the daughter to keep the father at a distance, and there follows a fantasy struggle against being invaded by
his tics, mucus, angry outbursts, and other intrusive activity. The
anal quality of the descriptions is evident and is clearly allied with
the idea of a sadistic murderous attack. The very concentration on
the father, his movements, sounds, and words, gives some indication
of the uneasy excitement attached to his image. One has the impression of a little girl in terror of being attacked or "penetrated" by
her father. The very intensity of her repudiation of him and her
emphasis on his dirty and noisy qualities give us an inkling of the

way she has used regression and repression to deal with any phallic-sexual interest attached to him.

This supposition is further corroborated by the observation that in the early stages of analysis there is rarely any reference to the father's sexuality or to his masculine activity. He is held to be ineffectual as a man. His sexual relation to the mother is denied and his achievements in the outside world are denigrated. The defensive value of this "impotent" father is clear: if he is castrated, there is less fear of desiring him as a love object.

Behind this "castrated" image is an even more deeply disturbing one of the father who had *failed in his parental role*. His paternal authority was often represented as having been undermined by the mother, though not because the mother was thought dominating or masculine. On the contrary, as we shall see, she is pictured as the essence of femininity, but is also reported to have secretly destroyed the father's importance as an authority figure. One mother, for example, was remembered as having plotted with her children to outwit the father in money matters. Another had helped her child alter her school marks before showing them to the father. A third was reported to have forbidden the father any access to the child during her early years on the grounds that she was delicate and nervous. The extreme threat evoked by this destruction of the paternal image was first revealed only in dreams, although it was detectable in certain symptoms of depersonalization.

> Karen dreams: "There was a little boy running in front of a car. A woman driver rides right over him and leaves him paralyzed. My father just stands there saying he doesn't know where to go for help. I scream 'You're a doctor, aren't you? You could be hanged for refusing to help someone in danger of death.' Then I take the baby to a woman doctor myself. She sprays it with ether but I keep on calling to my father to come and help me."

Karen's associations lead to angry vituperation against the father and to details which identify the damaged baby boy as a representation of herself. Further association and dream details lead her to recognize the woman doctor as standing for the analyst. Let us reconstruct the latent meaning of the dream insofar as it pertains to the present discussion. The accident to the little boy represents a castration on a rather wide scale (paralysis) which is caused by a woman driver. (Says Karen: "My mother's a terrible driver. Never looks where she's going!") But it is also a woman (analyst-mother) who is supposed to repair the damage of castration the father refused to worry about. (Homosexual relationships will bring the longed for completion.) However, the dangers of this latter solution are detected in Karen's associations with the word "ether." "Oh it either lulls you into insensibility so you feel no more pain—or else it kills you outright." [1] The analyst-mother can offer only two solutions to this damaged baby: She will lull it back into the fantasied bliss of the earliest mother-nursling relation, or again the same treatment might bring about its death. She is, in the long run, more dangerous with her dubious gifts than the rejecting father. On the other hand he is felt to have abandoned her to this overpowering, seductive mother, offering psychic death if he does not help to disentangle his daughter from her clutches. But the father does not heed the daughter's appeal. Her once phallic demand has regressed to a cry for help.

> A dream of Olivia's reveals a similar unconscious image. In her dream she watches a mother cat delivering kittens. The kittens are born with their eyes open, and she realizes that this means they are to die. She makes desperate endeavors to save the baby kittens, first putting them into a box too small for them, where they suffocate. She then puts them out with the mother cat in the snow, where they continue to fare badly. Her father is there, too, and she begs him for help. He replies that he is too busy, he has a business meeting. She runs back to her kittens and finds they are all dead. In recounting these details Olivia burst into tears and said the dream was like real life in that her father would not care if *she* died. The sequence of the kittens, doomed to die *because their eyes are open,* was actually a reference in primary-process thinking to an early primal scene memory. Olivia had watched her parents, when they thought she was asleep, and described her mother as "the cat who got the cream." What had died in the tiny's child's mind was hope that she might one day identify with the mother cat and have access to the genital father and the right to live kittens of her own. Her other associations all led to a feeling of being destroyed inside. (At this time she had been suffering for many months from amenorrhea, a symptom signifying the desire for a child; but Olivia's fantasy was that she was empty and finished. The dead kittens represented not only herself but her own unborn children doomed to die.) It is to her father that she turns in the dream to save the situation in which her

femininity is at stake. He does nothing and the end result is death.

This aspect of the father's having *failed* them, which all my homosexual patients displayed, was coupled with an image of the mother's forbidding any access to the father and frequently encouraging the daughter's avowed dislike for him, as though this hatred were a gift made to herself. Thus, any desire for the father, his love, or his penis was felt to be dangerous and forbidden by both parents—a desire which would entail the loss of mother's love and bring castration to father. This in turn gave rise to many conscious fantasies of a revengeful and persecuting father. Important at this point is some idea of the unconscious identification *with the father*, not as an object of libidinal investment but as a mutilated image possessed of disagreeable and dangerous (anal) qualities.

Self-Image and Father-Image

Olivia, always dressed in stained bluejeans topped by overlarge thick sweaters at the beginning of her analysis, complained about women in her environment who criticized her appearance and urged her to wear more feminine clothing. "I feel so miserable. Everyone looks down on me for being so scruffy. I am scruffy. And I don't look my age. And I look like a grubby boy. I'm convinced you're not interested in me. I don't suppose you even want to go on with my analysis." She then asked angrily whether there were lots of attractively dressed women who came to consult me. She started crying, saying that she was "dirty, clumsy, and disgusting," but that in any case it was impossible for her to be different. "I would feel so ridiculous dressed up like other women. Besides I can't bear to hear them cackling about fashions and make-up. All my life my mother made me get dressed up to go to receptions. I always felt angry and ill."

Here Olivia is communicating a number of important features about herself. To begin with, she now applies to herself many terms identical to those used to describe her father. Some of the features she described unconsciously represent *her only way of approaching him*. Largely lost to her as an object, her father is now, in a certain sense, embodied within herself. Yet this close identification with a regressed image of the father is felt, nevertheless, to be forbidden by the mother and to be despised by other women. But just as clearly she is determined not to be robbed of it, nor of its unconscious, all-important significance. Narcissistic identification with a father conceived of in anal terms is highly conflictual. This identification is displeasing to the mother, but guarantees the daughter an escape from a form of psychotic merging with her. In this session we see that Olivia also fears that the analyst will cast her out for those traits in which she unconsciously identifies with her father. These "anal" traits clearly represent a vital part of her identity, a part which she feels she must struggle to preserve.

She further identified with sadistic traits attributed to the father. Olivia wore a thick leather wristband, believing it gave her "an appearance of strength and cruelty." She also carried a large knife concealed in her handbag whenever she went out, ostensibly to protect herself from dangerous men (for example, taxi drivers) with whom she might come in contact. But the fact that it was she who wielded the knife and therefore might be considered dangerous was never conscious. Thus, Olivia identified with father's supposedly menacing strength and readiness to kill, as well as his dirtiness and his disgustingness.

While the unconscious identification with the "dirty, disgusting" paternal phallus was strongly disapproved by the mother, her manifest desire to keep all men at arm's length was not. Olivia had a store of horror tales, attributed to her mother, of brutal encounters with men. Consequently, she regarded her precautions not only as a necessary defense but as precautions her mother would approve. In this way the mother was felt to be against the heterosexual world both within (unconscious identification) and without (protection against desire on the grounds that men are dangerous).

> Here is Karen's self-portrait, painted in the same colors so to speak, but in her own inimitable style. "I'm just a piece of shit, and that's exactly how everyone treats me. But my friend Paula saw me quite differently. And that's how I knew she really loved me. She liked my craziness and she didn't treat me like shit!" She then added defensively (apparently wondering if the analyst will really love her too): "I haven't taken a bath for weeks and I don't give a damn. I smell like a skunk and I love it! Can you smell it?" To this clinging to her body products and odors, so highly invested narcissistically, Karen added a style of dress which carried out the same idea. Her appearance was that of a beatnik. When she was obliged by external circumstances to wear feminine clothing she felt anxious and uncomfortable. To my remark one day that she seemed to be telling me that it was neither

thinkable nor permissible for her to dress like a woman she shouted: "Are you crazy? Me—a woman? That's a good joke!" Her burst of loud laughter was immediately followed by uncontrollable sobbing.

Again we find a young woman describing herself exactly as she does her father, and in just those respects which, according to her, make it impossible that she love, trust, or respect him. She did not carry a knife around like Olivia, but in the same circumstances wove innumerable fantasies of killing men. "I'd like to kill some man, any man, and drive a knife right through his belly. Sometimes I'd like to strangle men with my bare hands." She made an expressive gesture in the air. "The other night I dreamed about R (a man who had exposed himself to her when she was five), and I was hacking him to pieces with an axe. There was a mess of blood, guts, and pus. I kept on chopping with my axe. And yet he wouldn't die." This dream, in which she chopped to pieces a man who subsequently came to life again, was a recurrent theme in Karen's dream life.

At other moments Karen projected these murderous impulses onto the men around her and was terrified to go out on the street, convinced that some man was plotting her destruction. These fears even spread to the inanimate world, and at such times Karen would keep her distance from tall buildings in panic lest they fall on her. She constantly anticipated that she would be the victim of plane crashes, earthquakes, or other uncontrollable disasters. They recalled vividly the fantasy that her father would sneak up behind her and cut off her head. It is not difficult to reconstruct the torturing fears meted out by her superego as punishment for any sexual wishes, no matter how disguised, toward the father. The originally phallic father through identification was now an anal-erotic possession—his whole being dominated by sadism.

We might note here that pregenital anal-eroticism has become detached from its aggressive component. While the unconscious anal-erotic link with the father has been retained as a narcissistic aspect of the ego of considerable intensity, it can in no way be linked with an active desire to absorb or receive anything from the father as a love object. What might have been fantasied as a desire to retain the father as an object of love coupled with a desire actively to incorporate his penis is replaced by the need to fend off anal-sadistic *attacks* from the father (projection of her own sexual desire). This served as a solid defense against any reawakening of heterosexual needs.

As might be anticipated, with the progress of analysis these patients were able to reveal in their dreams and fantasies a variety of anal-receptive wishes, the analysis of which permitted some integration of the infantile drives, leading in turn to the rediscovery of sexual desire and an intense wish in most cases to have a baby. Of course these wishes brought much anxiety and a resurgence of hypochondriacal fears in their wake and had to be analyzed in terms of the Oedipal danger (castration of one's sexual being) and the pre-Oedipal dimension (abandonment and death) if the tie to the maternal imago were to be dissolved.

A dream of Olivia's is evocative at this point, through its primitive Oedipal imagery as well as its anal-erotic symbols. "I dreamed I was running along the beach at X where I spent all my childhood holidays. I see that I have a penis attached to my body. A group of men come running after me and shoot bullets at me. The bullets all fly into my anus. Now I am very ill and I find my way to a place where a group of doctors examines me. My penis has disappeared. They study an X ray of my insides. In my rectum, and extending even into my abdomen, there is a huge black rat. It is very dark and still. And in a way it is beautiful. Like something graven in stone, like those stone carvings around the Château de Blois. I want to scream, nevertheless, when I see the rat, and try to hide it. The doctors tell me I must vomit it up or else it will poison me and I shall die. But at that moment I realize that I must not vomit it up. If I move I shall lose the rat—and then I shall die. I woke up paralyzed with fright and afraid to move."

Here the rat, likened to emblems (around the Château de Blois) and symbol of the father's phallic power, is now lodged in her anus. The dream provides one clue to her vomiting phobia (that she would vomit up this internalized phallus) and some insight into the conflict by which she felt torn inside. The doctors in the dream represented both the mother who had nursed her through interminable "intestinal" maladies in childhood and the analyst who at that time was believed, like the mother, to prohibit her keeping anything valuable inside her. Father and his penis were forbidden. Yet she cannot live if she loses the rat. Without her father she is nothing. She will die.

What light do these brief clinical excerpts shed on the relation of the homosexual to her father? In the first place we find no trace of what is regarded as normal or usual in the relation of the

girl to her father. None of the usual neurotic solutions to the conflict over id-wishes directed to the father is found. Even in dreams
the erotic aspects of the drives attached to him remain relatively
camouflaged. If we take Karen's dream of the baby boy, who is run
over while the father stands by helplessly, we see that the desire for
the phallic father has regressed to the need for a father who will
protect his child from the demands of the pre-Oedipal mother. In the
dreams the dangerous aspects of the latter are obvious. (It should
be recalled in this connection that consciously the desire is to eliminate the father, represented as an intruder in the mother-daughter
relationship. Anxiety about the father's exclusion is totally unconscious.)

What has happened to the father as a love-object in the internal object-world of the little girl hidden in the patients under
discussion? Not only has she been unable to deal with her primitive
wishes, but in her attempt to deal with her parents and their unconscious demands upon her, her ego has undergone profound modifications. Whatever the father's unconscious problems may have
been (frequently compounded by external events, such as his sudden return from the armed forces, the birth of a baby brother, the
death of a beloved nurse), the daughter appears to have abandoned
him as an object of libidinal wishes at the height of the classical
Oedipal period. This discarded paternal object was then incorporated into the little girl's ego-structure never to be given up. No
other man ever takes father's place in the homosexual girl's universe. The giving up of the father as an object of libidinal investment corresponds in no way to the relinquishing of the original object which we find in normal women, nor to the producing of
symptoms dealing with frustrated Oedipal wishes and castration
anxiety which we find in neurotic developments. Nor has the
father divested of his sexual attraction been retained as the only
possible object, as in the case of women with a "masculine" character. For the homosexual the father is lost as an object, and the relationship with him is replaced by a specific form of identification.
The ambivalence inherent in any identification is here immeasurea-
bly heightened; the ego will subsequently suffer merciless superego
attack for those identifications which form an essential part of its
identity. The depressive reproaches, which the homosexual heaps
upon herself, have the quality of the classic reproaches of the melancholic. They represent an attack upon the internalized father,
yet the narcissistically important and zealously guarded object is a
bulwark against psychotic dissolution. This "pregenitalized superego" results in ego fragility and in impoverishment and paralysis of

much of the ego's functioning. (Space does not permit a description of these impoverished lives.)

We are still faced with the question as to why the little girl, in her attempt to internalize something as vitally important to her growth and development as the phallic representation of her father, is able to do so only at the expense of object loss, ego impairment, and immense suffering. In describing the internalized image in its various aspects we have furnished only a partial explanation of the obstructions to harmonious integration. A fuller understanding requires us to investigate more closely the relation to the maternal imago (the more so since our division of the parental couple is an artificial one).

The Mother-Image

The mother is described in a highly idealized fashion—beautiful, gifted, charming, and so on. She is felt to be all that the daughter is not, but this unequal situation is apparently taken for granted. There is no conscious envy of the mother. Furthermore, she emerges as a figure of total security against the dangers of living which might face the patient. Yet at the same time the mother is felt to be in constant danger herself, and fears for her imminent death are common. In fantasy she is the victim of fatal accidents, the prey of brutal attackers, or she is threatened with imminent abandonment or excessive domination by the father. He is believed to make unfair demands upon her, both sexually and otherwise.

Identification with such an imago is difficult for two main reasons. First, any aspirations toward narcissistic identification with the mother are doomed to failure, because the mother is believed to possess gifts of beauty, intelligence, and talent which the daughter simply "was not born with." Unconsciously, idealization of the mother figure is necessary to repress a fund of hostile and destructive feelings toward her. It is therefore important that she be kept an unattainable ideal. Second, this attitude is reinforced by the belief that on the heterosexual plane the mother had an unhappy, if not dangerous, role. In no instance was there any conscious feeling that the mother was enhanced or made complete by her possession of the father as a love object. The wishful fantasy of each of these patients in the beginning of analysis could have been summed up as a desire for the total elimination of the father and the creation of a tender and enduring mother-daughter relationship. This latter desire was in most cases displaced onto women as sexual partners destined at the same time to be mother substitutes. Elaborations of the same wish were constantly reiterated in the early transference situation. Its aggressive elements, though transparent, were unconscious. Let us now listen to these women talking of their mothers.

> Olivia: "Mother was talented and beautiful. She was a star in the eyes of the public and everyone around her adored her too. . . . I always wanted to be near her. Whenever she went out I was haunted by the idea that she would get run over. . . . She is very pure and innocent, and can't imagine that anyone can have evil thoughts . . . the only trouble is that she can't understand what it is to be ill. She was never sick. . . . Somehow she was never there when I needed her. I wonder if all my stomach troubles weren't just a way of keeping her near me. . . ."
>
> Eva would say: "I loved her so much I used to save up all my pennies to buy her flowers." (Later she stole money from her father to give flowers to her girl-friends.) "When she was caring for my little sister I was almost ill with longing for her. Sometimes I would try to be ill so that she would keep me at home with her." Later, she reported: "But somehow it was as though you couldn't get close to her. She wasn't mean, but she gave things instead of love."

These two examples taken at random could be multiplied many times. All in all the mother has an even more stereotyped representation than the father. She is an ideal to be adored but never attained. She remains outside the daughter's ego identity in her idealized aspects. Added to her highly esteemed qualities are suggestions of coldness and aloofness and the feeling that one could not be secure in her love—except perhaps through illness. The vivid impression of all these patients that the mother secretly denigrated the father has already been stated. This contributed no doubt to the daughter's belief that the father was undesirable, if not dangerous, and should be distrusted and outwitted. There was a recurring fantasy, therefore, that without mother's collusion and protection daughter might be exposed to a specific danger from the father. In the early phases of analysis this danger was rarely made explicit; the accent was placed on mother's indispensability.

The majority of these patients maintained, on the basis of circumstantial evidence, that there was no sexual relation between the parents, supposedly because the mother refused to "submit to humiliations," "was tired of being brutally attacked," etc. One patient had been told by her mother that she had sexual relations with the father but that these took place while the mother was asleep. (This patient suffered from severe insomnia for many years and could not sleep in her Paris apartment alone. She had to have a woman friend nearby in order to sleep without fear. Thus, she recreated the situation of childhood in which the mother stood between the daughter and her unconscious desire for the father.) Stories of rape and other sexual violence were common in these analysands' sessions and were sometimes attributed to the mother. The overall impression was that the mother repudiated heterosexual feelings in herself and forbade them to her daughter.

Let us briefly recapitulate the parental images as they were revealed in the early analytic sessions. Father is the repository of all that is bad, dirty, and dangerous, while mother is maintained as a nonconflictual object. She is the fountainhead of all security—a security later sought in other women who become sexualized love objects. She is thought to possess many valuable feminine attributes, but these evoke no conscious jealousy. The daughter later on will hope to have access to some of these qualities by loving another woman. The one sour note in the lovely mother theme is the impression that she is cold, distant, lacking in understanding. However, this is in no way consciously resented by her daughter in her attempt to keep the idealized image intact. Instead, these women regarded *themselves* as unlovable children, disappointing to their mothers. How could such a mother accept such a daughter—untidy and unfeminine, frequently in ill health and almost invariably a failing student in spite of more than average intelligence?

From behind this discourse two very different themes gradually emerged: constant concern for the mother's health and safety, obsessive images of her falling fatally ill or of finding her dead or cut to pieces. Often these were displaced onto female sexual partners, and only as the analysis proceeded were they found to have existed for many years in childhood, attached to the mother. They required one's staying very close to the mother (or her later substitute) and covering her with solicitude, which often thinly veiled their underlying aggressive content. Although the fantasies of the loved one's falling victim to a fatal catastrophe were consciously considered as a total threat to the analysand and to her object-world she could not avoid coming to see that these were magical means of preventing dangerous impulses in herself from *destroying the maternal object.*

The second theme which turned up with surprising regularity was that of a rigidly controlling mother, meticulously preoccupied with order, health, and cleanliness. A remark from Karen typifies this image: "My mother hated everything to do with my body. When I defecated she treated it like poison. For years I believed my mother did not defecate. In fact I still find it hard to believe! Another patient was forbidden ever to mention hcr toilct needs. From an early age she was trained to cough politely in order to draw attention to such phenomena. She always felt dirty and ashamed because of her excremental/excretory functions. Another mother always referred to constipation as "back trouble" and forbade her daughter to look at her feces. These aspects of the mother's controlling anality and rejecting anal-eroticism and their effect on the non-integration of the anal components of the libido will be discussed later. Their displacement on the phallic image of the father has already been shown.

Material relating to the maternal imago as rigidly controlling and physically rejecting, whether it arose in the transference or in childhood memories, stirred up considerable resistance, since it was felt to be an aggressive attack on the maternal object and involved the risk of separating oneself from an object on whom there was a symbiotic dependence. The deep sense of rejection these women felt for their own bodies was painfully brought to light. It often expressed itself, to begin with, through fantasies of loving *another woman's body*. The homosexual patient frequently described in detail all the caresses, tenderness, and minute explorations she wishes to lavish on a female partner or to enact with the analyst. One learns that this intense sensuous appreciation of the body of another woman contains all the loving that these patients unconsciously demand for their own bodies, but feel they do not merit, since they sensed that their mothers did not love either the body or its functions. Two patients were convinced that their mothers' insistence on their wearing pretty clothes had been a desperate attempt to hide their bodies, believed to be ugly, deformed, and dirty (thus identifying with what they thought was the mothers' view of their own condition).

This is perhaps the moment to examine the role of penis envy and castration anxiety in the female homosexual structure, since such anxicty is obviously intcnsc and, indccd, might bc described as a feeling of being physically demolished or at best of being beset by fears of disintegration. We find none of the common expressions of castration anxiety or penis envy which enliven the material of most woman analysands. (And indeed of patients of both sexes.) In general, neurotic anxiety about female "castration" tends to be expressed, if not mutely evinced in symptoms, in a feeling that one is unlucky and damaged by the very fact of being a woman; the homosexual patient on the other hand shows clearly that for her certain women are endowed richly and magically and these become the ideal love objects. The unusual feature of penis envy is that the desire to have a penis of one's own is perfectly conscious. The homosexual patient frequently dreams that she has a penis, weaves sexual fantasies or masturbates around the idea of a penis of her own, and sometimes fabricates a penis which she attaches to her own body. Of course, there is no man attached to that penis; it is valued or desired as a thing in itself, divested of its masculine meaning, at least in consciousness. As far as its symbolic significance is concerned for which one might reserve the term "phallus"—the erect penis endowed from time immemorial with rich symbolic meaning, applying equally to both sexes as a symbol of power, of fertility, of desire—it has none of these meanings for her. Its particular importance as the psychical representative of the internalized father (on which we do not need to expand here) is equally missing, as we have seen. The father's penis has been divested of its phallic significance, the internalized paternal phallus having regressed to the status of an anal object. One patient gave a vivid illustration of this transfer of power from the penis to a fecal representation. On opening the door to the bathroom one day when she was six, she found her father there in the act of defecating. She was startled and incredulous since she had believed till then that men did not defecate. "You see he already had a penis, I couldn't understand that he would defecate as well," was her reflection. She left her father so to speak in possession of his penis, but castrated him anally instead. Only she and her mother possessed the valuable phallic power through the unique privilege of being able to defecate.

These brief examples of the attitude to the penis, and the unusual expressions of penis envy it gives rise to, show us that this can be achieved only through mechanisms of manic denial, disavowal, and as a consequence of a certain disturbance in reality-testing. Thus, the role of the penis is devalued and denied, not only in the primal scene but also in its symbolic meaning in the unconscious. Much of the homosexual girl's sexual activity is designed to prove that mother never desired father's penis and that it was not necessary for the sex act in any case. In this respect her fantasy is strongly reminiscent of what we find in fetishistic character formations. There are other similarities as we shall see; for example, a certain terror of the female genital is hidden in the homosexual woman's fantasies as it is in the structures of male perversion. Evidently, for a woman to have a deeply horrifying and terrifying idea of the vagina leads to a particular kind of disturbed body image which does not find its counterpart in the fetishist. Also the fabricated "play penis" of the homosexual girl has few of the qualities of the fetishistic object, the primary function of which is to enable sexual desire and sexual fulfillment. One of my patients during her adolescence wore a fabricated penis whenever she went out. At a certain point in the analysis, when she was exploring her feelings of guilt about this youthful behavior, she suddenly desired once again to make such a penis. It no longer seemed such a hideous crime, and she apparently was able to let her desire for the play penis come to the fore once more. "Last night I made myself a penis out of some bits of material; I caressed it on my body and felt flushed and excited. Then suddenly I had a strange urge to push it inside my body. It nearly frightened me to death." The vaginal sensations and the feeling of desire which she described filled her with anxiety, and the thought came to mind that if she were to give in to such crazy feelings she would explode or die. A dream which followed gave further insight into the interdiction of all sexual desire—she dreamed that her mother was about to die. In effect the prohibiting and cruel part of the mother-image would die if she allowed herself to become sexually alive. Up till this moment the make-believe penis had blocked both clitoral and vaginal sensation, thus contributing to the repression of genital desire.

When the homosexual claims that she is playing a masculine role to a woman, it is not to give her something like a penis, but it is to mask a deeper desire, to *take* from the partner something magic or phallic in the symbolic sense. The masculine role thus hides the wish to complete oneself at the expense of the other woman: a narcissistic recuperation. This "completion fantasy" takes many forms: one may become complete by being both mother and child, or by absorbing from the mother substitute her attributed feminine magic and secrets, or some representation of an internalized paternal phallus, and so on. At the same time the partner changes from an idealized, perfect object in which nothing is lacking, to an object suddenly seen as destroyed and incapacitated as the woman feels herself to be. At these moments the homosexual lives out the fantasy of *repairing* the other (basically this is a reparation of the mother). At those times she feels she has "something precious to offer a woman which no man could supply." This gift of herself, originally offered to the mother, was never thought of as being acceptable to the latter. What the mother rejected is gladly taken and indeed demanded by the partner. Thus, the relationship to her is felt to be an integral part of the patient's identity and a confirmation of her existence. Her fear of being abandoned by her friend readily gives rise to suicidal ideas, or may also be expressed in reverse: "If I leave her *she* will die."

This brings us back to another important aspect of the relation to the original object which comes to light in analysis. From being remembered as the one stable and integrating object in the daughter's life, the mother comes to be apprehended (in dreams, in fantasies, in the transference) as a dynamic force opposing all movement and all desire. Profoundly aggressive and hateful feelings accompany the changing imago. From being a sheltering wall the mother becomes a prison. But the desire to escape from her is swiftly followed by fear of total loss, of something resembling death. The loosening of ties to her also leads to a reawakening of interest in the father and stirrings of heterosexual desire. These changes in turn precipitate crises of anxiety for the same reasons. Two patients, at a period of analysis during which they were reliving early Oedipal wishes and were preoccupied with heterosexual fantasies and increased narcissistic interest in themselves as women, both fell ill for a period of weeks, one to inexplicable febrile attacks and the other to vomiting and malaise. Both complained of overwhelming fatigue and went through some weeks of acute mental and physical anguish, requiring delicate and persistent analysis in order to elucidate the conflict-laden fantasies which sought expression in such distressing body experiences.

This abbreviated description of the anxieties released with the first steps toward the recognition of sexual desire involves the body ego and sheds further light on the tenacious tie to the mother-image. Let us try to clarify the nature of this infantile tie. The homosexual patient unconsciously experiences her relationship to the mother as though she were an indispensable part or function of her. While it is tenable at one level to say that she regards herself as her mother's "phallus," we see that on another level she feels controlled by the mother like a fecal object. She functions to gratify and enhance the maternal ego. Early infantile memories reveal precociously established ego control and sphincter control which, far from liberating the tiny child, rendered it more dependent than ever on the mother. We might also say that such patients feel themselves to be the very arms or legs of the mother. I have borrowed this last piece of imagery from one patient who dreamed that she *was* her mother's legs. How can a leg separate from its body? And what sort of independent existence could it hope to enjoy? And again, how would the mother-body function if the legs decide to leave it? Such is the dilemma facing the homosexual patient when she begins to desire a loosening of this close body tie to the internalized mother. Two unacceptable solutions loom before her. Her fear of becoming nothing more than an amputated body part recedes, only to be replaced by nightmarish fears that the mother will seek revenge or will die.

Relinquishing the mother as an object of symbiotic completion and identifying with her instead places the patient in a new situation of danger: as an individual woman in her own right she is once more faced with her fears of the heterosexual world. A pertinent example regarding her own father was recounted by Olivia. She was to meet her father after a lengthy separation. She always had awaited his rare visits to Paris with distaste, but on this occasion she was excited in anticipation of seeing him and talking to him about herself. She took pains to dress elegantly for the dinner they were to have together. The father told her he had always considered her to be "psychologically retarded" and then went on to criticize her dress and her jewelry, saying these things did not suit her. She was seized with sudden vertigo and rushed to the cloakroom, where she clung to the mirror trying to capture her own image. In her own words: "The face I saw was the face of an utter stranger. I thought I would scream. I kept repeating my name over and over trying to get back into my own body." In analyzing the importance of this brief episode of depersonalization she asked with remarkable insight: "Can one say there is such a thing as the castration of a *woman?* I mean something that would be as terrible for a woman as for a man to lose his penis?" To feel barred forever from being an object of desire in the eyes of the father was a castration in that she felt her sexuality was rendered nugatory. The episode precipitated a period of severe depression in this young woman. Nevertheless, she was able to say some months later: "I can forgive my father for his hatred and rejection of me. In a way I think he was afraid of loving me too much. He has always made remarks like those of a jealous lover." Her reflection was in all probability profoundly true.[2] In any case she succeeded in correcting the reality impression which had been so destructive, thereby creating a paternal image from which she could draw support for her feminine identity.

Two remarks from patients express vividly the complex and primitive tie to the mother, along with the dangers of desiring to dissolve it, terrifying though its maintenance has been. "The feelings I have about you (the analyst) are insupportable. I have never loved nor hated anyone so much in my life. If I love you you will destroy me, and if I hate you you will throw me out." Loving

meant devouring, and it seemed important to this patient for a certain time that I hate her. Also if she could count on my hatred she
would be better able to accept her strongly aggressive and sadistic
feelings toward me. At other times she would say: "If you love me I
am lost; then you will either destroy me and throw me out like shit
—or you will tie me up to you forever like my mother did."

Another patient brings the following fantasy: "My mother
and I are fused together. At one end we are sealed by our mouths
and at the other by our vaginas. We make up a circle bound by
cold steel bands. If it breaks we shall both be torn apart." This fantasy continued through several sessions and underwent the following transformation: "I broke that circle when I first loved another
woman. But there was only one vagina before it broke—and my
mother got it. With her icy fingers she closed mine up forever."

As the terrifying oral-symbiotic universe shared with the
mother becomes elucidated in analysis and the murderous pregenital images of the introjected primal scene yield up the desires concealed within them, the deteriorated introject of the paternal phallus is transformed, strengthening feminine identification. While still
showing traces of the old fantasy fears, the fears which now have to
be faced in the new tentative relations with men have many similarities to the common neurotic fears of other women patients: the
fear that one is less attractive than other women now regarded as ri-
vals, or the fear of having nothing of equal value to exchange for
what is sought in a love relationship with a man. The homosexual
experiences come to be analyzed in a new and more superficial dimension. The common neurotic fear that one will never have sexual pleasure with a man because of masturbation is here expressed
as: "Because I have shared these clitorial, oral, and anal experiences
with women I am forever barred from experiencing orgasm with a
man." The homosexual woman is now saying that because she has
masturbated with guilty *Oedipal* fantasies (however deeply concealed in their homosexual form) she fears that she must forfeit her
right to heterosexual pleasure. At the same time she becomes preoccupied with her capacity to love. The oral-destructive and compulsive elements of her earlier love relations with women lead her to
feel that she has never really loved anyone. But with this realization
she is already approaching a relationship based on sexual identity
and mutuality.

Self-Image and Mother-Image
As we have already seen, at the beginning of analysis these patients
invariably thought themselves unlovable and physically unattrac-

tive. In feeling they lacked femininity; they compared themselves
unfavorably to their mothers, whom they remembered as attractive
to men by their beauty, intelligence, talents, etc. There was no identification with the mother in any of these respects. There was, however, a large measure of destructive *projective identification*. The
hostility projected onto the mother-image, along with sadistic fantasies of the primal scene, led them to fear constantly for the mother's
safety and also to see themselves, by identification with the unconsciously damaged imago, liable to catastrophic destruction, mysterious illnesses, and violent attack from men.

The primal scene envisaged in sadistic-oral and anal terms
then served the urgent need of these patients to *deny* the parents'
sexual relationship. This denial reinforced the compulsive need to
protect the mother and the patient from such "attacks." From these
fantasy threads the daughter wove a false identity: if mother had no
desire or need for a heterosexual relationship with the father, the
daughter could believe that she was not a replacement for him and
an essential part of the mother's being.

Behind this feeling of being the mother's very essence lay
many contradictory ideas, one of which was the perception that the
mother, for unconscious reasons of her own, demanded such a relationship. All these analysands brought to light the feeling of having
been emptied out and *robbed* by the mother, consequently they
were devoid of what was vital to their existence and deprived of
what was innately their own, their feminine sexuality. The possibility of having any good or valuable thing in oneself was refused
them. Recurrent fears of vomiting were in part a response to the
unconscious injunction to *render up everything* to the mother—the
introjected father as well as one's own essential femininity. Another
common fear with a similar meaning was that of having to urinate
or defecate in a public place, since these functions represented a
unique tie to the mother. This fear restricted the freedom to work
away from home, to travel, and in two cases had contributed to intense school phobias.

Abundant material of the mother-with-the-enema, the
mother who administered laxatives daily, or the mother who
stressed the dangers to health in going to sleep with an unemptied
bowel appeared here. Defecation was a crime. And to withhold defecation was a crime. The unconscious desire to reincorporate what
had been ejected (the paternal phallus) led one patient to hold her
breath throughout defecation, terrified that she might smell her
own excrement (the same patient who, years later, said in her analysis, "I smell like a skunk and I love it!") and convinced that her

mother had forbidden her to do this. The mother who refused the child the right to her own fecal matter merged with the mother who refused access to the father and his penis.

The feeling of having been robbed of all one's phallic and anal treasures led to the desire to steal back what had been lost. In some patients this desire was effected in part in the homosexual act, but in other patients of similar structure it led also to a *compulsion to steal*. A brief study of the significance of the kleptomaniac act might help us at this point to understand more fully the nature of homosexual identifications. Two kleptomaniac patients described identical *conditions* essential to their shoplifting. Said one: "It gives me no pleasure to steal from the little half-blind jeweler who lives near me, yet it would be so simple. But I take things only from large stores with well-trained male supervisors. What a triumph to take things under their very noses—you can't imagine!" (The half-blind jeweler is a castrated image. There is no phallic triumph, as with the strong store supervisors.) Another patient said: "I steal everything my father refused to give me—handbags, clothes, watches, . . . and I have stolen hundreds of dollars from his wallet without his ever suspecting it." At first glance we can recognize these thefts as phallic representatives, taken from the unsuspecting father (or his substitute) and as a secret castration of him. But the patients themselves came to realize that although they were engaged in the compulsive theft of a penis-substitute the articles stolen were rarely in themselves penis symbols; instead, they usually were articles which would enhance femininity (perfume, underwear, jewelry). Furthermore, they often were articles used by the mother (or her substitute), articles suggesting magical feminine attributes refused the daughter by her mother. These articles epitomized for the daughter everything that was needed *to attract the father*. That the objects stolen frequently represented a quality of *"stolen" from the mother against her wishes* was confirmed by the fact that often these stolen goods were subsequently given to another woman (and in one instance to the mother herself). This gift-giving revealed the compulsion to make reparation for the unacknowledged wish to absorb and steal from the mother (or mother-substitute) the essence of her femininity. This might be regarded as a condensation of values: the hidden power to attract the father, the ability to make babies, and the life-giving propensities of mother as the provider of food, warmth, and comfort. All these qualities are unconsciously represented *also as a phallus*—an exclusively feminine one. As Brunswick pointed out in the 1940 paper written in collaboration with Freud: "The term 'phallic mother'

. . . best designates the all-powerful mother, the mother who is capable of everything and who possesses every valuable attribute." If the right to identify with her is felt to be withheld, her daughter may feel compelled to attack and rob her of these qualities.

The stolen objects thus represented a paternal phallus which in turn masked a maternal one. In this respect the kleptomaniac acts reproduced exactly what the homosexual sought and symbolically recaptured in her sexual relations. The theft, therefore, has the following meanings: It is the father's penis, withheld from the little girl and offered to the mother. It is also the theft of the mother under father's very eyes, for the father, as a rival for the mother and her gifts, has become a figure to be outwitted. Finally, it is a symbolic theft from the mother of the essence of her femininity which the girl believes exists only *outside herself*. Should she make pretensions to possessing such qualities herself she would feel threatened by the mother, who inevitably would take them away from her. However, she is something like the Sorcerer's Apprentice with her stolen magic! It threatens to overwhelm her, and as often as not she gives the intensely symbolic objects to another woman who presumably is better able to cope with the dangerous desires hidden within; and the giver thus shares vicarious pleasure. The whole act of theft is seen to be a play within a play: an Oedipal drama which conceals a pre-Oedipal one. It is a desire to enact a fantasy of the primal scene and at the same time a desperate attempt to restore individual identity. In these dynamic respects it is the direct equivalent of homosexual perversion.[3]

The homosexual patient's "theft dramas" are often acted out directly on her own body and expressed through phobic and physical symptoms. One patient reconstructed one such "theft" when talking of a disastrous evening she had spent. She was the center of interest at a fashionable reception when an attractive man entered the group and took over the conversation. Immediately overwhelmed with feelings of nausea and suffocation, she was obliged to go home. On her way she reflected on the situation and realized that she had experienced a moment of murderous rage and jealousy just before the onset of the symptoms. She suddenly had imagined herself swallowing this man's penis without his noticing it and having to vomit it up when discovered. The underlying significance of this imagined drama was contained in a screen memory in which the patient, two years old, watched the father leaving the mother's bedside. Her mother "had a smile like that of the Mona Lisa—the sort of smile you see on the face of lovers who make it quite obvious that they have something of the other inside them. I remember crying as she picked me up out of the cot. She gave me a toy to play with, and I was supposed to be satisfied. But *she* had what I wanted." All her life this patient believed her mother possessed unusual feminine gifts which she had not received. She constantly demanded things from her mother, but was never happy with what she got. Eventually, the vomiting phobia and the physical sensations from which the patient suffered were found to have crystallized around memories of the mother's pregnancy symptoms, thus further clarifying their symbolic meaning in relation to the mother.

In summing up the self-image of the homosexual girl, we can say that identification with the mother was prohibited in almost every sense. Behind the image of the "anal" mother, who demanded that her daughter be clean inside and out, was another who decreed that the daughter not be attractive or seductive. The merest thought of rivalry with the mother figure created acute anxiety, and the one way of achieving an uneasy feeling of completeness was by clinging to her. To separate from her meant to lose one's identity. But once the fear had been revealed that this would also destroy the mother, one may well surmise that these unhappy children had to construct defenses in order to deal with their mothers' unconscious problems. Certain of their bodily symptoms and anxieties suggest a fragility of the body ego which must have its roots in earliest infancy. Several of these women described feelings of being physically confused and of not knowing where their bodies ended, as though they extended into a terrifying nothingness. One patient was sometimes seized with panic when she was alone and would bang her head on the wall in order to feel that she really existed. Another recounts that on one occasion the woman with whom she lived (and to whom she was as desperately attached as she had been to her mother) was obliged unexpectedly to be absent for three days. The patient, overwhelmed by feelings of depersonalization of psychotic dimensions, could control her anxiety only by stubbing out burning cigarettes on her hands. Of course, it is evident that at one level she wished to protect her love from angry destruction by turning these feelings against herself, but at another level this sadistic act of burning her hands brought her an intense feeling of relief because it defined her body limits. This definition dispersed the feelings of depersonalization and reestablished the lost cathexes of her body-ego boundaries. Psychically, the sudden loss of the mother-substitute had brought about a loss of her own sense of identity.

The patient who believed that men did not defecate had many ideas about her body which had never been subjected to reality-testing and which were connected with a poorly established body ego. In the first months of her analysis she constantly referred to her clitoris as her "penis" and to her vagina as her "arse-hole," without giving the slightest indication that she was using these terms in a figurative sense. On one occasion when she talked of the menstrual blood which came out of her "arse-hole" I drew her attention to the fact that she seemed to regard anus and vagina as equivalent organs. She replied: "Well what's the difference? Oh I suppose they aren't *exactly* the same—but they're connected on the inside aren't they?" Among other bodily misconceptions she believed that she urinated through her clitoris and that in coitus the penis penetrated directly into the uterus.

Both the above-mentioned patients suffered at times from dramatic loss of equilibrium (for example, when in crowds or walking downstairs), and both were beset by the fear that in trying to walk through a doorway they would walk into the wall. To the fear of losing control of one's orifices (vomiting phobia, body elimination rituals) was added the fear of losing the feeling of the body's physical limits, suggesting that behind the anxiety about losing the introjected father and its symbolic representation—losing one's anal contents—there lay the fear of regressing to an undifferentiated state in which only the presence of the mother could enable the patient to differentiate herself from the outer world.

Allied to the inability of these patients to maintain a stable body image was a character trait which directly related to the maternal imago: an inability to organize their lives in even the smallest details. They seemed to live in the midst of disorder and confusion to a punitive degree. The inability to work constructively, to arrange papers, or to pack a suitcase reflected the same indecision and incapacity to organize and master, or to make a cohesive whole out of any given activity. The feeling of being ill-defined, incomplete, incapable, and vulnerable was thus intensified. Independent ego activity was hampered because it was felt to be dangerous.

We see in these different examples how the relation to the mother-image has *precluded the integration of the anal components of the libido* in such a way as to be useful to the ego. Thus, nothing could be achieved—or if achieved, retained. These patients had to prove that they could sustain no effort without the constant aid of the mother or a substitute. To have done so would have involved a separation from the mother's unconscious demand and therefore was forbidden. The mother who fosters precocious control of all kinds in her child, often with the desire that the child should *perform for her,* thus deprives the child of the right to perform or to master her world for her own pleasure. The desire to fulfill the ideal expectations of the mother becomes the ego-ideal. This is an extension of the desire to play the role of paternal phallus to the mother, but its energetic cathexis is derived from the component impulses of the anal phase. From then on anything that is undertaken can be done only in the service of another, never for oneself. Conflict is avoided, and instead the ego seeks to become an essential part of another's ego. The feelings of emptiness, of inadequacy, of damaged body image, of confused sexual identity, the blocked libidinal and aggressive strivings, and the impoverished activity now seek solution in a homosexual relationship.

The Homosexual Relation and Its Significance

None of the limited number of articles on female homosexuality stresses the fact that the girl, in making a homosexual attachment, is making a bid for freedom from the real mother as an external obstacle. This venture is doomed to fail in its aim, however, since she really struggles with a terrifying internalized mother; all the unconscious wishes and fears attached to this imago are displaced with little modification onto the partner. There are, however, certain dynamic changes in the girl's psychic situation when she seeks overtly to fulfill homosexual desires. All my patients revealed in analysis that this was consciously felt to be a triumph over the mother—and less consciously, over the father. Fear of the mother's reaction, should she discover the relationship, masks a keen desire to let her know that she has been replaced. One patient remarked: "Somehow I deliberately let mother find out about my love affair with Susan. She was absolutely furious of course—and I was secretly glad, as though I wanted to punish her for something. When she learns I'm in analysis with a *woman,* it'll just kill her!"

A further source of triumph lies in the fact that the new relationship is an actively erotic one. Sexual wishes and masturbation, always felt to have been forbidden by the mother, are desired and demanded by the mother-substitute. Rivalry with father for mother's love is no longer to be feared. Although divested of all libidinal interest the father-image was constantly present; even though the mother was felt to disparage the father and to undermine his authority, she went to bed with him and she had babies! Through the homosexual relationship the daughter now "proves" that male sex organs and even men themselves are dispensable. In effect she triumphs over the primal scene and the Oedipal parents and short-circuits the integration of her own castration anxiety.

The typical character traits discussed in this study (traits which have been interpreted as manifestations of a certain type of identification with the father), have always been a source of conflict between mother and daughter. The mother has always complained about her unfeminine daughter, who refused to dress attractively, go to parties, or behave like other girls—mother has always complained about her being disorderly, crazy, irresponsible, original— yet these same characteristics are accepted by the homosexual partner and often highly valued. This acceptance becomes another binding feature of such relationships. Hidden in the ruthless, irresponsible, anal-erotic child which these patients present to the world lies not only deep anxiety and anguish but also the internalized father. This is what the mother and the rest of the young woman's environment have never accepted. And this is what the partner accepts with open arms.

A significant example of such acceptance and sharing was recounted by one of my patients. She lived at that time in a very close, dependent relationship with an older woman and had often talked with her about her intense vomiting phobia. One evening, following a digestive upset, the young woman realized that she really was about to vomit. She called her friend to come and do something—anything at all—in order to prevent the vomiting. In answer the friend held out her hands so that she might vomit into them. The event over, the young patient exclaimed: "Now you will never love me again!" The friend then buried her face in the regurgitated meal and kissed it as a sign of love and total acceptance. This unusual exchange had a profound effect on my patient, bringing her a feeling of security about her body and herself which she had not experienced before. To her unconscious it meant total acceptance of every repressed sadistic and forbidden fantasy.

Apart from the feeling of now being accepted for all that was rejected by the mother, the homosexual also seeks to know her own body through the body of another woman. Both in fantasy and in sexual practice she frequently has more interest in giving sexual pleasure than in receiving it. This is motivated in part by internal prohibitions and in part by fantasies of controlling and dominating the partner sexually.

Up to now we have been examining the positive aspects of the homosexual relationship. It is clear, however, that few of the basic conflicts are solved and that the new relationship inevitably will become another closed circle. The woman partner is still an unconscious mother figure, with her own unconscious problems which demand solution; and thus all the conflicts originally attached to the mother imago will slowly crystallize around the partner. Perhaps the most striking conflict is the ambivalence toward the loved one which comes to light in analysis. The hate, thinly disguised as an obsessional concern for the partner's safety, leads to a compulsion to overprotect her, to demand her every movement, and consequently to control and victimize her. This tendency to reduce the other to a partial object, which one can control and manipulate (and "punish with love"), is equaled only by the fear of becoming, oneself, a partial object again focused upon the partner. Thus, such a patient seeks constantly to play a role of essential importance to her friend. This leads to her undertaking many tasks and functions of her partner (and sometimes playing an important counterphobic role) simply to avoid becoming the dependent and dominated one. But such aims contain the seeds of their own destruction. Certain of my patients spent much of their energy, which they really wanted and needed for themselves, doing things for the other woman, much to the detriment of their own work and interests. So here the wheel came full circle: they found themselves back in the early infantile situation in which the little girl performed solely to fulfill the maternal demands and unconscious needs. (The revelation of these unconscious ties to the homosexual partner raises the question of whether their mothers were not also using their daughters as *counterphobic objects* in order to deal with their own sexual and social anxieties.)

Thus, the ego seeks to maintain its precarious identity along the lines traced out in childhood. But the fact that this is a mutual aim does result in a certain reinforcement of the ego for these analysands. The threat of object-loss under these conditions may lead to grave disturbances in the narcissistic ego libido and may give rise to suicidal impulses. The extent to which ego identity, and the cathexes of the boundaries of the self themselves, can be disturbed is exemplified in the incident of the woman who burned her hands with lighted cigarettes when she had to endure the unexpected absence of her friend.

While the ego is reinforced in the homosexual relation, bodily fears concerning sexual fantasy are on the whole unmitigated and are often projected onto the partner's body. One patient brought a vivid example of such projection. This patient was clitorally and vaginally frigid and felt confused about where her vagina was. She imagined that it could constrict and cut like a knife, and she had a recurrent fantasy of giving birth to a child which would come out in broken segments. She attributed both oral and anal functions to her vagina. But this same frightening idea was also projected onto the vaginas of other women. In her first homosexual experience (with an older woman when the patient was eighteen) she was excited when the other woman demanded clitoral stimulation and happy to give these caresses to her friend. But one day when the friend asked her to put her fingers into her vagina, the patient drew back in horror. "I was sure my fingers would get stuck inside her, and that it would require the services of a surgeon to separate us. I was so terrified I just couldn't do what she asked." This fear was attached also to an unconscious aspect of her relation to her mother: she might fuse with the mother in such a way that she would never get free. Her mother's vagina would demand that she remain perpetually attached to it like a phallic organ, and only a surgeon's knife could separate them. That this woman's father was a noted Parisian surgeon makes her remark extremely pertinent and rich in symbolic meaning. Only an effective father could protect her from the dangerous maternal desire to make her into a permanent phallus.

Concluding Remarks

What conclusions may be drawn from this clinical study regarding the psychodynamic and economic significance of female homosexuality?

When a woman builds her life around homosexual object relations she is unconsciously seeking to maintain an intimate relation with the paternal imago, decathected as a libidinal object but possessed symbolically through identification. At the same time she achieves an apparent detachment from the maternal imago, represented in the unconscious as dangerous, invading, and all-forbidding. The idealized aspects of the maternal imago are now sought in the female partner.

The identification with the father, which has alienated the young girl from her true sexual identity, is more disturbing to the ego structure because its erstwhile phallic significance has regressed to an anal-sadistic one. Nevertheless, this introjection acts as a protective shield against further regression and against a psychotic restructuring within the limitless oral universe of the primitive mother-child relation. The feelings of hate and terror, which become attached to the maternal imago in the struggle for individuation, are kept in repression by idealization.

As the analysis proceeds the peculiar nature of the "solution" to the Oedipal conflicts is revealed. The regressed phallic image, represented in the unconscious as a dangerously exciting anal part-object, comes to symbolize that object which, *par excellence,* belongs to the mother. In a double sense, from the Oedipal as well as the pre-Oedipal point of view, that object is apprehended as exclusively hers and is forever a guilty possession. The mother is felt to demand that everything be rendered up to her: sexual and affectionate feelings for the father, as well as self-mastery and independence. The daughter, however, does not simply renounce all involvement with the father and return without further ado to the object of her first love, the mother of babyhood. There is clearly a regression from the triangular Oedipal constellation to a dyadic one. But within this regressive movement the young girl's ego has incorporated the symbolic phallus, and to some extent she identifies herself with it as a whole. The recreated exclusive mother relationship, then, is significantly different from a truly symbiotic one. The paternal phallus is no longer felt to belong to the mother but has become the daughter's patrimony! As it signifies a stolen and guilty possession, the daugher will forever live in dread of its being detected by other men or of losing it to the mother. Her immense gain is that she no longer need fear a return to the fusion with the mother which spells psychic death. Indeed, she now can believe that she contains all that is essential to equal her mother. Unconsciously, she assumes the role of the mother's phallus—an anal-phallus that only the mother may control and manipulate. A devouring love for the mother and a phobic clinging to her in childhood is paralleled by unconscious wishes for her death.

In that decisive moment when the girl tied to her mother decides to leave her for the woman who will become her lover, she symbolically castrates the mother of her phallus-child. That moment is experienced, therefore, as a moment of intense triumph. It is to the other woman that she will finally offer herself as the incarnation of all that she has symbolically taken away.

The new situation, however, contains the seeds of new dangers. The homosexual relationship, heavily loaded with narcissistic, libidinal, and sadistic significance, becomes the scene for the old internalized drama. The homosexual pays dearly for a fragile identity which is not truly her own. Yet she is compelled to play this role, for the alternative is the death of the ego. The attempt to repair and complete her lover masks the hope of completing herself at the other's expense. To this end she attempts to reduce her partner to the status of a partial object, one which can be manipulated as she felt she herself was in her infantile relation to the mother. She hopes thereby to avoid the danger of becoming the total possession of the other.

From the point of view of clinical categories we are dealing neither with classical neurotic nor with truly psychotic structures but clearly with a "third structure" which might be described as a "perverse" one. This nomenclature would nevertheless be misleading: the problem does not, in the writer's opinion, belong only to the sexual perversions. It is characterized by a continual *acting-out* of an internal drama in the outside world in an attempt to maintain ego identity. There are many neurotic mechanisms at work, but they fail to protect the ego with regard to its sexual identity. Hysterophobic and obsessional symptoms are poorly structured. Psychotic mechanisms include negation (of sexual reality), disavowal (of the primal scene), and continual splitting of the parental imagoes with consequent projection. In the cases presented in this paper there is a pathological introjection of the father figure according to a depressive model. The consequent risk of losing the identity-emblems thus acquired makes the homosexual liable to severe depressive episodes, or when projective mechanisms dominate, to psychotic episodes of a paranoid type, thus confirming Freud's early hypothesis of the genesis of this disorder.

This splitting in the ego's defensive system, accompanied by splitting of the internalized objects, is characterized by a specific redistribution of the split-off fragments. The parental objects, apprehended as idealized on the one hand and destroyed or destroying on the other, are divided: the mother embodies idealized "good," while hostile aggressive feelings originally attached to her are projected onto the father, who becomes entirely "bad," that is, either destroyed (castrated) or dangerously destroying. In consequence anxieties, either depressive or persecutory, are likely to come to consciousness and to overwhelm the ego in its relation to the external world.

The distortion in sexual identity is inevitably accompanied by fragility of ego identity in general, disturbance of body-ego perceptions, and symptoms of depersonalization. The superego, regressed to an archaic pregenitalized formation, constantly threatens the ego so that depression or the loss of reality-testing may occur. Faced with manifold psychic dangers the young woman thus turns to a homosexual love as a bulwark against them.

If the danger inherent in the new relation itself does not disrupt this protective arrangement the ego will receive some much-needed support, though little fulfillment of sexual and narcissistic needs. In particular the deeply repressed desire for the father's love is always liable to return and to challenge the pact which the homosexual woman has signed with her parental imagoes, the pact which contains the clause of her own castration. For the price she must pay for her homosexual identity is the renunciation of all feminine sexual desire as well as of the children she consciously longs for.

In conclusion we might sum up the psychic economy of female homosexuality as follows: an attempt to maintain a narcissistic equilibrium in face of a constant need to escape the dangerous symbiotic relationship claimed by the mother imago, through conserving an unconscious identification with the father, the latter factor being an essential element in a fragile structure. This identification, costly though it may be, helps to protect the individual from depression or psychotic states of dissociation and thus contributes to maintaining the cohesion of the ego.

Notes

INTRODUCTION

1. C. J. Luquet: "The great majority of psychoanalytical studies on instinctual drives and the development of the ego have been made with reference to man's development, with merely a secondary adjustment when applying the same results to women."
2. The articles in this book do not intend to cover the whole problem of female sexuality but merely to study certain aspects of it.
3. Standard Edition (S.E.), Vol. VII. All quotations from Freud in this book from the *Standard Edition of the Complete Psychological Works of Sigmund Freud* (S.E.), ed. by James Strachey (London: The Hogarth Press). (Tr. note.)
4. (London, 1913).
5. *Collected Papers*, 4 (1925): 30–59.
6. S.E., Vol. XIX.
7. *Ibid.*
8. *Ibid.*
9. S.E., Vol. XXI.
10. S.E., Vol. XXII.
11. *International Journal of Psychoanalysis*, 9 (1928): 332–45.
12. *International Journal of Psychoanalysis*, 1 (1920): 125–49.
13. *Psychoanalytic Quarterly*, 2 (1933): 489–518.
14. *International Journal of Psychoanalysis*, 6 (1925): 405–18.
15. *International Journal of Psychoanalysis*, 11 (1930): 48–60.
16. Vol. 9, July, 1961.
17. Hélène Deutsch, *The Psychology of Women* (New York, 1944).
18. *Psychoanalytic Quarterly*, 9 (1940), 293–319.
19. Presse Universitaire de France (Paris, 1951).
20. *International Journal of Psychoanalysis*, 13 (1932), 361–68.
21. *International Journal of Psychoanalysis*, 13 (1932), 348–60.
22. *International Journal of Psychoanalysis*, 14 (1933), 57–70.
23. Melanie Klein, *Psychoanalysis of Children* (New York, 1932).
24. *International Journal of Psychoanalysis*, 9 (1928), 169–80.
25. This could be opposed to the Freudian equation:
    "Pleasure = instinctual discharge."

26. *International Journal of Psychoanalysis*, 8 (1927), 459–72.
27. *International Journal of Psychoanalysis*, 14 (1933), 1–33.
28. *International Journal of Psychoanalysis*, 16 (1935), 263–73.
29. *International Journal of Psychoanalysis*, 1 (1920), 371–95.
30. *Collected Papers*, 2 (1924), 255–68.
31. *International Journal of Psychoanalysis*, 9 (1928), 161–66.
32. *Collected Papers*, 2 (1924), 164–71.
33. *International Journal of Psychoanalysis*, 3 (1922), 1–29.

A MASCULINE MYTHOLOGY OF FEMININITY

1. Freud, indeed, wrote in the *Three Essays:* "It is perhaps in connection precisely with the most repulsive perversions that the mental factor must be regarded as playing its largest part in the transformation of the sexual instinct. It is impossible to deny that in their case a piece of mental work has been performed which, in spite of its horrifying result, is the equivalent of an idealization of the instinct."

OUTLINE FOR A STUDY OF NARCISSISM IN FEMALE SEXUALITY

1. "That is all I had to say to you about femininity. It is certainly incomplete and fragmentary and does not always sound friendly. But do not forget that I have only been describing women insofar as their nature is determined by their sexual function. It is true that that influence extends very far; but we do not overlook the fact that an individual woman may be a human being in other respects as well. If you want to know more about femininity, enquire from your own experiences of life, or turn to the poets, or wait until science can give you deeper and more coherent information" (Freud, *New Introductory Lectures on Psychoanalysis*, London, 1933).

2. Melanie Klein believes, similarly, that the oral desire for the penis is derived from the desire for the breast. But one could also say (see E. Jones and Karen Horney's criticisms) that sexuality is the permanent factor: the child experiences it at each stage of development and that the eroticization of suckling is an attempt to abreact what should properly be called sexuality, but for which the child is not yet ready.

3. "With the onset of puberty the maturing of the female sexual organs, which up till then have been in a condition of latency, seems to bring about an intensification of the original narcissism" (Freud, "On Narcissism, An Introduction," in *Collected Papers*, London, 1925).

4. Of course, every case is specific and these tendencies are generalized; yet they are common enough for their study to be interesting. Furthermore, in this study we envisage an attitude toward sexuality, observable in people from our own milieu and produced by today's civilization. The kind of person we shall study here is neither ill (like those we meet in psychoanalytical practice) nor perfectly

normal (who probably does not exist outside fiction) but halfway between: the common man or woman who has certain conflicts but who is considered normal from a social point of view.

5. R. A. Spitz, "Hospitalism: An Inquiry into the Genesis of Psychiatric Conditions in Early Childhood," *Psychoanalytic Study of the Child,* 1 (1945), 53–74.

6. Women are forced to assume a certain narcissistic autonomy from their dependence on their love objects, which rarely meet their expectations.

   Recognition of this need often brings women together, giving them solidarity. The mother can scarcely do other than help her daughter build up this autonomy. To some extent women do achieve this and manage to organize their lives alone.

7. During analytical treatment, one must follow all phases of this integration of the phallus in increasingly complex forms.

8. One could study the differences between the sexes from the point of view of narcissistic integrity as represented by the phallic image. Indeed, in the animal world the male usually has visible, seemingly narcissistic signs of this integrity (beauty, presence, adornments), but in our society these visual phallic representations belong to woman, who finds thus a phallic compensation for her dependence on man's penis.

9. Narcissism exists in its own right, for itself. Its very existence is gratuitous since it serves no purpose, which, according to Ella Freeman Sharpe, defines artistic creation. I agree: Creativity is essentially narcissistic.

FEMININE GUILT AND THE OEDIPUS COMPLEX

1. Sigmund Freud, "Female Sexuality," 1931.

2. Melanie Klein, *Envy and Gratitude* (New York, 1957).

3. "Our understanding of feminine frigidity . . . can be complete only if we take into consideration the fact that there is a constitutional inhibition that has no parallel in men" (*The Psychology of Women,* New York, 1944).

4. Sigmund Freud, *Beyond the Pleasure Principle* (London, 1950).

5. Sigmund Freud, *The Ego and the Id* (London, 1927).

6. Sigmund Freud, *Inhibitions, Symptoms, Anxiety* (London, 1936).

7. *Psychology of Women.*

8. *Collected Papers,* 4 (London, 1918), 217–35.

9. "I have had occasional opportunities of being told women's dreams that had occurred after their first experience of intercourse. They revealed an unmistakable wish in the woman to keep for herself the penis which she had felt."

   I believe that this desire, which Freud thinks is a regressive one, is, in fact, the manifestation of a desire more authentically feminine, that of keeping the penis in order to be *impregnated* by it. The female sexual desire to be penetrated seems to me to be in-

separably linked in the unconscious with the biological consequence
of that desire—impregnation, that is to say the desire, as E. Jones
said, to keep the penis in oneself in order to turn it into a child.
Also, the instinctual drive at the level of the primary processes is
absolute and unlimited and cannot be set in a spatio-temporal
framework. The complementary masculine desire is similar in that
it is not limited to penetrating one particular part of the woman's
body at a given moment, but, as Ferenczi said in *Thalassa,* it is a
desire to return one's whole body to the mother's womb.

10. *"Epouser"* = "to take the exact shape of" *and* "to marry." (Tr. note.)
11. It is not sufficient to give purely sociological reasons for women's difficulties in professional or creative fields; we need to seek out the
deep unconscious roots of these difficulties. But neither would it be
exact to say that there is no sociocultural factor. Women's internal
guilt is constantly encouraged by real external factors. Psychoanalysts rightly emphasize the role of these external factors in creating neuroses—by being particularly favorable to unconscious conflicts common to many people.
12. This assertion was maintained by Freud even in his "Short Account
of Psychoanalysis" (1924), after many people had opposed him in
theory and by clinical observation. Yet in the article Ruth Mack
Brunswick wrote with him ("The Pre-Oedipal Phase," 1940), he
seems to have more or less accepted that early sensations do exist
in the vagina.
13. I think this transfer of cathexis is due to the guilt associated with the
anal-sadistic incorporative drives.
14. The narcissistic cathexis of these characteristics is linked, according to
Grunberger, with the anal-sadistic phase, and thus the only objects
of value are those which can be measured, compared, and precisely
graded.
15. Freud not only ignores the vagina but, until the castration complex,
that is, the Oedipus complex, he believes the girl's sexuality to be
identical with that of the boy. She merely hopes for receptive satisfactions from her mother, but she does not expect them to be
phallic and denies the penis as well as the vagina. When she turns
to the father wanting a child by him, it is not yet a desire for incorporation of the paternal penis. For Freud, the girl's Oedipus complex occurs without interfering with incorporation desires (or
desires of being penetrated in any manner); in a similar way the
boy has no desire to penetrate the mother. He is ignorant of her
possessing an organ complementary to his own. It is only at puberty
that erection of the penis indicates a new aim—the penetration of
a cavity. Apart from numerous indications that there are early
desires of penetration (which many people have noted), erections
are frequent before puberty, and one finds babies having erections,
particularly while being suckled. E. Jones, Melanie Klein, Josine
Müller, Karen Horney, and, more recently, Phyllis Greenacre, in

discussing the girl's discovery of the vagina, stress the fact that we are used to talking about external and visible organs without taking deep coenesthetic sensations into consideration. Girl's ignorance of their vaginas does not prove the nonexistence of a genital desire to incorporate the penis, just as a congenital malformation obstructing the mouth would not deny the existence of hunger. Indeed, the impossibility of satisfying the instinct increases guilt, in face of the "condemned" vagina.

16. Once frustration has brought the primary narcissistic phase to an end.

17. Unconsciously, he has probably always known she had no penis just as, unconsciously, he always knew she had a vagina. But this does not exclude representations of a phallic or castrated mother, since the primary processes readily admit contradiction.

18. International Psychoanalytic Press, 1922.

19. Of course other causes also dictate a man's future attitude to women, one of which is an identification with the real father in his relation to the mother.

20. See Karen Horney, "The Dread of Women." The little boy feels an aggressive desire for his mother. In her role as educator she is obliged to dominate him and frustrate him. He desires to penetrate her, but feels humiliated at being small and incapable of achieving this, which leads to his feeling narcissistically wounded and immensely inferior, but he also feels a violently aggressive desire for revenge, which is projected, along with those desires caused by the first frustrations, onto the mother and her vagina.

21. One patient suffering from ejaculatio praecox was content in his first sexual relations at the age of twenty-two with merely external contact "because he did not know" that the vagina existed. Such "ignorance" is due to frightening sexual fantasies. For him the female organ was a threat, full of fecal content (crumbling caves full of garbage, cow's cloaca blocked with dung "as hard as granite," corpses found in rooms, crashed cars spread across an icy road, etc.). Therefore, penetration is dangerous: in order to avoid it one must "fill the vagina with powdered glass, use it as a chamber pot and fill it to the brim," think of it as a john where one puts the lid down before urinating or else tries to get rid of the contents first. Thus, at puberty, this patient spent a lot of time disembowelling flies; one of his favorite fantasies was the following: he was master of a harem and ruled women of all ages with a whip. He had established very strict rules in which the women had to defecate by orders and under close scrutiny. This illustrates the child's inversion of sphincter education and his victory over the anal penis of the intrusive mother. (This patient also had fantasies about excision of the clitoris.)

Men fear the mother's power, and her anal penis in particular. Later they try to stop women from using their anal impulses. As woman is guilty about her own anal wishes toward the father, she

becomes an accomplice to the man's defenses. This conjunction results in the visible inhibition of women's anality in society: a
woman must never swear, spit, eat strong food or wine, and until
recently was not allowed to discuss money or business. Charm and
grace are on the whole either reaction formations or sublimations
of anal impulses (the opposite of vulgarity). At the same time,
women are represented as illogical, vague, incapable of the rigors
of science, engineering, etc.—all signs of successful integration of
the anal components.

(Owing to the enforced repression it undergoes, the anal instinct may become somewhat "corrosive." The weaker muscular
structure of women also favors this corrosive aspect of feminine aggression, as it does not allow for adequate motor discharge. Women
are said to scratch, bite, or poison, whereas men punch or knock
down.) In fact this desire for victory over the omnipotent mother
is often displaced by men onto all women. An exception is the
daughter, perhaps because she is in a dependent situation. The father projects onto her an *idealized image* which is opposed to the
"normal lasting contempt" (Freud, Ruth Mack Brunswick, Hélène
Deutsch) he feels for other women. His daughter often represents
the best part of himself and of the good, primitive object. She is
tenderness, purity, innocence, and grace and represents for him a
privileged relationship which escapes his ambivalence.

Of course, this relation is not always there, as some men extend
their maternal conflicts onto their daughters, too. An obsessional
patient suffering from ejaculatio praecox was discussing his six-
year-old daughter who was working hard at school in order to attract his attention, a fact he was well aware of: "I push her away
from me but, being truly feminine, she still tries to attract my attention"; but the relation I have described exists frequently enough
for it to be noticeable. Three patients told me at the outset of
their treatment that one of their reasons for coming to analysis
was a desire to help their daughters.

22. In her article on "The Pre-Oedipal Phase" (written with Freud), Ruth
Mack Brunswick reconsiders the idea that the desire for a child is
a substitute for penis envy: the desire for a child expresses mainly
the desire to have what the mother possessed: a child.

I believe that if the child's desire is linked both with penis
envy and with the omnipotent mother, it is because of a certain
connection between penis envy and the omnipotent maternal
imago.

23. For Freud (in "Femininity," 1932), if a woman comes to analysis in
order to be more successful in her profession, she is by the same
token displaying her penis envy.

24. The same is true of men: for a man to achieve his professional ambitions is symbolically to have a penis *like the father.*

25. Protecting oneself from penetration is also a way of safeguarding the object. A whole series of aggressive acts toward the father can be understood as an attempt to protect him from *contact*.

26. Of course, this may also be due to regression.

27. Space prevents our considering here the child's role as a narcissistic support. Joyce McDougall noted that penis envy plays as important a role in mothers as in women who are childless.

    It is a fact that many mothers castrate their children psychologically, which indicates that their penis envy is not satisfied by maternity.

    It is no solution to the problem to say that in these cases the women have not been able to transform their desire for a penis into a desire for a child.

    Having a child may mean possessing what the omnipotent mother had (Ruth Mack Brunswick), but it does not yet mean having *something different* from what she had, and this, I believe, is the true aim of narcissistic achievements.

28. *Collected Papers,* 4 (1925), 39–59.

29. *Collected Papers,* 4 (1925), 60–83.

30. Taken anally in France. (Tr. note.)

31. This is similar to the situation described by Simone de Beauvoir in *The Second Sex* (New York, 1952).

THE SIGNIFICANCE OF PENIS ENVY IN WOMEN

1. Indeed, masturbation could appear later on with different fantasy content, but what has been repressed earlier leaves its negative mark on all future personality development.

2. It is worth noting that the hand as a means for the introjection of the primal scene always represents the genital organ of the opposite sex.

3. This is so true that the identification with the castrator, the one who forbids "autoeroticism," is necessarily part of a masturbatory fantasy. Without this identification, however paradoxical or neurotic it might seem, the interdiction is experienced as a true castration and is manifested by inability to do anything and by extreme tension. The psychotic autocastration has no meaning other than that of trying, in desperation, a paralyzing identification in order to remove an inhibition which is just as deadly.

4. There are two ways of compromising the child's maturing identifications. 1st, to forbid the orgasm which would confirm the validity of his efforts to fulfill himself. 2d, to suppress the fantasy by substituting an objective reality for it (seduction). In this case the fantasy identification is stopped by an effective but premature achievement, and the mutilating effects of inhibition which result from this trauma are similar to those of the other stringency. That is why people who are inhibited about masturbation have fantasies

to the extent of mythomania about scenes of rape, and these "precociously ravished" women behave in exactly the same way as those who are inhibited about orgasms.

5. BB means at the same time Brigitte Bardot and "baby" in French. (Tr. note.)

HOMOSEXUALITY IN WOMEN

1. The woman who sprays the child with ether also represented an important fixation. We learned later that "ether" stood for the mother's urine (an unconscious phallic equivalent for this patient). She had many erotic fantasies of drinking the urine of a female partner (linked to nourishing milk, a further female "phallus") coupled with ideas of its destructive and corrosive aspects. In a brief sexual relationship with a man Karen had asked him to urinate in her vagina in expectation of an ecstatic experience.

2. Olivia's intuition seemed confirmed some years later when—still in analysis—she was planning to marry. Her father wrote to tell me that the analysis had failed, since he would lose his daughter. After the birth of her little son two years later he wrote, this time to his daughter, saying there was no reason for them ever to communicate with each other again!

3. Melitta Schmideberg drew attention in 1956 to the relationship between delinquent acts and perverse acts, such as fetishism and exhibitionism, in two male patients.